The Rail Lines
of Southern
New England

NEW ENGLAND RAIL HERITAGE SERIES

The Rail Lines of Southern New England

A Handbook of Railroad History

RONALD DALE KARR

Branch
Line
Press

Pepperell, Massachusetts

Manufactured in the United States of America.
Printed by Braun-Brumfield, Inc., Ann Arbor, MI

Cover design by Diane B. Karr.

Library of Congress Card Number 93-90147

ISBN: 0-942147-02-2

Branch Line Press
13 Cross Street
Pepperell, Massachusetts 01463

*Frontispiece: A Central Vermont freight works the interchange at the
Conrail main line at Palmer, Mass., in September 1994 (photo by the
author).*

*Cover: Outbound from Boston, a passenger train on the Penn Central
(Boston & Providence) approaches Forest Hills, Mass., in September
1971 (photo by the author).*

10 9 8 7 6 5 4

Contents

Contents

Under the watchful eye of the conductor a Penn Central GG1 electric locomotive is coupled onto a New York-bound Amtrak train at New Haven in May 1973. The GG1s are long gone, and with completion of electrification from New Haven to Boston changes of motive power here will cease.

Preface

RAILROADS MAY NOT have played as important a role in New England history as in other parts of this country, but Yankees have a rail heritage worth commemorating. By the end of the nineteenth century the rail lines of Massachusetts, Connecticut, and Rhode Island formed one of the densest rail networks in America. Today, a good portion of this system is gone, and the surviving remnants shrink with each passing year.

In 1981, while a librarian at Northwestern University's Transportation Library in Evanston, Illinois, I set out to compile a comprehensive historical guide to the rail lines of New England past and present. The first draft of the sections on Connecticut and part of Massachusetts was completed by the time I left Illinois for Massachusetts in 1985. In 1989 some of this material was published as *Lost Railroads of New England*.

My primary goal in writing this handbook was to try to make sense out of New England's rail network by breaking it down into segments, then tracing the history of each segment from its origins to the present. To do this I consulted hundreds of sources, including published histories, maps, timetables and directories, contemporary magazines and newspapers, and local rail experts. As is true of most handbooks, much of the information here is derived from a large body of published research, in this case

The Boston & Maine's East Somerville yard outside Boston was still busy in September 1971 when this shiny SW-1 switcher posed for a portrait.

prepared by amateur and professional students of New England rail history.

Many persons assisted me in preparing this handbook. In particular I would like to thank Thomas J. Humphrey, J. Leonard Bachelder, and R. Richard Conard who generously shared their vast knowledge of New England rail history with me. Each reviewed the manuscript of this book in great detail and provided extensive critiques. They did their best to correct my errors, even though I did not always heed their advice. Len Bachelder provided an abstract of hundreds of passenger train schedules, which I hope he eventually will publish. Tom Humphrey graciously allowed me to spend a Saturday afternoon with his superb private historical collection. Thanks also to Richard W. Symmes, Curator of the Walker Transportation Collection, Beverly (Mass.) Historical Society and Museum, who guided me through the society's vast photo collection and provided photographs for this book.

Most of the historical photos in this book are courtesy of the Walker Transportation Collection, Beverly Historical Society and Museum, and are used with permission from the society. My good friend Roger Yepsen contributed photographs of Connecticut railroading in the early 1970s. Uncredited photos are my own.

A number of my fellow railfans provided information and materials on railroad lines with which they were familiar. I would like to thank: Mary Anthony, Alfred S. Arnold, Donald H. Brayden, Jr., W. George Cook, Prof. William L. "Toby" Dills, Seth Fisher, Arthur Gaudet, Richard M. Haywood, Paul Hotchkiss, Frank J. Labuz, Nelson H. Lawry, Ray McMurdo, Robert E. Moran, Donald F. Morrison, Donald S. Robinson, Alan B. Rohwer, William W. Schweikert, Ellis E. Walker, and H. Arnold Wilder.

Research for this book was conducted at a number of libraries and was aided by many of my fellow librarians, archivists, and curators. I would like to thank Russell Maylone, Curator of Special Collections, Northwestern University Library; Mary Fortney, Map Librarian, Northwestern University Library; Dorothy Ramm and Mary MacCredie, Librarians, Northwestern University Transportation Library; Marie Anne Drouin and Mary Beth McNeil, Interlibrary Loans, O'Leary Library, University of Massachusetts Lowell; and Martha Mayo, Special Collections Librarian, Center for Lowell History, University of Massachusetts Lowell.

Above all, this book would not have been possible without the enormous help of my wife, Diane. She served as editor, critic, proofreader, typist, and cover designer, and performed countless other tasks. Thanks also to my two younger children, Jeannine and Matthew, for keeping me company on some of my photography expeditions and all three children for enduring years of research, writing, and train-chasing detours during family trips.

Finally, any errors are my responsibility. Despite my best efforts to make this book as accurate as possible, a few have undoubtedly been overlooked. I would greatly appreciate these being brought to my attention for possible future editions.

Introduction

HAVE YOU ever come across an active rail line or abandoned right of way and wondered about its history? Who built it and when? Where did it go? What was its original name? What type of traffic did it see? When was it last used? Who operates it now?

If the rail line is located in Massachusetts, Connecticut, or Rhode Island, this book will help answer these questions. This handbook provides a brief history of every common-carrier railroad line in southern New England. (Excluded are electric and tram lines, including those that survived as diesel-powered freight spurs; cog railways and inclines; industrial, military, mining, and logging railroads; lines constructed but never operated; and most urban industrial spurs and branches. Some of these, however, are listed in Appendix A.)

In order to survey the history of all of southern New England's railroads, past and present, I have arranged the thousands of miles that composed the region's rail network into eighty-three systems, ranging in size from a few miles to more than a hundred. Each of these segments is based on an historical railroad, in most cases the first company to construct the line. Most, but not all, of

.B&M locomotive number 1008 pauses at Essex, Mass., at the end of the 5.5- mileEssex Branch in 1939, three years before the line was abandoned. Until 1927 the rails extended another half mile to Conomo. (Photo courtesy Walker Transportation Collection, Beverly Historical Society & Museum.)

these segments were once operated as independent railroads before becoming absorbed into larger systems. Each segment is identified by a number and a name, the latter usually reflecting either the original name or another name by which the line was known when it was operated independently. Shorter branch lines (around fifteen miles or less) are usually grouped with the main line to which they connect, while most longer branches are listed separately. Exception is made for a few short lines that were operated independently for long periods.

Present-day railfans will be more familiar with many of these segments under more recent names. In an historical guide such as this, however, I wanted to emphasize the origins and evolution of the individual components that came to make up New England's rail system. Many if not most of our present-day branch lines are truncated remnants of former through routes, which were built for reasons that often had little to do with their present use.

The Southern New England Rail Network

By 1900 one of the nation's densest networks of rail lines crisscrossed southern New England, leaving few centers of population unserved. In hundreds of rural villages in Massachusetts, Connecticut, and Rhode Island the depot had replaced the Meetinghouse as the focal point of town activity. Stores, banks, hotels, taverns, and coal and grain dealers in most towns clustered around the railroad. From the local station, trains departed several times each day for Boston, New Haven, Hartford, Providence, Springfield, or Worcester, as well as more distant points such as New York, Albany, and Portland. Intercity routes linked all of these cities together, making it easy—for those who could pay—to travel throughout southern New England or to ship or receive goods to or from anywhere.

Since it opened in 1899 Boston's South Station has been the most important passenger depot in New England. Only part of the facade shown in this September 1971 view survives today.

This network took more than half a century to build. The first New England railroads, a trio of lines radiating from Boston, were completed in 1835. Each of these, the Boston & Lowell, the Boston & Worcester, and the Boston & Providence, was initially intended only to provide Boston with direct service to three important interior cities. Over the next few decades scores of additional railroads were chartered, either to connect cities together or as branch lines to provide service to communities left off direct routes.

As time passed railroad tycoons slowly assembled these various short lines into larger railroad systems. As late as 1865 southern New England still had more than 30 independently operated railroads, many of them locked in heated competition with each other for freight and passenger traffic. This rivalry produced many miles of additional rail lines as companies sought to raid customers from other systems and protect their own markets from competitors seeking to expand. Decades of unfettered competition took their toll, however, and railroad investors and bankers wearied of paying for it. A process of consolidation began in the 1870s, gathered steam in the 1880s, and was completed by the century's end.

By 1880 most of the region's rail lines were encompassed in 18 systems: the New York, New Haven & Hartford (the New Haven); Housatonic; Naugatuck; New Haven & Northampton; New York & New England; Central Vermont; Connecticut Western; New York, Providence & Boston; Providence & Worcester; Boston & Providence; Boston & Albany; Connecticut River; Old Colony; Worcester & Nashua; Fitchburg; Boston & Lowell; Boston & Maine; and the Eastern. A decade later, there were just 11: the New Haven; Housatonic; New York & New England; Central Vermont; Central New England & Western (successor to the Connecticut Western); New York, Providence & Boston; Boston & Albany; Connecticut River; Old Colony; Fitchburg; and Boston & Maine.

In 1892 the New Haven acquired the Housatonic and the New York, Providence & Boston systems. The year following it obtained the extensive Old Colony system, and in 1895 the even larger New York & New England, giving it a near monopoly in Connecticut and Rhode Island. The Boston & Maine captured the Connecticut River RR in 1893, and in 1900 it absorbed the Fitchburg. The New York Central system bought control of the Boston & Albany at the same time. Thus by 1900 virtually all of the rail lines of southern New England formed part of just three large systems: the New Haven, the New York Central (Boston & Albany), and Boston & Maine Railroads. Except for a few short lines there were only two other railroads of consequence in the region: the Central New England (finally acquired by the New Haven in 1903) and the Central Vermont (which in 1899 had come under the control of the Grand Trunk Railroad of Canada).

Despite two world wars, several bankruptcies and near failures, widespread track abandonment, and enormous technological change, these three rail systems survived until 1969. In that year the New Haven, bankrupt and exhausted, was taken over by the Penn Central Railroad, the successor to the Boston & Albany. In the two decades that followed, the rail scene in Massachusetts, Connecticut, and Rhode Island became increasingly complex as transit authorities in Connecticut and Massachusetts acquired trackage, and the bankrupt Penn Central gave way to federally-funded Conrail, which retained only the Boston & Albany and a few other lines. The bulk of the old New Haven was transferred to Amtrak, the Boston & Maine, and new short lines.

Today railroad service in southern New England is provided by several major carriers, as well as a number of short lines. These include Guilford Transportation Industries (GTI or Guilford), which provides freight service over most of what remains of the Boston & Maine in Massachusetts under the name of Springfield Terminal; Conrail, whose most important operation in this region is the old Boston & Albany main line in Massachusetts, and who also operates some ex-New Haven lines in Massachusetts and Connecticut; the Providence & Worcester, a short line which grew into a system providing freight service throughout Rhode Island and much of Connecticut, as well as operating an ex-Boston & Maine branch to Gardner, Mass.; Amtrak, which not only owns and operates the ex-New Haven shore line between the Massachusetts-Rhode Island boundary and New Haven, but also provides intercity rail passenger service between Boston and New York, Boston and Albany, and Boston and New Haven via Hartford, and operates under contract commuter service out of Boston; the Massachusetts Bay Transportation Authority (MBTA), which owns and manages the numerous rail lines out of Boston (currently being operated by Amtrak under contract to the MBTA); and Metro North, which provides commuter service out of New York over ex-New Haven lines in Connecticut.

How to Use This Book

Locator maps for the three southern New England states are at the beginning of this book. Each of the lines shown on the maps is identified by a route number. Abandoned routes are indicated by *dashed* lines. The various lines are arranged in this guide by the route numbers.

For each line the following information is provided:

Map: The map provided for each entry is *not* drawn to scale. It is included to show the relationship of the entry to other rail lines. As with the locator maps, abandoned portions of lines are indicated by *dashed* lines.

Stations: For each main and branch line an all-time list of all known public passenger and freight stations, as well as junction

Technology and cost-cutting have made cabooses as obsolete as steam locomotives. In the spring of 1971, however, they were still a common sight at the end of nearly every freight train. These ex-New Haven cabooses are shown at Readville Yard south of Boston.

points that did not have service, is given. These are taken from *Official Guides*, employee and public timetables, and other sources. I have generally excluded towers, engine houses, and other points used only by railroads for their own use and not open to the public. The most commonly used name (usually, but not always, the most recent) is shown first, and other names are listed in parentheses. I have not included minor variations in spelling. As an editorial policy apostrophes have been removed from station names. In the nineteenth century it was common to include apostrophes in station names (i.e., Grout's Corner), but in more recent times railroads have abandoned them. The numbers indicate distance in miles from the starting point.

Built: This represents the years that the main line was constructed, followed by the dates of construction of branches.

Operators: This represents the actual operator of the line (as opposed to the owner), for the period listed. In most cases this is the name that appeared on locomotives and passenger cars, tickets, and time tables. In recent years freight and passenger operations are often provided by different carriers. I have departed from this scheme in two instances. The MBTA is shown as providing passenger service, which in fact was provided by railroads and Amtrak under MBTA contract (but using MBTA equipment). Also, I have used the name Guilford for those lines operated after June 1983 by either the Boston & Maine or Guilford Transportation's Springfield Terminal subsidiary, which gradually took over operation of B&M lines in the 1980s in order to reduce the power of rail labor unions. The name Springfield Terminal has never caught on with either railfans or the general public, who usually call the company simply Guilford or GTI.

Daily Passenger Trains: Some indication of the relative importance of the line in the past is the number of passenger trains operated. The numbers used here represent scheduled weekday through passenger trains (between the endpoints of the main line of each system), as taken from the following issues of the *Official Guide of the Railways*: June 1869, June 1893, August 1919, September 1935, July 1950, July 1960, April 1971, and October 1981. Public or employee timetables were used to supplement listings in the *Official Guide*.

Abandonments: This information is taken from my *Lost Railroads of New England*, as supplemented by news sources and readers' reports. Note that these are dates of legal abandonment; often the segment was out of service before formal abandonment.

Historical narrative: The brief history of each line was compiled from numerous historical sources and confirmed by field checks wherever possible. Much of the information on recent operations came from readers of my *Lost Railroads in New England*, as acknowledged in the preface.

Sources: Major sources are provided for each entry (complete citations can be found in the bibliography). Among the other sources most often consulted were *Official Guides of the Railways*; various editions of *Poor's Railroad Manual*; Poor, *History of the Railroads*; *Chronological History of the New Haven Railroad*; annual reports of railroads and state railroad commissions; Cornwall and Smith, *Names First—Rails Later*; maps and atlases; various newspapers and magazines, most notably the *Boston Globe, Trains, Railfan & Railroad, Shoreliner,* and *B&M Bulletin*. Finally, much information was provided by fellow railfans, not all of whom I was able to acknowledge in the preface.

Further Hints

Tracking down rail lines in the field, especially those long abandoned, will require maps with greater detail than can be provided in a guide such us this. The initial edition of Mike Walker's, *Steam Powered Video's Comprehensive Railroad Atlas of North America: North East U.S.A.*(Kent, England: Steam Powered Publishing, 1993; available through Carstens Publications, Newton, N.J.) is attactive but riddled with errors. It can still be useful if used with caution.

Greater detail can be found on local street maps for cities and towns, such as those published by Universal Publishing Company and available at most local bookstores. Many of these maps show abandoned lines. For those with computers and CD-ROM drives, DeLorme's *Street Atlas USA* shows railroads as well as roads.

The ultimate in detail is provided by the 7½ and 15 minute quadrangle topographic maps published by the U.S. Geological Survey. Highly detailed, these charts show roads, streams, vegetation, contour lines, buildings, place names, and active and most abandoned railroads. Unfortunately, the maps are large and somewhat unwieldy, which reduces their usefulness in the field. Topographic maps may be obtained directly from the USGS (call 800-872-6277 to order) or from local dealers, or may be consulted at many public and college libraries.

Railroads, it should be emphasized, are private property. Trespassing on railroad facilities can result in arrest or serious injury. Railfans should observe from public areas such as grade crossings and highway or pedestrian bridges. With abandoned railroads it is best to assume the land is privately owned unless you know otherwise. I have attempted to identify in this guide those former railroad right-of-ways that now are open to the public, but I make no guarantee of the accuracy of this information. When in doubt, ask locally (check at town hall—the assessors will know who owns the right-of-way).

National railfan magazines such as *Trains* and *Railfan & Railroad* often feature articles and news stories on New England railroads. The single best source for news about Massachusetts, Connecticut, and Rhode Island railroads, however, is *Railpace Newsmagazine*, a monthly exclusively focused on railroading in the northeastern United States (for subscription information, write to P.O. Box 927, Piscataway, NJ 08855). For those with access to the Internet, fast-breaking rail news can be found on the rec.railroad Usenet group. Even more information can be gained by joining one of the many railroad historical societies or railfan groups listed in Appendix B.

Maps

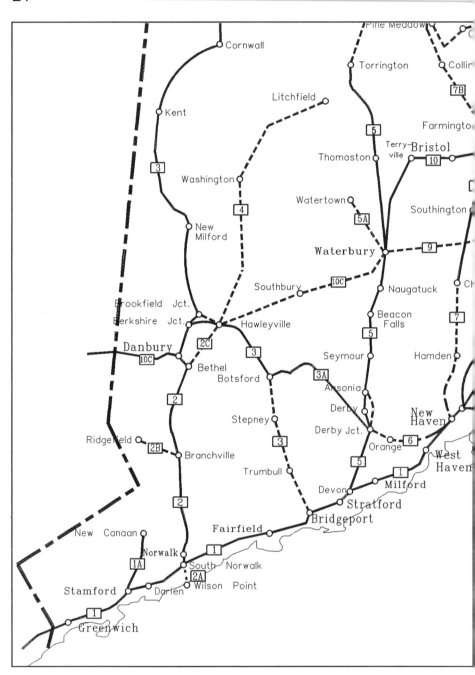

Southwestern Connecticut

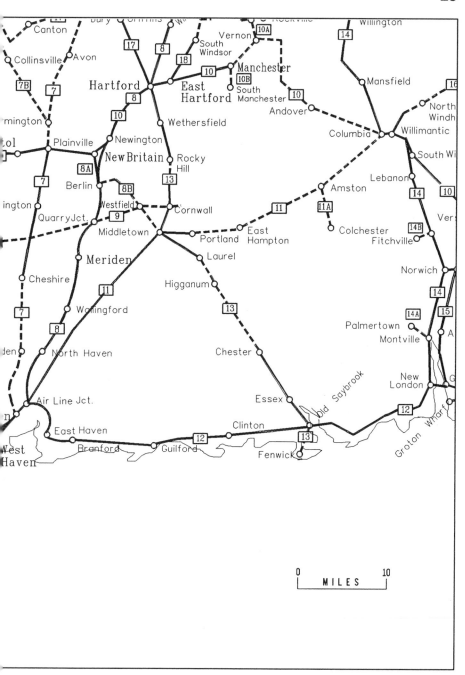

Southeastern Connecticut

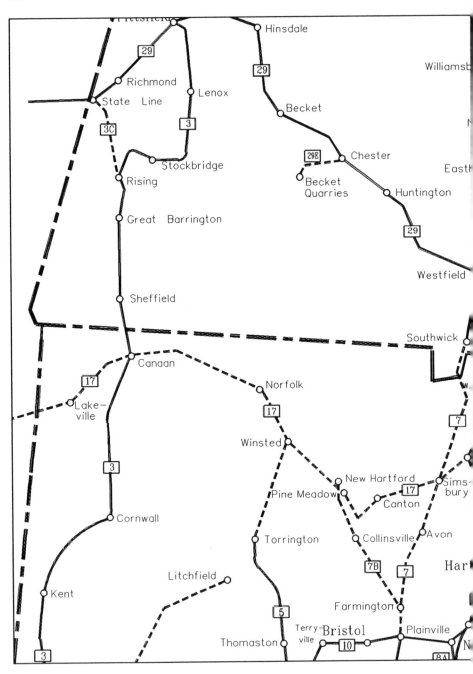

Northwestern Connecticut/Western Massachusetts

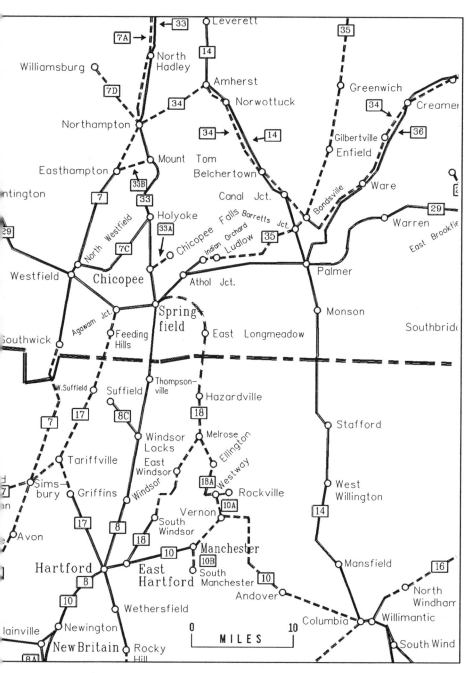

Central Connecticut/South Central Massachusetts

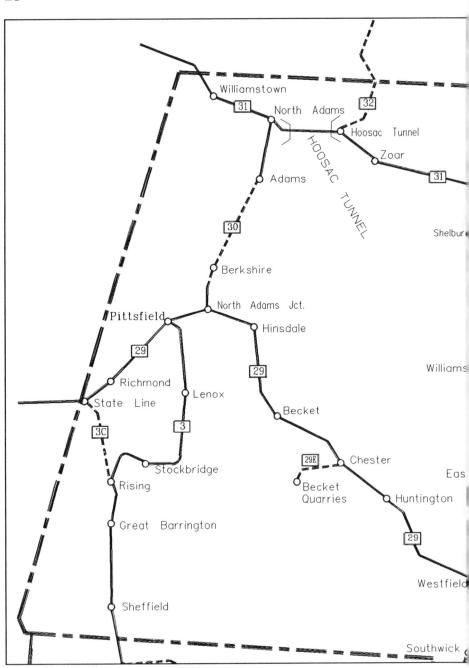

Western Massachusetts

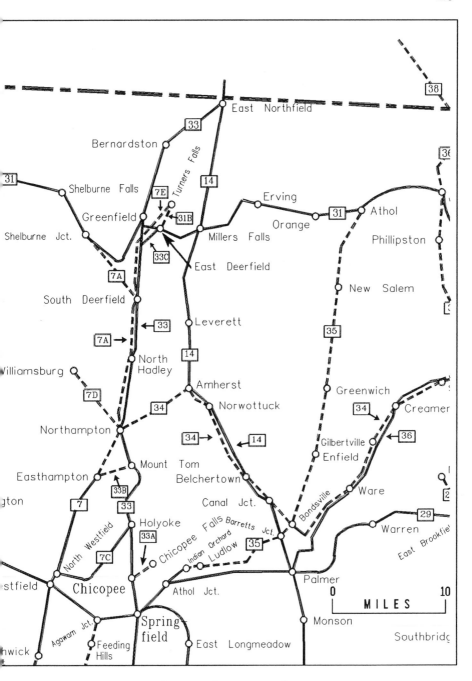

West Central Massachusetts

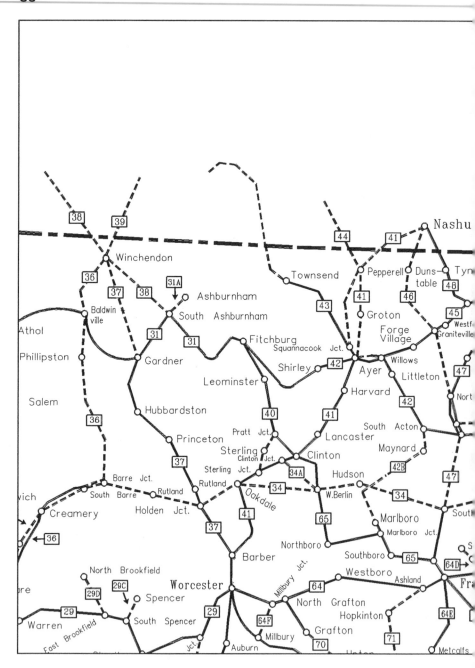

North Central Masschusetts

Northeastern Massachusetts

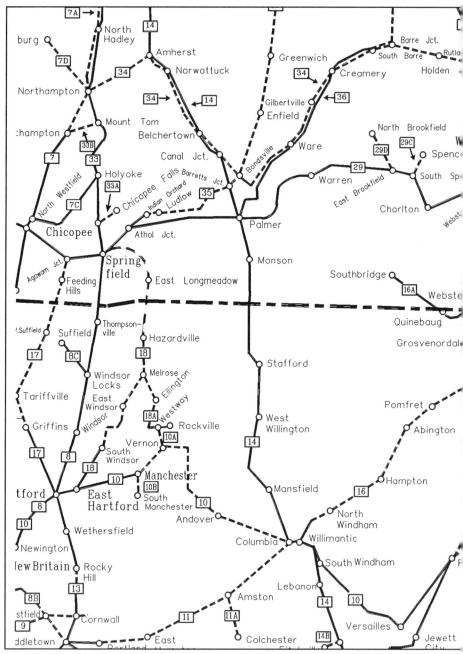

South Central Massachusetts/North Central Connecticut

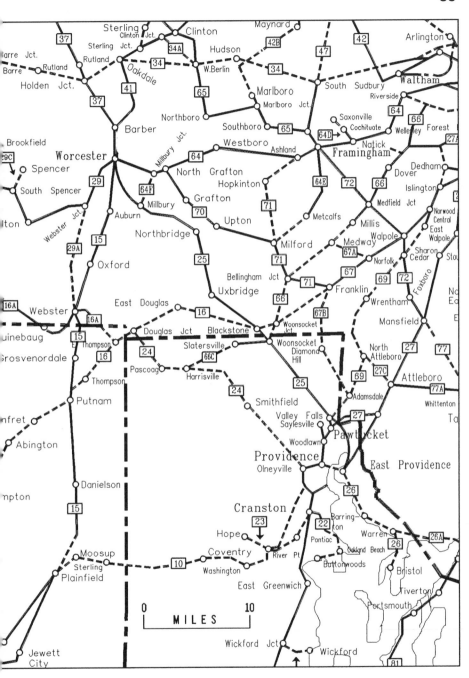

Southeastern Massachusetts/Northern Rhode Island

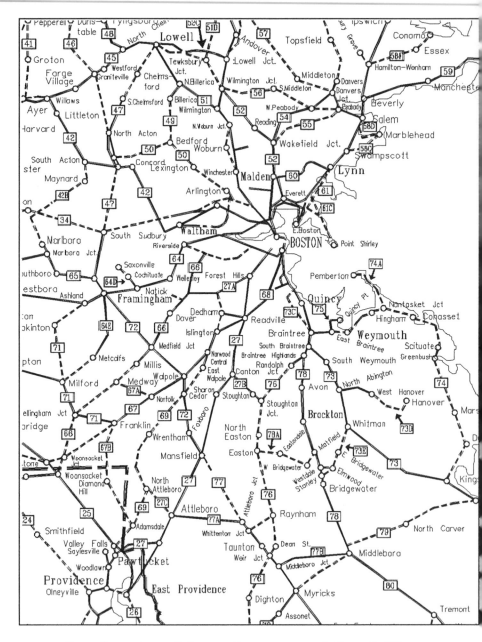

Southeastern Massachusetts and South Shore

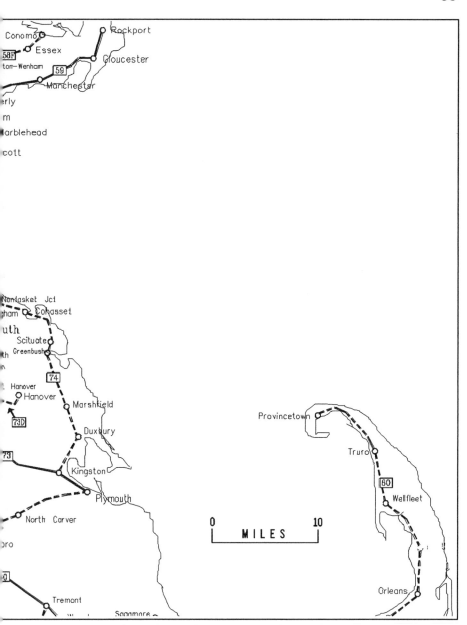

Outer Cape Cod, Massachusetts

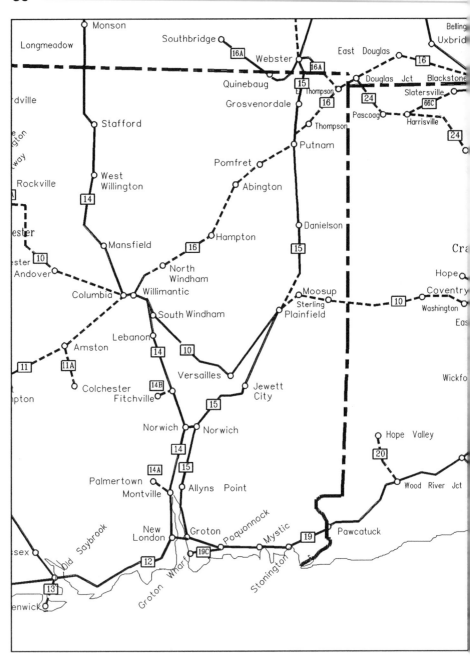

Eastern Connecticut

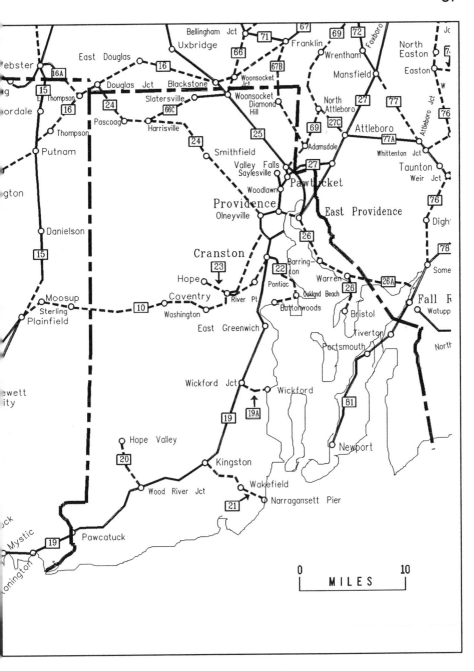

Rhode Island

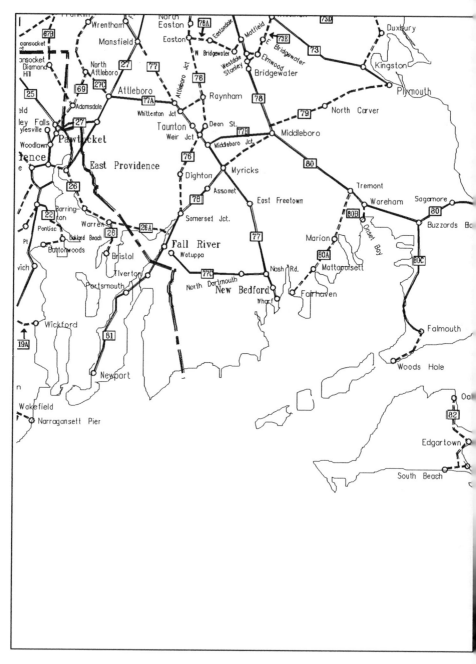

Southeastern Massachusetts

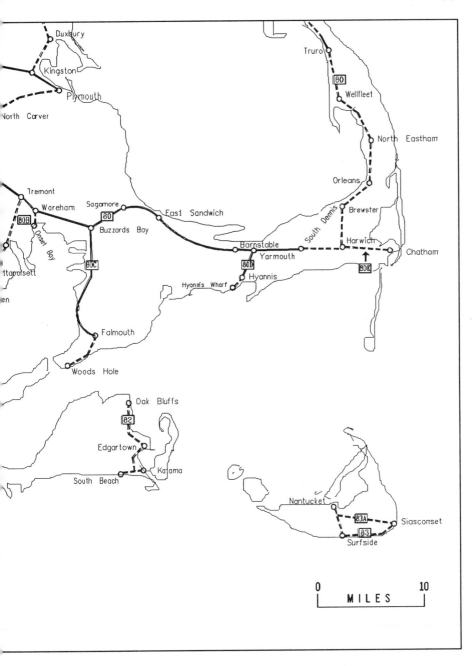

Cape Cod and the Islands, Massachusetts

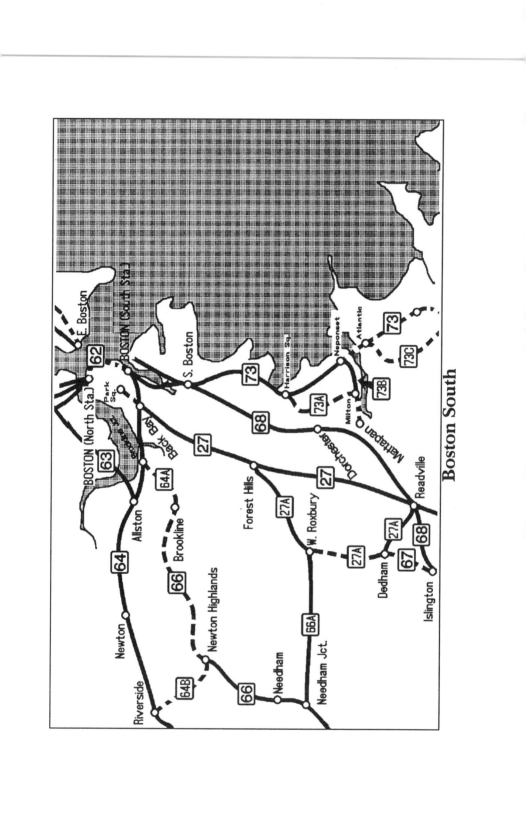

Boston South

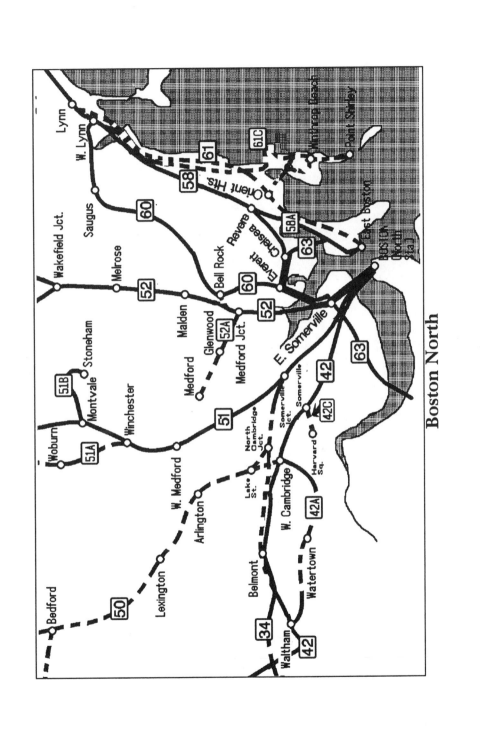

Boston North

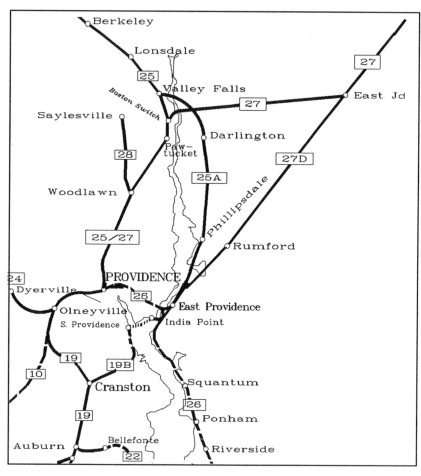

Providence, R.I.

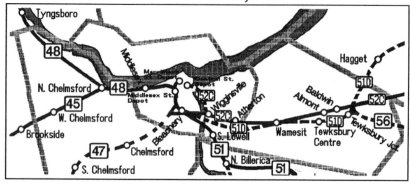

Lowell, Mass.

Abbreviations

B&A	Boston & Albany Railroad
B&M	Boston & Maine Railroad
ca.	circa
CV	Central Vermont Railway
I.C.C.	U.S. Interstate Commerce Commission
Jct.	Junction
MBTA	Massachusetts Bay Transportation Authority
MTA	Metropolitan Transit Authority
NY&NE	New York & New England Railroad
NYNH&H	New York, New Haven & Hartford Railroad
RDC	Rail Diesel Car
RR	Railroad
RY	Railway
USRA	United States Railway Association

1. New York & New Haven

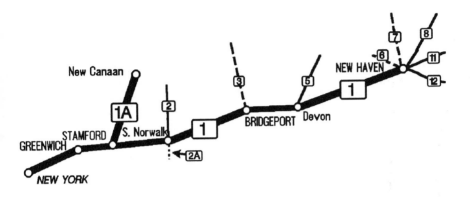

0 *New York, NY (Grand Central)*	39 Rowayton (Five Mile River)	67 Woodmont
28 Greenwich, CT	41 South Norwalk (Norwalk)	70 West Haven
29.5 Cos Cob (Cos Cob Bridge)	42 East Norwalk	72 New Haven, CT
30 Riverside	44 Westport (and Saugatuck)	**1A. New Canaan Branch**
31 Old Greenwich (Sound Beach)	47 Greens Farms	
33 Stamford	49 Southport	0 Stamford, CT
35 Glenbrook (Glen Brook)	51 Fairfield	2 Glenbrook
37 Noroton Heights (Noroton)	56 Bridgeport	3 Springdale
38 Darien	59 Stratford	4 Springdale Cemetery
	61 Devon (Naugatuck Jct.)	5 Woodway
	63 Milford	6 Talmadge Hill
		8 New Canaan, CT

BUILT: 1847-49; New Canaan Branch, 1868.

OPERATORS: *New York & New Haven, 1849-72; New York, New Haven & Hartford, 1872-1968; Penn Central, 1969-76; Conrail (freight), 1976- ; Amtrak (intercity passenger), 1971- ; Metro North (commuter passenger), 1983- . Providence & Worcester (overhead freight), 1993- .*

DAILY PASSENGER TRAINS: *1869:* 20, *1893:* 57, *1919:* 62, *1935:* 69, *1950:* 79, *1960:* 75, *1971:* 67, *1981:* 70, *1994:* 90.

In May 1973 a veteran GG1 locomotive is hitched onto a southbound Amtrak train at New Haven station.

ABANDONMENTS: None.

The busiest rail line in New England was not among the pioneer railroads of the region. The New York & New Haven RR received its charter in 1844, nearly a decade after the first steam railroads began operating in Massachusetts. A rail link between New York and New Haven would face stiff competition from the many steamship lines that plied the sheltered waters of Long Island Sound. The Connecticut shore was marked by frequent inlets and rivers that a prospective railroad would have to bridge. But as rail transportation began to prove itself, the potential traffic for this line was too much to resist. Among the promoters who finally launched the road were New York capitalists Robert and George L. Schuyler, Anson G. Phelps, and Elihu Thompson, who raised most of the money; Joseph E. Sheffield, New Haven's most prominent businessman and civic leader and the major force behind the New Haven & Northampton RR; and Samuel J. Hitchcock, president of the Hartford & New Haven RR.

With a giant GG1 electric locomotive in the lead, an Amtrak Boston to New York train roars past Norwalk circa 1971. (Photo by Roger Yepsen.)

Yale professor Alexander C. Twining, who plotted the paths of many early New England railroads, surveyed the course. Although inland routes had sometimes been proposed, Twining located the railroad along the shoreline, despite the numerous bridges that would be required. The route extended from New Haven to William's Bridge, in the Bronx, where connection was made with the New York & Harlem RR. Contractors, George Schuyler, Sidney J. Miller, and Alfred Bishop, began construction in September 1847. The entire line was opened in January 1849, although full freight service was not provided until several years later.

The original line was hastily built, and as traffic increased, it was continually reconstructed. The NY&NH opened as a single track road throughout. A second track was installed in 1854. The NY&NH became the funnel through which nearly all New York-bound traffic out of New England eventually passed. Other lines came under its sway: the New Haven & Northampton was leased in 1848, even before the NY&NH was completed. In 1870 its operations were coordinated with its long-time link to Boston, the Hartford & New Haven. Two years later the two merged to form the New York, New Haven & Hartford, the nucleus of southern New England's greatest rail system.

In 1866, an independent line, the New Canaan RR, was chartered, and in July 1868, it was opened from Stamford on the NY&NH, eight miles to New Canaan. This short line went bankrupt in 1879 and was reorganized in May 1883 as the Stamford & New Canaan RR. The NYNH&H leased it six months later, and it has been operated ever since as a branch of the NY&NH.

The most dramatic incident in the early history of the NY&NH occurred on May 6, 1853, when an eastbound express train ran off an open swing drawbridge at South Norwalk and plunged into the Norwalk River. Forty six people died in the wreck, by far the most serious rail accident in the United States to that time, and to this day the worst rail disaster in New England. Other notable accidents on the NY&NH occurred early in the twentieth century as the NY&NH began to suffer from overexpansion and mismanagement: excessive speed at interlockings caused derailments at Bridgeport, in which fourteen died, July 11, 1911, and at Westport, October 3, 1912, which saw seven perish; a collision at Stamford, June 12, 1913, killed six, and another at Milford, February 22, 1916, took ten more lives.

Throughout the nineteenth century various promoters attempted to construct lines parallel to the NY&NH, but the railroad managed to quash all such schemes. As a result, the New York-New Haven segment was the only major route in New England with but a single rail line. Thus nearly every famous train in southern New England has traversed this route: the *Merchant's Limited*, the *White Train*, the *Yankee Clipper*, the *Federal*, the *Montrealer/Washingtonian*, and the rest. Traffic over the NY&NH became so great that in the 1890s third and fourth tracks were added and all grade crossings, except in Bridgeport, were eliminated.

In 1899, the NYNH&H strung trolley wire over the tracks of the New Canaan branch and substituted electric streetcars for steam locomotive-hauled trains, a prelude to full scale electrification of the NY&NH. In 1903, the New York State Legislature outlawed the use of steam locomotives on Manhattan Island after July 1, 1903, which prompted the NYNH&H to undertake a massive electrification project. The railroad adopted an overhead 11,000-volt, 25-cycle single-phase system, with locomotives and self-propelled cars drawing current from catenary wires. Since local generating capacity was inadequate, the railroad built its own generator station at Cos Cob. The first segment, New York City-Cos Cob, was completed in April 1907, and the second, from Cos Cob to Stamford—then the terminus of most New York-bound commuter trains—was ready in October. In June, 1914, the electrification was extended to New Haven. The New Canaan branch was restrung with 11,000-volt catenary in 1908 and operated as an extension of the New York to New Haven main line.

Even before electrification the NY&NH was one of the nation's busiest commuter lines. Traffic continued to climb. By the 1920s western Fairfield County had become an elite suburban extension of New York City. Ridership on these trains peaked in the late 1920s, declined during the depression years, and rose to a new high during the war. After the Second World War the suburbs beyond Stamford—Darien, Westport, Fairfield, and the rest—also grew rapidly. Despite the post-war suburban boom, however, passenger counts fell, particularly following the opening of the parallel Connecticut Turnpike. Meanwhile, as the New Haven slid toward its second bankruptcy (which finally occurred in 1961), both commuter and long-distance passenger service deteriorated.

A southbound Amtrak express crosses the Saugatuck River on a lift bridge circa 1971. (Photo by Roger Yepsen.)

Relief did not come until the early 1970s. In 1969, the long-bankrupt New Haven was merged into the Penn Central, only to see that line in turn file for bankruptcy a year later. The Penn Central's failure spurred both federal and state lawmakers into action. In January 1971, the state of Connecticut, in conjunction with the state of New York, leased the NY&NH and hired the Penn Central to operate commuter service. The state purchased new self-propelled cars, the first of which entered service in 1973. Meanwhile, through passenger service had been taken over by Amtrak in 1971, and the NY&NH became an integral part of Amtrak's busy Boston-Washington Northeast Corridor. In 1976, Conrail, the successor to the Penn Central, assumed operation of the commuter trains; in January 1983 the Metro-North Commuter RR took over from Conrail.

Freight has always been secondary to passengers on the NY&NH. Still, the route has seen heavy freight traffic, and after electrification electric locomotives hauled long drags down from New England to the

The NY&NH main line once carried heavy freight traffic, as shown in this First World War-era view (collection of author).

docks in Brooklyn. After the Penn Central merger, however, diesels took over from electrics and through traffic was diverted to other routes. Particularly west of Devon, through freights were seldom seen by the early 1970s. In 1976, Conrail became the operator of freight service on the NY&NH. The Providence & Western obtained trackage rights in 1993 between New Haven and Devon to reach Derby and Danbury. In 1986 Amtrak converted the NY&NH from 11,000 to 12,500 volt, 60 cycle electric power and the old Cos Cob generating station was abandoned.

Sources: Baker, *Formation*, 71-75, 80-85; Grow, *On the 8:02*, 61-75; Harlow, *Steelways*, 180-81; Kirkland, *Men, Cities, and Transportation*, 1:258-65; 2:106; Middleton, *When the Steam Railways Electrified*, 428-29; Poor, *History*, 210; *Poor's Railroad Manual*, 1890, 55; Shaw, *History of Railroad Accidents*, 189-92, 297-98; Turner and Jacobus, *Connecticut Railroads*, 25-34, 203-300; Weller, *New Haven Railroad*.

2. Danbury & Norwalk

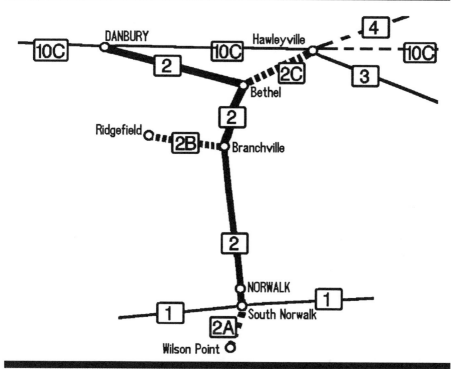

0	South Norwalk (Norwalk), CT	
0.5	Dock	
1	Norwalk	
1.5	Wall St.	
2	Catherine St. (Fair Grounds)	
3	Winnipauk (Winnepauk)	
3.5	Merritt 7	
4	Norwalk Mills	
5	Kent Rd. (South Wilton) (Hopkins) (Kent)	
7.5	Wilton	
9	Cannondale (Cannon) (Cannons)	
12	Georgetown	
13	Branchville (Ridgefield)	
14	Couchs	
15	Topstone (Sanford) (Sanfords)	
17	Redding	
21	Bethel	
22	East Danbury	
24	Danbury, CT	

2A. Wilsons Point Branch

0	South Norwalk, CT
3	Wilsons Point (Wilson Point), CT

2B. Ridgefield Branch

0	Branchville, CT
1	Florida
2	Cooper
4	Ridgefield, CT

2C. Hawleyville Branch

0	Bethel, CT
6	Hawleyville, CT

BUILT: 1851-52.

OPERATORS: *Danbury & Norwalk,* 1852-86; *Housatonic,* 1886-92; *New York, New Haven & Hartford,* 1892-1968; *Penn Central,* 1969-76; *Conrail,* 1976-93; *Metro-North (passenger),* 1983- ; *Providence & Worcester (freight),* 1993- .

DAILY PASSENGER TRAINS: *1869:* 7, *1893:* 13, *1919:* 19, *1935:* 8, *1950:* 12, *1960:* 10, *1971:* 14, *1981:* 14, *1994:* 18. Passenger service ended on Wilsons Point branch 1894; Hawleyville branch, 1907 or 1908; Ridgefield branch, 1925.

ABANDONMENTS: Hawleyville branch, 1911; Ridgefield branch, 1964; Wilsons Point branch, 1938, 1972.

Danbury interests chartered the Fairfield County RR in 1835 from Danbury to Norwalk or Fairfield. Although a route was surveyed, this road was never constructed, and in 1849 its charter was regranted to the Danbury & Norwalk RR. Construction began in 1851 and was completed between its namesake cities in February 1852.

After more than three decades of successful independent operation the D&N was leased to the Housatonic RR in 1886. Six years later, when the Housatonic was swallowed by the New Haven, the D&N

In 1971 a Danbury-to-Norwalk commuter train passes Cannondale station in the town of Wilton. (Photo by Roger Yepsen)

Bethel station as it appeared in July 1971.

became an integral part of the New Haven system. Freight was secondary to frequent commuter passenger service. Until 1971 through passenger trains from New York City to Pittsfield, Mass., were run over this route, bypassing the Housatonic's original Bridgeport-Danbury line which ultimately was abandoned.

In 1925 the New Haven electrified the D&N, using the same 11,000-volt a.c. catenary system employed on the NY&NH's New York-New Haven line. The wires were removed in 1961. In recent years commuter service to New York has generally used locomotive-hauled trains, some running through to Grand Central Terminal.

The D&N passed to the Penn Central in 1969 along with the rest of the New Haven system. Conrail assumed operation of the line under subsidies in 1976 and provided freight and passenger service until 1983 when the Metro-North Commuter RR took over operation of the commuter trains. Conrail continued to provide freight service under contract to the Connecticut Department of Transportation, who now owned the line. During the 1980s Conrail operated one daily local

Danbury-South Norwalk freight. In 1993 the Providence & Worcester RR replaced Conrail as freight service provider.

In July 1884 the D&N extended its tracks southward from South Norwalk to Wilsons Point on Long Island Sound, reputed one of the finest harbors on Long Island Sound. In conjunction with the New York & New England RR the D&N now formed part of a through route from Boston to New York City, with freight cars departing on barges from Wilsons Point to terminals in New York, Oyster Bay, Long Island, and even New Jersey. Traffic over this route halted abruptly in 1892 when the New Haven took over the D&N, and the Wilsons Point branch was used only for local freight service. The last remnent of this branch was given up in 1972.

The D&N constructed two other short branches: a four-mile line to Ridgefield, opened in June 1870 and abandoned in 1964; and a six-mile extension to Hawleyville, completed in July 1872. The latter line was built in conjunction with the Shepaug RR to enable Shepaug trains to reach Norwalk. After 1884 it was also used by Boston-Wilsons Point through trains. With the end of this service in 1892 the branch was little more than an extension of the Shepaug, to whom the New Haven leased it from 1892 to 1897. Around 1908, ten years after the New Haven acquired the Shepaug, Litchfield-to-Norwalk trains were rerouted via Danbury and the Hawleyville branch was taken out of service. The New Haven did not get around to formally abandoning the line until 1911; even so, it was one of the earliest abandonments of the New Haven system.

Sources: Baker, *Formation*, 72, 89-91; Cornwall, "Danbury & Norwalk"; Gladulich, "Exploring Metro-North"; Harlow, *Steelways*, 177-78; Kirkland, *Men, Cities, and Transportation*, 2:98; Turner and Jacobus, *Connecticut Railroads*, 100-03; Woodworth, "Shepaug, Litchfield & Northern"; 224 I.C.C. 227.

3. Housatonic

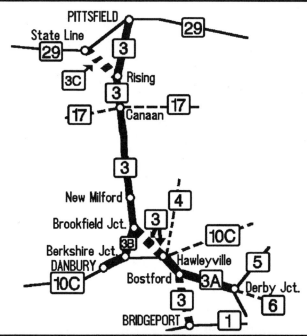

3A. Derby Branch	3B. Danbury Branch	3C. State Line Branch
0 Botsford, CT	0 Brookfield Jct., CT	
2 Monroe	2 Stearns	0 Rising, MA
5 Stevenson	3 Berkshire Jct.	5 Gross
13 Shelton	4 Danbury, CT	7 West Stockbridge
14 Derby Jct., CT		11 State Line, MA

BUILT: 1837-50; State Line Branch, 1841-43; Danbury Branch, 1874; Derby Branch, 1888.

OPERATORS: *Housatonic,* 1842-92; *New York, New Haven & Hartford,* 1892-1968; *Penn Central,* 1969-76; *Conrail,* 1976-93; *Boston & Maine,* 1982-83; *Guilford,* 1983-91; *Housatonic,* 1984- ; *Providence & Worcester,* 1993- .

DAILY PASSENGER TRAINS: *1869:* 4, *1893:* 8, *1919:* 4, *1935:* 4, *1950:* 4, *1960:* 4, *1971:* A single weekly train, northbound Fridays and southbound Sundays. Passenger service ended April 30, 1971. Service between Hawleyville and Bridgeport ended in 1931 or 1932. State Line Branch service ended 1928; Derby Branch, 1925. Some excursion trains since 1971.

ABANDONMENTS: Bridgeport-Stepney, Brookfield Jct.-Hobarts, 1940; Stepney-Botsford, 1963; New Milford-Canaan, 1976 (restored to service 1984); State Line Branch (State Line-West Stockbridge, 1961; West Stockbridge-Rising, 1964).

In 1836 the Connecticut legislature issued a charter to the "Ousatonic RR" to build southward from the Massachusetts line to a terminal on Long Island Sound, following the route of a canal proposed in the 1820s. The rail line was intended to tap the marble and granite quarries and the iron, lime, and clay works along the route, as well as through traffic.

Bridgeport interests gained control and secured for their city the southern terminus. Alfred Bishop of Bridgeport became the road's contractor and builder, and the city itself subscribed to stock. Roswell B. Mason—later mayor of Chicago—surveyed the route. Construction began in 1837, was completed between Bridgeport and New Milford (including a tunnel at Hawleyville) by 1840, and opened from Bridgeport to the state line in December 1842.

In 1837 the Housatonic's owners obtained a Massachusetts charter to build the Berkshire RR to extend the Housatonic northward to West Stockbridge. Here the line would link up with the four-mile West Stockbridge RR (chartered in 1836, completed 1838) to reach the New York border, where it met the Hudson & Berkshire RR and the new

Western RR, which continued on via a New York-chartered subsidiary to the Hudson River. Work on the Berkshire RR began in February 1841, and the line opened simultaneously with the Housatonic less than two years later. In 1843 the Housatonic leased both the Berkshire and the West Stockbridge.

The Housatonic formed part of the first all-rail line from New York to Albany, as well as part of a route to Boston via the Western. In 1847 the Housatonic obtained a charter to build the Stockbridge & Pittsfield RR to reach Pittsfield (on the Western). Started in 1848, this line was completed in January 1850. The Housatonic leased the new line even before it was opened, and the route immediately became part of its passenger main line, the segment from Rising to West Stockbridge and State Line now becoming primarily a freight cutoff.

In its early years the Housatonic faced financial difficulty, much of which fell on the taxpayers of Bridgeport. By the late 1860s, however, the railroad was shipping 100,000 quarts of milk a day to New York City, and the line was moderately profitable. New feeder lines brought traffic, and the Housatonic grew by absorbing other short railroads. After years of competition the New Haven RR took over the Housatonic in 1892, the line becoming that railroad's Berkshire division.

Following the merger, the New Haven reduced parts of the Housatonic main line to branches and upgraded former secondary routes to main lines. In 1921 the New Haven rerouted all New York to Pittsfield trains via the Danbury & Norwalk and the Danbury Branch, and discontinued passenger service on the main line between Hawleyville and Brookfield Junction. The main line south of Hawleyville saw local passenger service until late 1931 or 1932, and by 1940 two segments of the old main line—Bridgeport to Stepney and Hawleyville (Hobarts) to Brookfield Junction—had been abandoned. By the time the Penn Central took over the New Haven in 1969 the Housatonic was a minor secondary route. Through freight trains had stopped running early in the 1960s and passenger service had dwindled to a single weekend round trip before ending altogether in 1971. By 1973 even local freight service had virtually ceased on much of the line: less than one train a week worked the segment between New Milford and Canaan.

When the Penn Central ceased operating its rail lines in 1976 Conrail took over the Housatonic. The thirty-five-mile segment be-

One of the landmarks of New England railroading, the Canaan, Conn., depot is located where the Connecticut Western crossed the Housatonic (July 1990, looking north).

tween New Milford and Canaan was abandoned (with the tracks remaining in place), despite attempts to establish a short line railroad to operate it. In 1982 the Boston & Maine took over operation of the Canaan-Pittsfield segment, while Conrail continued to operate the line south of New Milford.

Two years later a newly formed Housatonic RR leased the abandoned trackage between Canaan and Boardmans Bridge (just north of New Milford) from the state of Connecticut. The line was reopened first for seasonal tourist excursion service and then in 1989 for freight, interchanging at Boardmans Bridge with Conrail. Meanwhile the hard-nosed labor policies of Guilford Transportation, which had succeeded the B&M as operators of the old Housatonic north of Canaan, had provoked a series of strikes which shut down the line for a time. By the time the line reopened most customers were gone and service fell to one train a week. Thus in January 1991 Guilford was quite ready to yield to the Housatonic.

At the end of 1992 the new Housatonic expanded once more, obtaining from Conrail the remainder of the old Housatonic into

Danbury. For the first time in 30 years through freight trains appeared on the Housatonic. Today the largest customer on the line is a paper mill at New Milford.

In addition to the State Line branch the Housatonic had two other branches. In 1864 the New York, Housatonic & Northern RR was chartered to build from Brookfield to White Plains, N.Y. The first five miles of the line between Brookfield (Brookfield Junction) and Danbury were opened in September 1868. The line was always operated by the Housatonic, which leased the line in 1872 and formally absorbed it in 1882. In the twentieth century this became part of the main line.

In 1887 the Housatonic gained control of the New Haven & Derby RR by purchasing the interest of the city of New Haven in that short line. The sale was conditional on the Housatonic building a link between itself and the New Haven & Derby, terms with which the Housatonic lost no time complying. In November 1888 the Housatonic Valley RR opened between Botsford and Derby Junction, under control of the Housatonic.

After the New Haven takeover this new branch formed part of the through route to the west via the Poughkeepsie Bridge over the Hudson River to Maybrook, N.Y. (The New Haven, however, preferred using the Naugatuck RR via Bridgeport instead of the New Haven & Derby). This remained a major freight route until May 8, 1974, when fire severely damaged the bridge at Poughkeepsie. (The bridge remains standing but has not been used since the fire.) Through freights no longer used the route, but local traffic on this double-tracked line remained heavy into the 1980s. Flood damage at Derby in 1982 severed this line for several years, but the route was reopened in November 1988, and direct freight service between New Haven and Selkirk Yard (south of Albany, N.Y.) for a time resumed. The new Housatonic RR obtained control over this branch in 1992 with Conrail retaining trackage rights to reach the Tilcon asphalt plant in Danbury. In 1993 these rights passed to the Providence & Worcester.

Sources: Baker, *Formation*, 62-63, 72-73, 89-93; Harlow, *Steelways*, 178-80; Kirkland, *Men, Cities, and Transportation*, I:240-42; Patch, "Housatonic Railroad Story"; Schermerhorn and Armstrong, "Housatonic Railroad Story"; Turner and Jacobus, *Connecticut Railroads*, 48-60; U.S. Railway Association, *Preliminary System Plan*, 2:388-89; U.S. Railway Association, *Final System Plan*, 2:38-39; 224 I.C.C. 477; 240 I.C.C. 129.

4. Shepaug

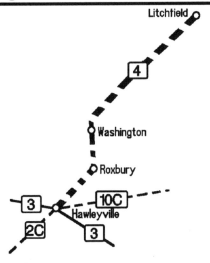

0 Hawleyville, CT	12 Roxbury	24 Romford
3 Hanover Springs	15 Judds Bridge	26 Norris
5 Shepaug	17 Valley Sta.	29 Bantam
6 West Shore	19 Washington	30 Lake
8 Roxbury Falls	20 New Preston	32 Litchfield, CT

BUILT: 1870-72.

OPERATORS: *Shepaug Valley,* 1872-73; *Shepaug,* 1873-87; *Shepaug, Litchfield & Northern,* 1887-98; *New York, New Haven & Hartford,* 1898-1948.

DAILY PASSENGER TRAINS: *1893:* 4, *1919:* 5. Passenger service ended 1930.

ABANDONMENT: Entire line, 1948.

The Shepaug Valley RR was chartered in 1868, and construction began in October 1870 from Hawleyville. A year later the tracks reached Roxbury, and by this time building crews were at work south from Litchfield. The job was completed in January 1872. Traversing the typically rugged Connecticut terrain of rural Litchfield County, the twisting path of the Shepaug used thirty-two miles of track to connect points crows would find only twenty-three miles apart. When it first opened the Shepaug Valley connected with the Housatonic RR at

Hawleyville. Six months later the Danbury & Norwalk opened its own branch to Hawleyville, giving the fledgling Shepaug Valley a more direct route to New York City. Even this advantage was not enough to prevent the bondholders from foreclosing on the financially troubled line, and in 1873 the Shepaug Valley RR was reorganized as the Shepaug RR. In the 1880s the Shepaug operated as an independent short line, an increasing rarity in Connecticut. It operated four locomotives, two passenger cars (in the 1890s it even added a parlor car!), three express and baggage cars, forty-two freight cars, and a caboose. Locally owned and operated, its headquarters was in Litchfield, where a third of its directors resided. Milk, ice, marble, iron, granite, and silica formed the bulk of its outgoing traffic.

The beginning of the end of the Shepaug's independence came in 1887 when bondholders once more foreclosed and caused the line to be reorganized a second time as the Shepaug, Litchfield & Northern RR. By the time the New Haven RR finally took over in 1898 Shepaug was one of the last remaining independently operated short lines in the state. It now became the New Haven's Litchfield branch.

For the first few years under New Haven control, little changed except the name on the rolling stock. In 1905, however, direct service was introduced between New York City and Litchfield (discontinued in 1913). In 1908 the New Haven rerouted all traffic between Litchfield and Norwalk via Danbury, allowing the abandonment of the Danbury & Norwalk's Bethel to Hawleyville branch over which this service had previously operated.

Passenger traffic on the Shepaug declined in the 1920s, and the last passenger trains ran in 1930. The increasing substitution of concrete for stone and the growing use of artificial ice reduced freight traffic. In 1937 the New Haven applied to abandon the entire line, but the I.C.C. bowed to complaints from shippers and refused the request. The Commission noted that "the rugged character of the territory has retarded the development of improved highways closely paralleling the branch." Ten years later, however, the New Haven applied once more, citing the expense of rebuilding a trestle across the Housatonic River, and in 1948 it was permitted to abandon the entire line.

Sources: *Chronological History of the New Haven Railroad*; Turner and Jacobus, *Connecticut's Railroads*, 111-12; Woodworth, "Shepaug, Litchfield & Northern"; 228 I.C.C. 415.

5. Naugatuck

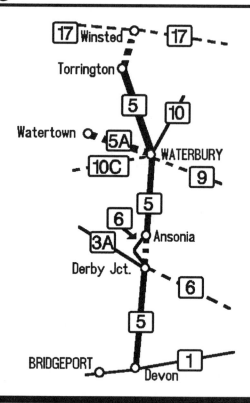

0 Devon (Naugatuck Jct.), CT	27 Waterbury (Freight St. Jct.)	47 Torrington (Wolcottville)
2 Baldwins	27.5 Highland Jct. (Watertown Jct.)	52 Burrville
7.5 Turkey Brook		56 Winsted, CT
8 Derby Jct.	30 Waterville	
9 Derby	33 Jericho	**5A. Watertown Branch**
11 Ansonia	34 Reynolds Bridge	
15 Seymour	36 Thomaston (Plymouth)	0 Highland Jct. (Watertown Jct.), CT
16 North Seymour (Rimmon)	39 Fluteville	1 Browns
18 Beacon Falls	41 Campville (Camps Mills)	2 Oakville
22 Naugatuck		3 Weltons
23 Union City	44 East Litchfield (Litchfield)	5 Watertown, CT
24 Platts Mills		
26 Bank St. Jct.		

BUILT: 1848-49; Watertown Branch, 1870.

OPERATORS: *Naugatuck,* 1849-87; *New York, New Haven & Hartford,* 1887-1968; *Penn Central,* 1969-76; *Conrail,* 1976-93; *Boston & Maine (freight),* 1982-83; *Guilford (freight),* 1983- ; *Metro North (passenger),* 1983- ; *Providence & Worcester (freight),* 1993- .

DAILY PASSENGER TRAINS: *1869:* 6 (Devon-Waterbury, 8), *1893:* 10 (Devon-Waterbury, 13), *1919:* 9 (Devon-Waterbury, 15), *1935:* 4 (Devon-Waterbury, 12) *1950:* 4 (Devon-Waterbury, 12) *1960:* 8 (Devon-Waterbury), *1971:* 8 (Devon-Waterbury), *1981:* 8 (Devon-Waterbury), *1994:* 12 (Devon-Waterbury). Passenger service Waterbury-Winsted ended 1958; Watertown Branch, ca. 1925.

ABANDONMENTS: Derby Jct.-Ansonia, ca. 1912?; Torrington-Winsted, 1963; Watertown Branch, 1973.

Bridgeport's Alfred Bishop, the builder of the Housatonic RR, was also responsible for the Naugatuck. In 1845 Bishop obtained a charter to build a line from Long Island Sound northward through the Naugatuck River valley. The towns of this valley, from Derby to Winsted, already were thriving industrial centers, specializing in the production of brass and metal goods. Bishop was able to convince the towns and businesses along the route to support the project, although New Haven balked at subscribing to the $75,000 worth of stock that Bishop demanded if the latter city were to be the line's southern terminal. Instead the line began at Naugatuck Junction (later Devon) on the New York & New Haven RR five miles east of Bridgeport.

Construction did not begin until April 1848. The railroad required considerable engineering skill, since the line crossed the river at several points, flooding occurred frequently, and the river banks were rugged and rocky. The line was completed from Naugatuck Junction (later Devon) to Seymour in May 1849; from Seymour to Waterbury in June; and from Waterbury to Winsted in September. Trackage rights over the New York & New Haven from Naugatuck Junction to Bridgeport enabled the Naugatuck to reach that city, which has ever since served as its de facto southern terminal.

Unlike the Housatonic, the Naugatuck carried little through traffic. Even so, the line thrived, thanks to freight traffic generated by the industrial towns it served. The Naugatuck prospered under successful independent operation for nearly forty years until leased by the New Haven RR in April 1887. After consolidation, part of the Naugatuck main line along the south bank of the Naugatuck from Derby Junction to Ansonia was rerouted over the parallel route of the New Haven & Derby along the north bank. The original Naugatuck main line was downgraded to an industrial spur and gradually abandoned. Flood control projects have since obliterated nearly all signs of this railroad.

The Naugatuck was operated by the New Haven until 1969. Passenger service north of Waterbury ended in 1958, and the segment from Torrington to Winsted was abandoned in 1963. The Penn Central took over operation of the remaining freight and passenger service in 1969. At this time the only portion of the Naugatuck to see substantial freight traffic was the first eight miles of the route from Devon to Derby Junction, this being part of the through route to the West via the Poughkeepsie Bridge. The rest of the line was served by a daily freight. The burning of the Poughkeepsie Bridge on May 8, 1974, permanently closed that through route to the west. Penn Central turned the line over to Conrail in 1976. In 1982 the Boston & Maine assumed operation of freight service on the Naugatuck north of Derby Junction, and the following year passenger service was transferred to the Metro-North Commuter RR, under the auspices of the Connecticut Department of Transportation. In 1993 the Providence & Worcester RR took over freight operations from Conrail between Devon and Derby Junction.

By the 1970s passenger service over the Naugatuck had been cut to four daily round trip passenger trains between Bridgeport and Waterbury, usually self-propelled RDC cars. From June to December 1982 the line was out of service due to flood damage. Recently the old RDC cars have been replaced by modern Metro-North push-pull units, and service has been boosted to six daily round trips, the highest number of trains to operate on this line since 1956.

The branch to Watertown was chartered in 1869 as the Watertown & Waterbury RR and opened in the fall of 1870. The Naugatuck immediately leased and operated the line, and it afterwards remained a branch of the Naugatuck. Passneger service ended in the mid-1920s. It was abandoned by the Penn Central in 1973.

Sources: Baker, *Formation*, 71-73, 89; Harlow, *Steelways*, 183-84; Kirkland, *Men, Cities, and Transportation*, 1:241; Turner and Jacobus, *Connecticut Railroads*, 88-98; 228 I.C.C. 117.

6. New Haven & Derby

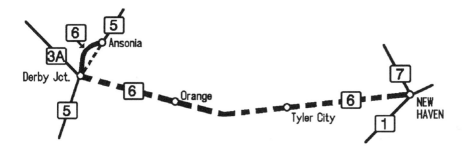

0 New Haven, CT	10 Derby Jct.	13 Ansonia, CT
2 West Haven	11 Derby-Shelton	
5 Tyler City	(Birmingham)	
7 Orange	(Derby)	

BUILT: 1868-71.

OPERATORS: *New Haven & Derby*, 1871-89; *Housatonic*, 1889-92; *New York, New Haven & Hartford*, 1892-1968; *Penn Central*, 1969-76; *Conrail*, 1976-82; *Boston & Maine*, 1982-83; *Guilford*, 1983- ; *Metro North (commuter passenger)*, 1983- .

DAILY PASSENGER TRAINS: *1893:* 15, *1919:* 4, *1935:* 12 (Derby Jct.-Ansonia), *1950:* 6 (Derby Jct.-Ansonia), *1960:* 8 (Derby Jct.-Ansonia), *1971:* 8 (Derby Jct.-Ansonia), *1981:* 8 (Derby Jct.-Ansonia), *1994:* 12 (Derby Jct.-Ansonia). Passenger service New Haven-Derby Jct. ended 1925.

ABANDONMENTS: West Haven-Orange, 1938; Orange-Derby Jct., 1941.

New Haven interests secured a charter for the New Haven & Derby RR in 1864, but the project did not get underway until 1867 when the city government was persuaded to purchase the majority of its stock. Its promoters hoped that this short line would enable New Haven to tap the rich traffic of the Naugatuck at Derby Junction and divert some of it away from Bridgeport. Furthermore, it was intended that the line would eventually be extended westward to a connection with the Erie

RR by way of a Hudson River bridge. Neither of these goals was realized.

Construction of the NH&D began in 1868 and the line was opened in August 1871. Although the route was short, the country was rugged and the line twisting. The intended traffic never materialized and the NH&D responded by undercutting the rates of the Naugatuck. The latter railroad reached a pooling agreement with the NH&D in 1879 which ended the competition. but when the New Haven RR leased the Naugatuck in 1887, the NH&D was once more on its own. Its owners, the city of New Haven, put the line out for bids. The New Haven offered $300,000, the Housatonic, $275,000. The city accepted the latter's low bid because the Housatonic promised to build the long-awaited extension west from Derby Junction. The NH&D passed to the Housatonic (a formal lease was signed in 1889) and the branch from

Led by Metro North 801 (an ex-Conrail GEB23-7), a commuter train leaves Derby Jct. for Waterbury in August 1992. The line between Derby Jct. and Ansonia is virtually the only remaining part of the New Haven & Derby.

Derby Junction to the Housatonic main line at Botsford was opened November 1888.

Operation by the Housatonic was brief, since that system was in turn absorbed by the New Haven in 1892. Under the New Haven, the NH&D was another excess line. Passenger service from New Haven to Derby Junction ended in 1925, as well as freight service between Orange and West Haven. In 1937 the New Haven requested permission to abandon the NH&D between West Haven and Derby Junction, but protests from shippers in Orange persuaded the I.C.C. to allow abandonment of only the inactive track between West Haven and Orange. In 1941 shipper objections were unable to prevent the abandonment of the stretch from Orange to Derby Junction.

After the New Haven absorbed both the NH&D and the Naugatuck it found itself with two parallel lines between Derby Junction and Ansonia: the NH&D along the north bank of the Naugatuck River, and the Naugatuck line along the south bank. The New Haven decided to utilize the NH&D as its main line to Waterbury, and downgraded the original Naugatuck route to an industrial spur. Both Guilford freights and Metro North passenger trains still use three miles of the NH&D between Derby Junction and Ansonia. A short portion of the New Haven-West Haven segment also survives as a spur servicing a few industrial customers.

Sources: Baker, *Formation*, 72, 89-91; Turner and Jacobus, *Connecticut Railroads*, 104-110; 224 I.C.C. 235; 228 I.C.C. 117; 247 I.C.C. 41.

7. New Haven & Northampton

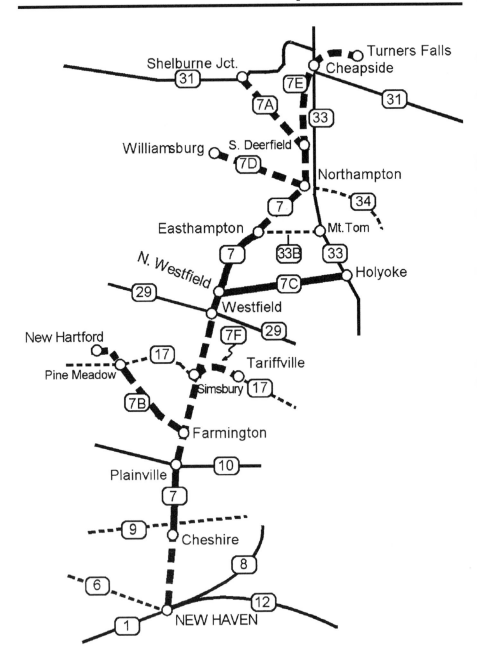

0 New Haven, CT	68 Southampton	1 Ingleside
0.5 Fair St.	72 Easthampton	2 Lanes Quarry
3 Highwood (Stock Yard)	77 Northampton, MA	9 Holyoke, MA
4 Hamden Plains		**7D. Williamsburg Branch**
6 Centerville (Ives)	**7A. Shelburne Falls Extension**	
8 Mount Carmel		
10 Bradleys	0 Northampton, MA	0 Northampton, MA
12 Brooksvale (Brooks)	4 Hatfield	1 Williamsburg Jct.
15 Cheshire	8 Whately	3 Florence
20 Milldale (Hitch-cocks)	12 South Deerfield	5 Leeds
21 Plantsville (South-ington Corners)	16 Conway	7 Haydenville
22 Southington	18 Shelburne Jct. (Conway Jct.), MA	8 Williamsburg, MA
27 Plainville		**7E. Turners Falls Branch**
31 Farmington	**7B. New Hartford Branch**	
37 Avon		0 South Deerfield, MA
40 Weatogue	0 Farmington, CT	4 Deerfield
42 Simsbury	3 Unionville	6 Cheapside
46 Floydville	6 Burlington	8 Montague City
47 Granby, CT	8 Collinsville	9 Turners Falls, MA
53 Congamond, MA	13 Pine Meadow	
55 Southwick	14 New Hartford, CT	**7F. Tariffville Branch**
61 Westfield	**7C. Holyoke Branch**	
62 North Westfield		0 Simsbury, CT
64 Brick Yard	0 North Westfield, MA	3 Tariffville, CT

BUILT: 1847-56; New Hartford Branch, 1849-50, 1870, 1876; Tarriffville Branch, 1849-50; Williamsburg Branch, 1867-68; Holyoke Branch, 1871; Shelburne Falls Extension, 1881; Turners Falls Branch, 1882.

OPERATORS: *New York & New Haven*, 1848-69; *New Haven & Northampton*, 1869-87; *New York, New Haven & Hartford*, 1887-1968; *Penn Central*, 1969-76; *Conrail*, 1976-82; *Boston & Maine*, 1982-83; *Pioneer Valley*, 1982- ; *Guilford*, 1983- .

DAILY PASSENGER TRAINS: *1869: 4, 1893: 8, 1919: 4.* Passenger service ended New Haven-Northampton ca. 1928; New Hartford Branch, ca. 1928; Williamsburg Branch, 1921 or 1922; Turners Falls Branch, 1918 or 1919; Holyoke Branch, 1920 or 1921; Shelburne Falls Extension (Conway-Shelburne Jct., 1917 or 1918; Northampton-Conway, 1918 or 1919).

ABANDONMENTS: Easthampton-Northampton, 1969; Simsbury-Westfield, 1976; Avon-Simsbury, 1981; New Haven-Cheshire, 1987; Plainville-

Avon, 1991. New Hartford Branch (New Hartford-Collinsville, 1956; Collins-ville-Farmington, 1968); Tarriffville Branch, ca. 1869 (then sold to Connecticut Western RR; abandoned 1932); Williamsburg Branch (Williamsburg-Florence, 1962; Florence-Easthampton, 1969); Shelburne Falls Extension (Shelburne Jct.-South Deerfield, 1923; South Deerfield-Northampton, 1943); Turners Falls Branch (Northampton-Cheapside, 1943; Cheapside-Turners Falls, 1985), .

On the fourth of July in 1825, accompanied by a gala parade and lengthy speeches, ground was broken for the Farmington Canal. New Haven interests chartered the canal in 1822 to tap the trade of the upper Connecticut River valley. Despite a passage made difficult by numerous falls, most traffic took the river to Hartford, where it was loaded onto ships that sailed down the rest of the river into Long Island Sound without stopping in New Haven. Benjamin Wright, who had supervised the construction of part of New York's Erie Canal, surveyed the route of the canal northward from New Haven through Plainville and Farmington to the Massachusetts line; the Hurd brothers completed the route to Northampton on the Connecticut River.

The Farmington Canal deliberately bypassed the largest city in its vicinity, Hartford, since the canal was intended to take business away from there. In 1829 the canal was completed north to Farmington, Conn., and in 1835 finally reached Northampton. Unfortunately for its backers in New Haven, the canal—seventy-eight miles, the longest in New England—was a failure. Thanks in part to improvements to navigation on the Connecticut above Hartford, and to the canal's low-budget construction, the anticipated traffic never materialized. The Farmington Canal went bankrupt in 1836 and was reorganized as the New Haven & Northampton Company. The new management proved no more successful than the old, and the canal barely managed to operate into the 1840s. The completion of the Hartford & New Haven RR in 1839 gave New Haven a more practical route to the Connecticut valley.

In the early 1840s the canal came under the influence of Joseph E. Sheffield, the New Haven businessman and civic leader who was at this time promoting the rail link to New York that would become the New York & New Haven RR. Sheffield, its largest stockholder, proposed that the canal be converted into a railroad. Alexander C. Twining surveyed the route and reported that a railroad would be more successful than the canal. In 1846 Connecticut authorized the transformation of the canal company into a railroad, and construction began north from New Haven. Operation of the canal ceased at this time. The rails reached Plainville in December 1847, and the railroad began operating the following month. By March 1850 the line was opened to Granby, just south of the Massachusetts line. Although the railroad generally followed the route of the canal, much of the line between New Haven and Hamden (Centerville) ran alongside or even on the Cheshire Turnpike, which resulted in frequent collisions with road vehicles. This route was not relocated onto its own right of way until 1880.

The ultimate northern terminus of the NH&N had never been decided. The railroad's Connecticut charter did not give it authority to build in Massachusetts, and rival railroads, particularly the parallel Hartford & New Haven, sought to block its entry into the Bay State. Three possible routes were considered: west to Pittsfield, north to Northampton, or northeast to Springfield. At the time of its completion to Granby in 1850, the NH&N also opened branches to Collinsville (in March) and Tariffville (in January), the former aimed at Pittsfield and the latter at Springfield. (The three mile Tariffville branch was abandoned and then transferred to the Connecticut Western RR around 1870 and incorporated into its main line.)

Early in 1848 the New Haven & Northampton was leased to the New York & New Haven, primarily to reinforce the position of the latter road in its dealings with the Hartford & New Haven by giving it potential access of its own to Springfield and to the Western RR, the source of most of the H&NH's traffic. The H&NH soon came to terms and the NY&NH agreed that the NH&N would stop at Granby. But within a few years ostensibly independent companies were formed to extend the NH&N northward. The Farmington Valley RR was chartered in Connecticut to run from Granby to the Massachusetts line, and in 1852 the Massachusetts legislature authorized the Hampden RR to build from the Farmington Valley's terminus to Westfield and the Northampton & Westfield RR into Northampton. The through route from Granby to Northampton opened in July 1856, and the three small railroads, which had merged in 1853 to form the Hampshire & Hamden RR , were taken over by the NH&N.

In 1869 the lease of the NH&N by the NY&NH expired, and the NH&N resumed independent operation. Various branches and extensions were built in hopes of increasing traffic. The Williamsburg branch had opened in February 1868. The Holyoke branch was chartered as the Holyoke & Westfield RR in 1870 and was completed in October 1871. Also in 1870, the branch to Collinsville was extended to Pine Meadow, and six years later to New Hartford. In 1881 the NH&N pushed northward from Northampton, constructing a line alongside the tracks of the Connecticut River RR to Conway Junction (later Shelburne Junction), where connection was made with the Vermont & Massachusetts. The railroad crossed the South River at Conway on a 175-foot steel bridge, purportedly the highest in New England. Trackage rights were secured over the V&M to North Adams via the Hoosac Tunnel, giving the NH&N a gateway to the west and the opportunity to compete with the New Haven. The line was opened to Conway Junction in July 1881, and the branch to Turners Falls the following October. In 1887 these trackage rights ended when the state of Massachusetts sold the Hoosac Tunnel to the Fitchburg RR. As a consolation the NH&N obtained trackage rights between Shelburne Junction and Shelburne Falls.

The New Haven responded to this challenge by buying control of the NH&N—at a cost above market value—from Joseph Sheffield, who had retained ownership of much of the stock. In 1887 it leased the entire NH&N system. As a part of the New Haven, the NH&N was parallelled by other routes, including the New Haven-Hartford-Springfield main line and the Boston & Maine's Springfield-Northampton-Deerfield route. Through passenger service was cut and then eliminated altogether in the late 1920s. Operations on the Shelburne and Turners Falls extension were suspended in 1919 and the Turners Falls extension resumed only in the early 1920s. In 1925 the extension from South Deerfield to Shelburne Junction (Conway Junction) was abandoned. The remainder, from Northampton, was given up in 1943, after being out of service for over a decade. In 1947 the B&M acquired the final four miles of the Turners Falls branch (over which it had obtained trackage rights in 1925), from Cheapside to Turners Falls, and abandoned its own parallel line. The Turners Falls branch survived until October 1981, when operation was discontinued. Formal abandonment came in 1985.

More branches were pruned after the Second World War. The outer end of the New Hartford branch, from Collinsville to New Hartford, was abandoned in 1956; the rest of the line went in 1968. In 1962 the Williamsburg branch was cut back to Florence. The main line from New Haven to Northampton remained intact until 1969 when the Penn Central took over operation of the NH&N from the New Haven. In that year the segment from Easthampton to Northampton was abandoned along with the rest of the Williamsburg branch. The rest of the line saw little traffic, except on the two lines north of Westfield. In 1973 three day a week freight service was provided between New Haven and Simsbury; between Simsbury and Westfield only fifteen trains were run the entire year. A few years later the connection with the Northeast Corridor main line at the south end of the line at Fair Street in New Haven was discontinued when low bridge clearances would not permit the passage of modern boxcars. Henceforth, New Haven customers had to be served by way of Plainville and Cheshire.

In 1974 the U.S. Department of Transportation declared the entire segment from New Haven to Westfield potentially excess trackage. The following year the USRA heard pleas that the line from New Haven to Farmington was needed for emergency rail service in case flooding closed alternative routes, and that traffic justified retention of the Farmington-Simsbury segment. The USRA heeded these rather dubious arguments and ordered all but the portion from Avon to Westfield be included in Conrail. The state of Connecticut agreed to subsidize the operation of freight service from Avon five miles north to Simsbury.

In the 1980s freight service on the Connecticut portion of the NH&N consisted of daily trains operating north and south from Plainville, while the Massachusetts lines out of Westfield saw trains three times a week. In 1982 the Boston & Maine assumed operation of the Connecticut line to Avon (the continuation to Simsbury was abandoned), and the Massachusetts branches were taken over by the Pioneer Valley RR, a new short line controlled by the Pinsly Company. In 1991 the B&M abandoned eight miles from Plainville to Avon. The lower portion of the main line from New Haven north to Cheshire, saw its last trains in the early 1980s and was abandoned in 1987.

Sources: Baker, *Formation*, 72-8; Harlow, *Steelways*, 181-83; Kirkland, *Men, Cities, and Transportation*, 1:237-39; Kistler, *Rise of Railroads*, 18-25, 142-44; Lee, "More North of Northampton"; Lee, "North of Northampton"; Stanford, *Lines of the New York, New Haven and Hartford*; Turner and Jacobus, *Connecticut Railroads*, 60-66; 82 I.C.C. 45.

8. Hartford & New Haven

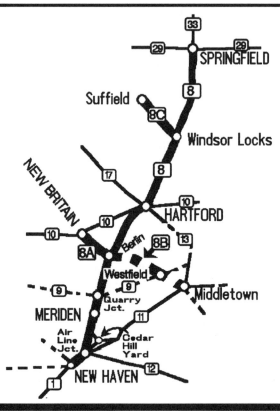

8C. Suffield Branch	1 Woods	4 South St.
0 Windsor Locks, CT	2 Boston Neck	5 Suffield, CT
	3 Airport Switch	

BUILT: 1836-44; Middletown Branch, 1848; New Britain Branch, 1865; Suffield Branch, 1870.

OPERATORS: *Hartford & New Haven,* 1838-72; *New York, New Haven & Hartford,* 1872-1968; *Penn Central,* 1969-76; *Conrail,* 1976- ;*Amtrak (passenger),* 1971- ; *Boston & Maine,* 1982-83; *Guilford,* 1983- ; *Connecticut Central,* 1987- .

DAILY PASSENGER TRAINS: *1869:* 10, *1893:* 30, *1919:* 31, *1935:* 29, *1950:* 34, *1960:* 24, *1971:* 6, *1981:* 28, *1994:* 16. Passenger service ended Suffield branch, 1925; Middletown branch, ca. 1932; New Britain branch, ca. 1935.

ABANDONMENTS: Middletown Branch (Berlin-East Berlin, 1940; East Berlin-Newfield, 1961).

The Hartford & New Haven, one of Connecticut's earliest railroads, was chartered between its namesake cities in 1833. Promoted both by New Haven and Hartford interests, as well as intermediate towns, the line was intended to provide New Haven with access to the rich Connecticut River valley and give Hartford an outlet to Long Island Sound when the river froze. The route was surveyed by Alexander C. Twining, the Yale professor who plotted the paths of many early Connecticut railroads. Directed to run the tracks through Middletown, Twining rejected this hilly route in favor of an easier one to the west through Meriden. Middletown and other communities left off the route protested; ultimately, in 1850, a branch was built linking Middletown to the main line at Berlin.

Construction of the Hartford & New Haven began at New Haven in 1836, but was halted the following year because of financial panic. Although attempts to obtain state aid came to naught, enough funds were gathered to resume building, and the segment from New Haven to Meriden went into operation in December 1838. One year later, in December 1839, the line was completed to Hartford. Southbound traffic at New Haven, both passenger and freight, transferred to steam boats for New York and beyond, since the all-rail route to Manhattan did not open for another decade.

From the beginning the railroad's promoters had planned eventually to extend the H&NH into Springfield, Mass., where connection would be made with the Western RR to Boston (then nearing completion), as well as with projected lines traversing the Northern Connecticut valley. Once the H&NH was a going concern its directors secured charters from Connecticut and Massachusetts and started construction north from Hartford in 1842. The line was completed to Springfield in December 1844. At Warehouse Point the railroad spanned the Connecticut River on a 1500-foot wooden bridge, one of the largest in New England. In October 1846 a storm swept the bridge off its piers; a new one was ready just forty-five days later. Twenty years later this bridge was in turn replaced by one of New England's first iron bridges, supposedly the longest yet built in the U.S.

With the completion of the Springfield extension, the H&NH rapidly developed into one of the region's most important trunk lines. (By 1872 it was double tracked.) With the completion of the New York & New Haven RR in 1849 it became part of the first (and for many years the only) all-rail route between Boston and New York City. In 1870 the operations of the Hartford & New Haven were combined with the New York & New Haven, and two years later the two railroads were merged to form the New York, New Haven & Hartford, soon to be New England's dominant carrier.

Three branches were added to the H&NH about this time. When the Connecticut River port of Middletown was left off the main line, some of its citizens chartered the Middletown RR in 1848, and in 1849 they constructed a branch line to Berlin. The H&NH took over the branch in 1850. In 1860 it was extended another mile to the river. The short line from Berlin to New Britain was built in 1865 as the independent New Britain & Middletown RR, but operated by the the H&NH, which purchased it in 1868. The Suffield branch line, built as the Windsor Locks & Suffield RR, was completed in 1870 and operated by the New Haven.

At the end of the nineteenth century the New Haven began to experiment with electric traction. In 1898 the New Britain branch was electrified using a 600-volt D.C. third rail system. Electric operation of this branch was short-lived; the state of Connecticut won a law suit claiming that the unexposed third rail was too dangerous to be allowed. Steam powered locomotives were recalled in 1906 and the third rail was removed. That same year, however, trolley wire was strung above the Middletown branch. Passenger service was provided by electric cars until the 1920s when the wires were taken down.

The darkest moment in the history of the H&NH occurred in the early morning of September 2, 1913. On this foggy day southbound traffic was extremely heavy because of large numbers of vacationers returning from northern New England to New York City. Delays had bunched several passenger trains together. A slow local train had caused two sections of the southbound *Bar Harbor Express* to halt just south of Wallingford. A few minutes later the first section of the *White Mountains Express*, going 50 mph, crashed into the rear of the second section of the *Bar Harbor Express*, smashing its old wooden Pullman cars into splinters. A total of 21 passengers died. A deadly combination of excessive speed, an obsolete signaling system, and the failure of the rear brakeman to adequately cover his train had produced the tragedy.

By this time the completion of the all-rail shore line route from New Haven to Boston through Providence in 1889 had diverted traffic from the H&NH route. As the twentieth century progressed, the

Amtrak 477 pulls out of Windsor Locks on its way soutbound from Spring-field toward New York and Washington, D.C., in September 1994. Until recently two tracks carried passenger and freight traffic along this route.

various financial and management troubles of the New Haven RR took their toll. Through passenger service to Boston and northern New England via this route declined, so that by the time the New Haven turned the H&NH over to the Penn Central in 1969 only Springfield-Hartford-New Haven-New York trains remained. The Middletown branch was lopped off in two segments: the stretch from Berlin to East Berlin was abandoned in 1940, and the rest of the line went in 1961.

The assumption by Amtrak of all passenger operations over the H&NH in 1971 led to improved service. Passenger service was restored north of Springfield to Montreal and a through train, the *Bay State*, used the H&NH to connect New York and Boston. More Springfield to New Haven trains were added. In 1976 Amtrak bought the H&NH along with other parts of the Boston-Washington Northeast Corridor. Unfortunately, Amtrak's deteriorating finances in the late 1970s and early 1980s eroded much of this gain. The *Bay State* was discontinued in 1975, a victim of minimal advertising, frequent schedule changes, slow running times, and strong bus competition. After a nine-year hiatus, the *Bay State* was finally restored in October 1984. In 1990 Amtrak began removing the second track along the H&NH, making it a single track line for the first time since the 1850s.

Under the Penn Central the H&NH became Connecticut's most important freight line. With the closing of the Poughkeepsie Bridge route and the elimination of car float service across New York Harbor in the early 1970s, nearly all Connecticut rail traffic entered and left the state via this route. Freight from the South and the West was routed to Selkirk Yard, near Albany, and then over the Western (Boston & Albany) to Springfield. In 1976 Conrail assumed operation of freight service on the H&NH from the Penn Central, and in 1982 the Boston & Maine also received trackage rights over the line, as well as becoming the operator of the New Britain branch.

In 1987 the newly formed Connecticut Central RR took over operation of the remaining one mile of the former Middletown branch in Middletown. Conrail continues to operate the Suffield branch as its Suffield Industrial Track serving several freight customers.

Sources: Baker, *Formation*, 72-81; *Chronological History of the New Haven Railroad*; Cornwall and Smith, *Names First*, 77; Harlow, *Steelways*, 172-77; Kirkland, *Men, Cities, and Transportation*, 1:234-37; Shaw, *History of Railroad Accidents*, 243-44; Turner and Jacobus, *Connecticut Railroads*, 25-34; Weller, *New Haven Railroad*; 242 I.C.C. 163.

9. Meriden, Waterbury & Connecticut River

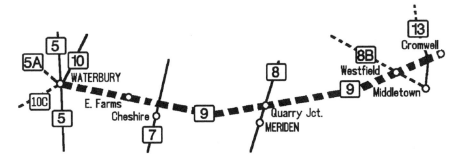

0 Waterbury, CT	13 Southington Rd.	21 York Hill Quarry
3 Dublin St.	15 Cheshire St.	24 Highland
6 East Farms	16 Hanover (Houghs	26 Smiths
8 Summit	Mill)	27 Westfield
10 Prospect	18 Meriden (Quarry	28 West Cromwell
11 West Cheshire	Jct.)	31 Cromwell, CT

BUILT: 1883-88.

OPERATORS: *Meriden & Cromwell*, 1885-88; *Meriden, Waterbury & Connecticut*, 1888-92; *New York & New England*, 1892-95; *New England*, 1895-96; *New York, New Haven & Hartford*, 1898-1968; *Penn Central*, 1969-76.

DAILY PASSENGER TRAINS: *1893:* 6. Passenger service ended Westfield-Cromwell, 1896; Meriden-Westfield, 1908 (replaced by electric trolley service, which continued until 1932); Waterbury-Meriden, 1917.

ABANDONMENTS: Westfield-Cromwell, 1904; East Farms-Meriden, 1924; Westfield-York Hill Quarry, 1938; Waterbury-East Farms, 1958; Meriden-York Hill Quarry, 1969; at Meriden, 1976.

Even though central Connecticut was covered by a dense network of rail lines by the 1880s, manufacturers in Meriden decided they needed yet another railroad. Although a major manufacturing center, Meriden had but a single rail line, the H&NH segment of the New Haven RR. The manufacturers, led by Horace C. Wilcox, obtained the dormant charter of the Meriden & Cromwell RR (granted in 1871), and began building in September 1883. In April 1885 they completed the line from a depot at Center Street in Meriden to dockside at Cromwell, on the Connecticut River, where connection was made with river steamers.

No sooner was the line opened than it was proposed to extend it westward to Waterbury. The citizens of the latter city were persuaded to subscribe to $125,000 worth of stock in this venture. A charter for this extension, as the Meriden & Waterbury RR, was obtained in 1887, and construction began. The line was opened to Waterbury in July 1888. Just before completion the two lines were consolidated into the Meriden, Waterbury & Connecticut River RR. The station in Meriden was relocated and the old Central Street depot became a freight house. The Waterbury extension proved to be much more expensive than anticipated, in part because the state railroad commission would not allow crossing of roads at grade.

In 1889 the MW&CR owned 5 locomotives, 7 passenger cars, and 154 freight cars. Its existence as an independent line was brief. Although unprofitable, the MW&CR became part of the struggling New York & New England system in October 1892, and with the rest of the NY&NE was transferred to the short-lived New England RR, a New Haven subsidiary, in 1895. Since the entire reason for building the MW&CR was to provide rail access for Meriden independent of the New Haven, the line no longer served any purpose. Thus the MW&CR became one of the earliest railroads to be abandoned in Connecticut. The New England RR suspended service on the entire line in 1896 when the bondholders of the MW&CR foreclosed. Service did not resume until after the line was reorganized as the Middletown, Meriden & Waterbury and leased to the New Haven RR. Operation of the segment between Westfield to Cromwell, however, was never resumed, and this line was formally abandoned in 1904.

In 1898 the state threatened to revoke the railroad's charter unless the line resumed operation, and in December 1898 and January 1899 the New Haven once more put the MW&CR west of Westfield back into service. The New Haven introduced New Haven-Waterbury passenger trains using the New Haven & Northampton line and the MW&CR between Cheshire and Waterbury in 1904, but these were discontinued a few years later. In 1906 the New Haven strung trolley wire over the line between Meriden and Westfield and provided Meriden-Middletown passenger service with electric cars. Shortly after America entered the First World War in June 1917 service was suspended between Waterbury and Meriden (except for local freight to East Farms). Passenger service consisted of a single round-trip mixed freight and passenger train (i.e., either a single passenger car hitched onto the back of a local freight or a freight train that carried passengers in the caboose). In 1924 the New Haven abandoned the line from East Farms to Meriden (except for the last mile and a half into the latter city). Trolley service from Meriden to Westfield survived until 1932. In 1938 the five-mile stretch between Westfield and York Hill Quarry, on the outskirts of Meriden, was given up.

After 1938 only two short remnants of the MW&CR remained at Waterbury and Meriden. The tracks from Waterbury to East Farms were cut back to central Waterbury in 1958 in conjunction with the building of Interstate 84, which follows part of the right of way of the MW&CR. The two-mile segment from Meriden to the York Hill Quarry was abandoned in 1969 after having been out of service for at least three years. After this, about three miles remained in service, east and west of the old Meriden station (Quarry Junction), where connection was made with the New Haven & Hartford line. This, too, was finally abandoned in 1976 with the coming of Conrail. A railroad that never should have been built, the Meriden, Waterbury & Connecticut River has left almost no trace of its brief existence.

Sources: *Poor's Manual of Railroads, 1890,* 43; *Railroad Gazette,* April 10, 1885, 240; *Railroad Gazette,* May 6, 1887, 311; Snow, "Meriden, Waterbury & Connecticut River R.R."; Turner and Jacobus, *Connecticut Railroads,* 195; U.S. Railway Association, *Final System Plan,* 2:35-36; U.S. Railway Association, *Preliminary System Plan,* 2:386; 86 I.C.C. 471; 224 I.C.C. 187.

10. Hartford, Providence & Fishkill

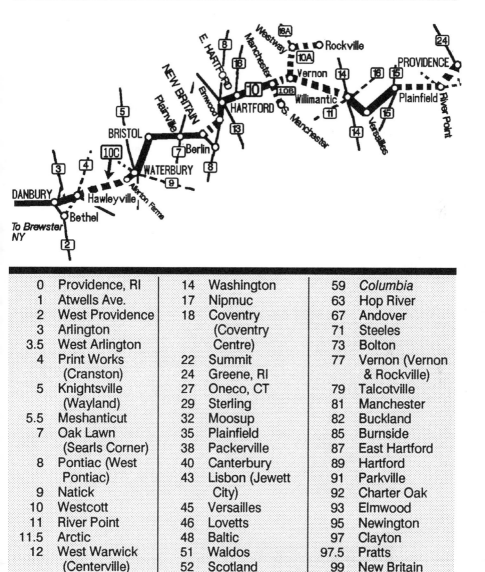

0	Providence, RI	14	Washington	59	*Columbia*
1	Atwells Ave.	17	Nipmuc	63	Hop River
2	West Providence	18	Coventry	67	Andover
3	Arlington		(Coventry	71	Steeles
3.5	West Arlington		Centre)	73	Bolton
4	Print Works	22	Summit	77	Vernon (Vernon
	(Cranston)	24	Greene, RI		& Rockville)
5	Knightsville	27	Oneco, CT	79	Talcotville
	(Wayland)	29	Sterling	81	Manchester
5.5	Meshanticut	32	Moosup	82	Buckland
7	Oak Lawn	35	Plainfield	85	Burnside
	(Searls Corner)	38	Packerville	87	East Hartford
8	Pontiac (West	40	Canterbury	89	Hartford
	Pontiac)	43	Lisbon (Jewett	91	Parkville
9	Natick		City)	92	Charter Oak
10	Westcott	45	Versailles	93	Elmwood
11	River Point	46	Lovetts	95	Newington
11.5	Arctic	48	Baltic	97	Clayton
12	West Warwick	51	Waldos	97.5	Pratts
	(Centerville)	52	Scotland	99	New Britain
13	Quidnick	55	South Windham	103	Plainville
13.5	Anthony	58	Willimantic	105	Forestville

Conrail 1985, a GE-built B23-7 locomotive, switches at the end of the line in Manchester, Conn., in July 1992. Once part of the Providence-Waterbury main line, this nine-mile segment is now Conrail's Manchester Secondary Track.

107	Bristol	4.5	Rockville, CT	14	Southbury
112	Terryville				(Pomperaug
115	Tolles	**10B. South Manches-**			Valley)
115.5	Hancock	**ter Branch**		15	
116.5	Wheatons				South Britain
117	Greystone	0	Manchester, CT	19	Sandy Hook
	(Hoadleys)	1	Middle Turnpike	21	Newtown
119	East Waterville	2	South	22	North Newtown
	(Waterville)		Manchester, CT	24	Hawleyville
121	Highland Jct.			30	Danbury
122	Waterbury, CT	**10C. Danbury Exten-**		32	Fair Grounds
		sion		35	Mill Plain, CT
10A. Rockville				40	*Brewster*
Branch		0	Waterbury, CT		*(Brewsters), NY*
		2	Allerton Farms	*77*	*Poughkeepsie*
0	Vernon, CT	3	Union City	*117*	*Campbell Hall,*
1	Vernon Centre	4	Bradleys		*NY*
3.5	Westway	8	Towantic		
	(Spring St.)	11	Oxford (South-		
			ford)		

BUILT: 1847-55; Rockville Branch, 1863; South Manchester Branch, 1869; Danbury Extension, ca. 1866-1881.

OPERATORS: *Hartford, Providence & Fishkill*, 1849-78; *New York & New England*, 1878-95; *New England*, 1895-98; *New York, New Haven & Hartford*, 1898-1968; *Penn Central*, 1969-76; *Conrail*, 1976- ; *Boston & Maine*, 1982-84; *Providence & Worcester, 1982- ; Guilford*, 1984- ; *Housatonic*, 1993- .

DAILY PASSENGER TRAINS: *1869:* 2 (Providence-Hartford, 4; Hartford-Waterbury, 4); *1893:* (Providence-Willimantic, 7; Willimantic-Hartford, 14; Hartford-Waterbury, 14); *1919:* (Providence-Willimantic, 6); *1935:* (Willimantic-Hartford, 4; Hartford-Waterbury, 17); *1950:* (Willimantic-Hartford, 6; Hartford-Waterbury, 10) Passenger service ended Willimantic-Plainfield, 1927 or 1928; Plainfield-Washington, 1930 or 1931; Washington-Providence, ca. 1932; Hartford-Willimantic, 1955; Hartford-Waterbury, 1959; Rockville Branch, ca. 1929; South Manchester Branch, 1933; Danbury Extension (Danbury-Brewster, ca. 1928; Danbury-Waterbury, 1932).

ABANDONMENTS: Plainfield-Washington, 1967; Manchester-Columbia, 1970; Washington-Providence, 1990. Rockville Branch, 1970; Danbury Extension (Allerton Farms-Southbury, 1937; Hawleyville-Southbury, 1948); South Manchester Branch, 1986; Elmwood-New Britain, 1992.

Across southern New England the tortuous path of the Hartford, Providence & Fishkill RR winds its way. Providence businessmen in 1846 launched the Providence & Plainfield RR to extend from Rhode Island into eastern Connecticut. Even before construction began, the western terminus was pushed to Willimantic, then Hartford, and finally Waterbury, with the eventual intent of reaching the Hudson River. The Connecticut portion was chartered as the Hartford & Providence RR in 1847, and in 1849 was merged with another unbuilt railroad to form the Hartford, Providence & Fishkill. It was consolidated with the original Rhode Island corporation in 1851.

The idea of a rail link between Providence and Hartford, two of New England's most important cities, would have made good sense, had it not been for the miserable topography of southern New England. In Connecticut, all major rivers flow from north to south, and constructing a rail line in this direction is not particularly difficult. East-west lines are another matter. As the crow flies, the distance between Providence and Hartford is but sixty-five miles; the rivers and rugged hills of eastern Connecticut forced the HP&F to build ninety miles of twisting track between the two.

Construction of the Hartford & Providence began at Hartford in 1847, simultaneously building westward toward Waterbury and eastward toward Providence. On December 1, 1849, the initial segment of the HP&F between Hartford and Willimantic opened. The following June the line was extended to Bristol. At this point the railroad ran out of money. The city governments of Hartford and Providence were persuaded to swap their own municipal bonds for the railroad's, and with these funds the line was completed to Providence in October 1854 and to Waterbury in July 1855.

Never profitable, the HP&F finally slid into bankruptcy in the wake of the financial panic of 1857. In 1863 the newly-formed Boston, Hartford & Erie RR acquired title to the HP&F, but the trustees representing creditors refused to yield control until they were paid. Thus the HP&F continued to be operated independently until 1878, when it was finally absorbed by the New York & New England RR, which had succeeded the Boston, Hartford & Erie in 1875.

The HP&F never became one of the region's more important lines, but its lack of success could not be blamed on excessive branch line construction, since it never built any. Two branches were added by later operators of the line. The four and a half mile Rockville RR between Vernon and Rockville (chartered in 1857), opened in 1863. Upon completion it was taken over by the BH&E and afterwards was operated as a branch of the HP&F. The South Manchester RR was chartered in 1866 and completed its two-mile line in June 1869. Owned by the Cheney Brothers to service their South Manchester silk mills, the line was operated as an independent short line. Passenger service came to an end in January 1933, and shortly afterwards the road was taken over by the New Haven. Conrail suspended freight service in 1981 and the line was abandoned in 1986 and the tracks removed.

From the beginning the promoters of the HP&F had dreams of extending their line westward from Waterbury to the Hudson River at Fishkill (Beacon). Although the HP&F and its successors excelled at losing money, private investors—including the notorious Jay Gould and others of the Erie RR ring—and state governments alike were persuaded to invest millions to secure this extension. Work on the extension to Danbury and beyond began in the 1860s under the direction of Sidney Dillon, chief contractor of the Union Pacific. Cutting through the rugged hills of western Connecticut was slow work, and the extension to Brewster, N.Y., did not open until the summer of 1881. The following January the rails finally reached Fishkill via a subsidiary line.

The extension west of Danbury proved to be the most successful portion of the HP&F. The completion in 1892 of an extension from Hopewell Junction, N.Y., to the Poughkeepsie Bridge across the Hudson, opened a new all-rail route to the coal fields of northeastern Pennsylvania. This new route was not enough to save the New York & New England from its arch-rival, the New Haven. The latter finally swallowed the entire NY&NE system, including the HP&F, in 1895. Reorganized under New Haven direction as the New England RR, the system was formally leased in 1898 and made an integral part of the New Haven. Under the New Haven, heavy through coal trains crossed the Poughkeepsie Bridge and ran via the HP&F's extension through Danbury to Hawleyville, and then south over the Housatonic to Derby Junction

These massive piers once carried the tracks of the Danbury Extension across the Housatonic River near Southbury, Conn. The line was abandoned in 1948.

The New Haven came to use the HP&F less as a through route, except for the portion of the extension west of Hawleyville. In an attempt to boost local traffic the New Haven electrified portions of the line near Hartford. Work started between Hartford and New Britain in December 1896 and was extended to Bristol by 1898. Although the line was double tracked, only one set of rails was electrified. Electricity was distributed to self-propelled cars by means of a third rail centered between the tracks. In 1906 electrification was discontinued, after a successful law suit brought by the State of Connecticut alleging that the exposed third rail was a threat to public safety. The following year trolley wire was strung over the main line from Burnside station in East Hartford to Vernon, and then to Rockville via the Rockville branch. Trolley cars were run over this route until the 1920s. Passenger service on the extension west of Danbury ended in the latter part of the 1920s and ended between Danbury and Waterbury in 1932. Passenger trains between Providence and Hartford also stopped running in the 1920s, service ending first on the segment between Willimantic and Plainfield in 1927 or early in 1928, and between there and Providence a few years later. Passenger service between Willimantic and Waterbury continued for another three decades, as part of a route that extended to Boston. This ended abruptly in August 1955 when flash floods destroyed part of the line between Willimantic and Boston near Putnam, Conn. The New Haven suspended passenger service from Blackstone, Mass., to Hartford and never resumed it. Hartford-Waterbury service survived until the end of the decade.

In 1937 the portion of the extension from Waterbury west to Southbury was abandoned; the track beyond Southbury to Hawleyville went in 1948. In 1967 the New Haven abandoned the main line between Washington (Coventry), R.I. and Plainfield, Conn. The Penn Central assumed operation of what remained of HP&F in 1969. The following year the segment between Manchester and Columbia, just outside of Willimantic, was abandoned, along with the Rockville branch. Twenty years later the unused tracks remained in place.

Under the Penn Central the HP&F became a series of unconnected branch lines. The seventeen-mile segment from Providence to Washington saw daily local freight service, with an average of fourteen cars per train. Between Plainfield and Willimantic trains ran only twice a week, with Versailles the busiest station. The USRA recommended that the line between Versailles and Willimantic not be included in Conrail. The line between Manchester and Hartford had somewhat heavier traffic, with Manchester generating most shipments. From Hartford west to Bristol traffic was similar, but between Bristol and Waterbury service had declined to only a single freight train a week. Finally, the extension west of Hawleyville, part of the Poughkeepsie through route, continued to see several through freights a day until fire closed the bridge and ended most traffic via this route on May 8, 1974.

In 1976 Conrail assumed operation of the remaining HP&F lines, except for the segment between Plainfield and Willimantic, which was transferred to the Providence & Worcester RR. In 1982 the latter railroad took over operation of the HP&F from Providence to Washington, and the Boston & Maine acquired the segment from New

Britain to Waterbury. Freight service in recent years has consisted of daily weekday locals in most places (twice daily between Manchester and East Hartford), except for a single through freight over the extension west of Hawleyville. Service from Providence to Washington ended by 1988, and the line was abandoned in 1990. Although the tracks remain, the line between Versailles and Willimantic has not been in service since around 1985. In late 1992 the extension west of Hawleyville was sold to the Housatonic RR, and the following year the Providence & Worcester obtained trackage rights to service the Tilcon asphalt plant in Danbury.

Sources: Baker, *Formation*, 51-55; *Chronological History of the New Haven Railroad*; Corwall and Smith, *Names First*, 49; Harlow, *Steelways*, 197; Kirkland, *Men, Cities, and Transportation*, 2:32-34; Middleton, *When the Steam Railroads Electrified*, 428; Turner and Jacobus, *Connecticut Railroads*, 173-202; U.S. Railway Association, *Final System Plan*, 2:36-37, 39-41, 486; U.S. Railway Association, *Preliminary System Plan*, 2:382-83, 386-87, 391, 804; 193 I.C.C. 219; 221 I.C.C. 698.

11. Air Line

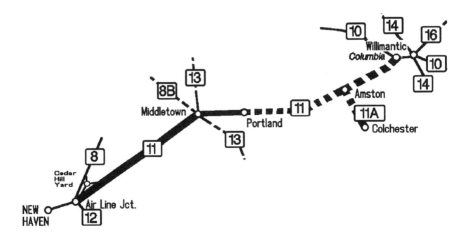

0	Air Line Jct. (Cedar Hill Jct.), CT	
2	Montowese	
6	Northford	
11	East Wallingford (Wallingford)	
15	Reeds Gap (Reeds)	
17	Middlefield (Middlefield & Durham)	
18	Middlefield Center	
19	Rockfall	
23	Middletown	
24	Portland	
28	Cobalt (Cobalt and Middle Haddam)	
31	East Hampton	
35	Lyman Viaduct	
37	Westchester (West Chester)	
42	Amston (Turnerville)	
45	Leonards Bridge	
48	Chestnut Hill (Liberty Hill)	
51	Columbia, CT	

11A. Colchester Branch

0	Amston (Turnerville), CT
4	Colchester, CT

BUILT: 1868-73; Colchester Branch, 1877.

OPERATORS: *New Haven, Middletown & Willimantic, 1870-75; Boston & New York Air-Line, 1875-82; New York, New Haven & Hartford, 1882-1968; Penn Central, 1969-1976; Conrail, 1976- ; Connecticut Central, 1987- ; Providence & Worcester, 1993- .*

DAILY PASSENGER TRAINS: *1893:* 8, *1919:* 6, *1935:* 2 (New Haven-Amston, Saturdays only). Passenger service ended Willimantic-Amston and Colchester Branch, ca. 1927; remainder of line 1936 or 1937.

ABANDONMENTS: Portland-Columbia, Colchester Branch, 1965.

The Air Line, like many other New England railroads, looked better on paper than it proved to be when constructed. During the 1850s and 1860s a series of short railroads were built with an eye to forming a direct route between Boston and New York. Although three major routes had been opened by 1860—via Springfield and Hartford, along the shore through Providence and New London, and by train to Fall River and thence by steamer—all were circuitous; only the Springfield route was entirely by rail. Would not, countless promoters argued, a direct route between the two cities make more sense?

It would have, had it not been for the deceptively rugged topography of eastern Connecticut. But the steep grades and sharp curves the route demanded could not deter the promoters. They consolidated the various short lines in Massachusetts and Rhode Island under the banner of the Boston, Hartford & Erie RR (later the New York & New England), then began pushing their line west from Putnam, Conn., toward Willimantic, and thence to New Haven and New York.

As early as 1846 the New York & Boston RR had been chartered to connect New Haven with Willimantic, but despite surveys and fund raising, the line never materialized. Connecticut interests, led by David Lyman of Middlefield, succeeded in 1867 in obtaining a charter for the New Haven, Middletown & Willimantic RR along the same path. The Connecticut River proved a major obstacle, with various interests opposed to the bridge that would have to be built at Middletown. Not until the Connecticut legislature authorized the crossing in 1868 did the project really get under way.

With investors wary of investing in the line, the railroad turned to local governments along the route. New Haven, Middletown, and other cities opened their municipal coffers to the fledgling railroad. With this aid and with investments from private individuals, the line was pushed through to completion, opening from New Haven to Middletown in 1870 and from there to Willimantic in 1873. (The branch to Colchester was built in 1876-77.) The connecting link from Putnam to Willimantic had been opened the year before, completing the long-sought direct inland route to Boston. The line was poorly constructed and the company slid into bankruptcy in 1875. The New Haven, Middletown & Willimantic was once more renamed, this time emerging as the Boston & New York Air-Line RR, though of course it reached neither city.

As built, the Air Line was handicapped by steep grades, curves, and viaducts that limited train size, especially between Portland and Willimantic. At East Hampton the 1100-foot long Lyman Viaduct towered more than 100 feet and the 1380-foot Rapallo Viaduct 60 feet above the valley. At first constructed of steel, these viaducts were covered by earth fill during the First World War. These viaducts remain accessible to hikers today, although the trains have been gone for nearly 30 years. Erosion is said to be uncovering the old steel girders. The Air Line crosses the Connecticut River at Middletown on a massive drawbridge, still in use, that remains an imposing sight.

As was typical of weaker railroads, the Air Line was driven to rate cutting and other desperate ploys to gain traffic. In 1879 the New Haven reached agreement to pool traffic with the Air Line. Three years later the New Haven leased the entire Air Line, not because of its intrinsic value, but because of the damage it could cause in the hands of a rival company. The early New Haven years were the best the Air Line (now the New Haven's Air Line Division) ever saw. Considerable freight came over this prime bridge route between the New Haven and the NY&NE. In 1884 the NY&NE introduced its crack express passenger train, the *New England Limited*, which travelled between Boston and New York by way of the Air Line. The *Limited* made the run in a mere six hours, stopping only at Willimantic, Middletown, New Haven, and Bridgeport. In 1891 the train was painted white (except the locomotive), soon acquiring the nicknames "White Train" and "Ghost Train." Despite its popularity the train proved too much trouble to keep clean. It was discontinued in October 1895, only to be replaced by the *Air Line Limited*, which made the run between Boston and New York in even faster time with only a single stop, at Middletown, for a change of engines.

With the opening of the rail bridge across the Thames at New London in 1889, the Air Line faced competition from two all-rail routes to Boston. The line's numerous curves and steep grades rendered it inferior to the other routes, and its importance diminished even further after the New Haven absorbed the NY&NE system in 1898. Through Boston-New York passenger service via the Air Line ended in 1924. Local service continued for a few years before being cut back to Middletown-Amston. Even this truncated service was eliminated in the early 1930s, only to be restored as a New Haven to Amston

Saturday-only round trip which was gone by October 1937. Through freights were routed onto other routes and even local freights were few by the onset of the Second World War, especially east of Portland. The New Haven did not get around to abandoning part of the Air Line until 1965, however, when the line between Portland and Willimantic was given up, including the Colchester Branch.

In 1969 the Penn Central took over operation of the remaining Air Line, New Haven to Portland. Several stations, including East Wallingford, Middletown, and Portland, still generated moderately heavy traffic. Conrail acquired the Air Line in 1976 and operated freight trains between New Haven and Portland until 1987, when operations between Reeds and Portland were transferred to the newly-formed Connecticut Central RR. Conrail continued to operate the segment between Cedar Hill Junction and Reeds until 1993, when it sold this operation to the Providence & Worcester RR. The Central Connecticut at this time also acquired trackage rights over the entire Air Line to the Conrail's Cedar Hill Yard in North Haven.

Sources: Baker, *Formation*, 56, 72, 82-3; Harlow, *Steelways*, 207, 211-14; Kirkland, *Men, Cities, and Transportation*, 2:83-5; Turner and Jacobus, *Connecticut Railroads*, 116-28.

12. Shore Line

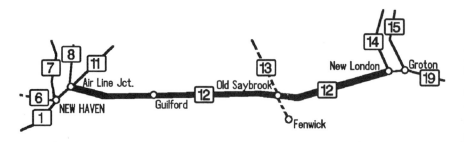

0 Air Line Jct. (Cedar Hill) (Fair Haven), CT	19 Madison	36 Sound View
	23 Clinton	37 South Lyme
	25 Grove Beach	41 Crescent Beach
4 East Haven	27 Westbrook	42 East Lyme & Niantic (East Lyme)
7 Branford	31 Old Saybrook (Saybrook Jct.) (Saybrook)	
9 Pine Orchard		43 Millstone
10 Stony Creek		46 Waterford
12 Leetes Island	32 Connecticut River	49 New London, CT
14 Sachems Head	34 Lyme & Blackhall (Lyme)	
15 Guilford	35 Black Hall	
17 East River		

BUILT: 1850-52.

OPERATORS: *New Haven & New London, 1852-57; New Haven, New London & Stonington, 1857-58; New York, Providence & Boston, 1858-62; New Haven, New London & Stonington, 1862-64; Shore Line, 1864-70; New York & New Haven, 1870-72; New York, New Haven & Hartford, 1872-1968; Penn Central, 1969-76; Amtrak (intercity passenger), 1971- ; Conrail (freight), 1976-91; Providence & Worcester (freight), 1982- ; ConnDOT (commuter passenger), 1990- .*

DAILY PASSENGER TRAINS: *1869: 10, 1893: 24, 1919: 32, 1935: 31, 1950: 34, 1960: 29, 1971: 20, 1981: 22, 1993: 22 (40, New Haven-Old Saybrook).*

ABANDONMENTS: None.

Today the tracks between New Haven and New London carry some of the heaviest intercity passenger traffic in the United States. The Shore Line forms part of the Northeast Corridor connecting Boston, New York, and Washington, D.C. But during its early years this line was only a modestly successful minor road.

The New Haven & New London RR was chartered in 1848 to connect its namesake cities, and Alexander Twining surveyed the route along the shore of Long Island Sound. Construction began in 1850 and the road was completed in July 1852. As built, the line was divided in two by the wide Connecticut River at Old Saybrook, and for many years entire trains were loaded aboard ferries at this point. Despite a large expenditure of borrowed funds, the line was not well constructed and traffic was disappointing.

The opening of the NH&NL in 1852 completed the direct rail route to Boston along the Sound, except for a short segment between Stonington and New London. The New London & Stonington RR was chartered in 1852 to close the gap. In 1857 the NL&S was merged into the NH&NL under the name of the New Haven, New London & Stonington, and was completed between Stonington and Groton at the end of 1858. At this point the entire line was taken over by the New York, Providence & Boston, which now operated from New Haven to Providence. But the shore route to Boston did not live up to expectations. Two ferry crossings, at the Connecticut and the Thames, prevented direct rail service and reduced the popularity of this route. In 1862 financial difficulties prompted the bondholders of the NHNL&S to retake control of the segment between New Haven and New London. In 1864 the NHNL&S was split into two new railroads, the Shore Line RY from New Haven to New London and the New London & Stonington RR, from Groton to Stonington. A few months later the latter road was bought by the New York, Providence & Boston.

The fortunes of the Shore Line began to turn in 1868 when, after years of unsuccessful efforts, permission to bridge the Connecticut was finally secured. In 1870 the two segments of the Shore Line were linked by a drawbridge at Old Saybrook, although the remaining ferry across the Thames at New London still prevented the Shore Line from becoming part of an all-rail line to Boston. But the Connecticut crossing was enough to interest the New York & New Haven, then in the process of consolidating with the Hartford & New Haven. The NY&NH leased the Shore Line in 1870, and the road remained an integral part of the New Haven system for nearly a century.

The Shore Line finally came into its own when the New York, Providence & Boston completed its massive steel bridge over the Thames between New London and Groton in October 1889. Within a few years this route vanquished its competitors to emerge as the undisputed primary rail path between New York and Boston. Over its rails ran many of the most celebrated trains of twentieth century New England: the *Merchants Limited*, the *Federal*, and many others. The Penn Central began operating the Shore Line in 1969, and two years later Amtrak took charge of passenger service. In 1976 Amtrak acquired the Shore Line as part of its takeover of much of the Northeast Corridor.

During the 1970s ambitious plans were drawn up by Amtrak and the U.S. Department of Transportation to upgrade the corridor to allow high speed rail service between Boston and New York. The many curves of the Shore Line were to be straightened, grade crossings eliminated, and ultimately, the route electrified. Grim economic reality overtook these grandiose schemes, however, and the plans were scaled back. Some improvements were made, but electrification was post-poned indefinitely. The distinctive Turbotrains, perhaps the most colorful innovation, were a daily sight on the Shore Line in the 1970s until operating difficulties forced their retirement.

Currently Amtrak operates twenty-two round trips over the route each day. Freight service has always been secondary to passenger operations over the Shore Line. Under the Penn Central, freight traffic was moderately heavy. When Amtrak acquired the Shore Line in 1976, Conrail assumed operation of freight service via trackage rights. Through trains no longer used this route, freight traffic to and from eastern New England having been shifted to the H&NH. A local freight train out of Cedar Hill Yard provided daily weekday service. In 1982 the Providence & Worcester RR took over Conrail's trackage rights between New London and Old Saybrook; in August 1991 the P&W replaced Conrail over the remainder of the Shore Line to New Haven. Daily service is provided Mondays through Fridays. In May 1990 the Connecticut Department of Transportation (ConnDOT) introduced commuter service between New Haven and Old Saybrook, and despite a tight budget was operating eighteen daily trains by 1993.

After more than twenty years of planning and delay, it now appears that electrification is finally coming to the Shore Line, and before too many years electric locomotives may yet run to Providence and Boston.

Sources: Harlow, *Steelways*, 185; Kirkland, *Men, Cities, and Transportation*, 2:83, 95, 105; Patch, "Connecticut's Shore Line East"; Roy, "Providence & Worcester Succeeds on Service"; Turner and Jacobus, *Connecticut Railroads*, 2-16.

13. Connecticut Valley

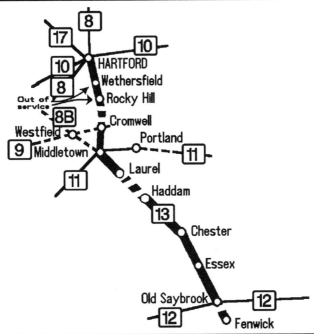

0	Hartford, CT	17	Middletown	35.5	Chester
2	State St.	21	Laurel	36	Deep River
6	Wethersfield	22	Maromas	40	Essex
7	Spring Brook	25.5	Higganum	44	Saybrook Jct. (Old
	(South Wethers-	26	Walkley Hill		Saybrook)
	field)	26.5	Haddam	46	Saybrook Point
9	Rocky Hill	28	Arnolds	47	Fenwick, CT
11	Dividend	32	East Haddam		
14	North Cromwell		(Goodspeeds)		
15	Cromwell		(East Haddam &		
16.5	Middletown Jct.		Moodus)		
	(Middletown)	34.5	Hadlyme		

BUILT: 1869-72.

OPERATORS: *Connecticut Valley, 1871-80; Hartford & Connecticut Valley, 1880-87; New York, New Haven & Hartford, 1887-1968; Penn Central, 1969-76; Valley (tourist), 1971- ; Conrail, 1976-1987; Boston & Maine, 1982-83; Guilford, 1983- ; Connecticut Central, 1987- .*

DAILY PASSENGER TRAINS: *1893:* 12 (Hartford-Saybrook Point), *1919:* 4 (Hartford-Saybrook Point; 10, Hartford-Saybrook). Passenger service ended Saybrook Point-Fenwick, 1917; Saybrook-Saybrook Point, ca. 1922; Middletown-Saybrook, 1930 or 1931; Hartford-Middletown, 1933.

ABANDONMENTS: Saybrook Point-Fenwick, 1917; Old Saybrook-Saybrook Point, 1922; Laurel-Old Saybrook, 1968 (reopened Old Saybrook-Haddam after 1971); Cromwell-Rocky Hill, 1972.

The Connecticut River valley had served as one of the earliest paths for rail lines in New England; all, that is, except for the final stretch of the river below Hartford. Here steamboats held sway. Not until 1868 did Hartford interests led by James Walkeley secure a charter to construct a line along the lower river. In that year the Connecticut Valley RR was organized with the intent of building a line along the west bank, passing through Middletown and reaching Long Island Sound at Old Saybrook, near the river's mouth. The fledgling railroad received aid from both the state and the city of Hartford.

Construction got under way in 1869 and the Connecticut Valley opened for business from State Street in Hartford to Old Saybrook in the summer of 1871. The line was extended to the then popular resort of Fenwick in 1872, and later at its northern end a connection was made with the Hartford, Providence & Fishkill RR in Hartford. Coal, which was unloaded at the railroad's docks at Saybrook Point, was the primary traffic on the new line. The Connecticut Valley had the misfortune of opening just prior to the great depression that began in 1873, and it soon found itself in financial straits. The bondholders took control of the line in 1876, and in 1880 the Connecticut Valley was reorganized as the Hartford & Connecticut Valley RR. The new management, sensing that prospects for a line that bypassed most of industrial Connecticut were poor, sought to sell their line. To boost the sale price the operators made physical improvements and talked of expanding northward via trackage rights or a new line to Springfield, where connections could be made with the Boston & Albany. Alarmed, the New Haven took the bait and bought control of the Connecticut Valley in the fall of 1882 at a price apparently well in excess of its potential worth. The New Haven took a formal lease in 1887.

The Valley Division, as the Connecticut Valley was renamed, formed a minor part of the far-flung New Haven system. Steamship traffic declined on Long Island Sound after the turn of the century and the coal ships no longer unloaded at Saybrook Point. The tracks from Saybrook Point to Fenwick were abandoned in 1917 and those from Saybrook Point to Saybrook Junction (Old Saybrook station) were abandoned in 1922 and removed in 1924. As part of a major campaign to upgrade local Connecticut service, the New Haven strung trolley wire over a short stretch of the Connecticut Valley between Middletown and Cromwell in 1906. Trolleys operated over this segment until around 1929, and conventional passenger trains stopped running in 1933.

By the final years of the New Haven in the 1960s few trains were seen on the Connecticut Valley. In 1968 the line between Saybrook and Laurel was abandoned. The following year the Penn Central took over the remaining portion of the Connecticut Valley. Around 1972 it abandoned the segment between Rocky Hill and North Cromwell. On the remaining segments, Hartford to Rocky Hill and Middletown to North Cromwell, freight trains were run only once a week. The USRA recommended that the segment from Wethersfield to Rocky Hill not be transferred to Conrail, but in 1976 Conrail assumed operation of the entire remaining Connecticut Valley. The state of Connecticut leased the Wethersfield-Rocky Hill segment and contracted with Conrail to provide freight service. In the early 1980s local freight trains were operated twice weekly on the Hartford-Rocky Hill section out of Hartford; the North Cromwell-Middletown segment was served as needed by a train out of Cedar Hill yard (near New Haven). The Boston & Maine in 1982 took over operation of the Hartford-Rocky Hill portion of the Connecticut Valley. Recently the line has been out of service south of Wethersfield. In 1987 Conrail transferred its remaining operations in the Middletown area to a new short line, the Central Connecticut RR.

In June 1971 the Valley RR, an operator of steam-powered excursion trains, reopened the abandoned trackage between Essex and Deep River. By 1980 trains were running from Old Saybrook to Chester, and the Valley RR was a popular tourist attraction. Today trains operate from April to October, some as far north as Haddam.

Sources: Baker, *Formation*, 72, 85-6; Harlow, *Steelways*, 193; Turner and Jacobus, *Connecticut's Railroads*, 156-70; 72 I.C.C. 250; U.S. Railway Association, *Final System Plan*, 2:32-34; U.S. Railway Association, *Preliminary System Plan*, 2:383-85.

14. New London Northern (Central Vermont)

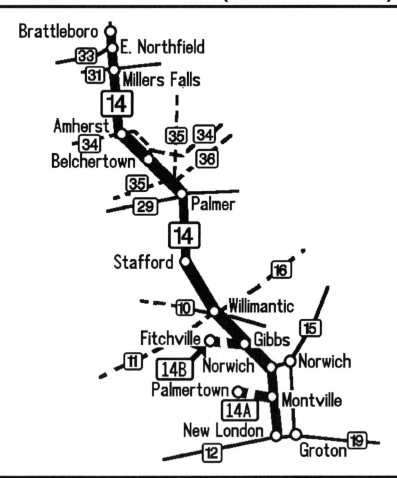

52 Orcutts (Orcutt)	88 Cushman (North	121 Brattleboro, VT
54 Ellithorp, CT	Amherst)	
56 State Line, MA	90 Leverett	**14A. Palmertown**
60 South Monson	93 Mt.Toby	**Branch**
61 Monson	96 Montague (South	
65 Palmer	Montague)	0 Montville, CT
68 Three Rivers	100 Millers Falls	2 Palmertown, CT
(Three Bridges)	(Grouts Corner)	
69 Barretts (Barretts	103 Northfield Farms	**14B. Fitchville Branch**
Jct.)	106 Gill	
75 Belchertown	109 Northfield	0 Gibbs (Fitchville
80 Dwight (Dwights)	111 East Northfield, MA	Jct.), CT
82 Norwottuck (South	111.5 South Vernon, VT	2 Fitchville, CT
Amherst)	114 Central Park	
85 Amherst	116 Vernon	

BUILT: 1848-67; Fitchville Branch, 1880; Palmertown Branch, 1899.

OPERATORS: *New London, Willimantic & Palmer,* 1849-61; *Vermont & Massachusetts,* 1850-70; *New London Northern,* 1861-71; *Amherst & Belchertown,* 1853-58; *Amherst, Belchertown & Palmer,* 1858-64; *Vermont Central,* 1871-73; *Central Vermont,* 1873-1995; *New England Central,* 1995- .

DAILY PASSENGER TRAINS: *1869:* 4, *1893:* 4, *1919:* 2 (New London-Palmer, 6), *1935:* 4, *1994:* 2. Passenger service discontinued 1947; resumed 1989.

ABANDONMENTS: Fitchville Branch, ca. 1980; Palmertown Branch, 1983.

Foremost among the New London Northern's claims to fame is that it was the only significant rail line in Connecticut never to come under the control of the New Haven RR. Indeed, it is virtually certain that this long line, which bypasses both Worcester and Springfield, would now be at least partially abandoned had it not retained its independence.

The NLN dates back to 1847 when a Connecticut charter was secured for the New London, Willimantic & Springfield RR. New London interests were largely responsible for the road. Hard times had befallen the nation's third-largest whaling port, and it was hoped a railroad might bring prosperity back to New London. An attempt had been made to have the Norwich & Worcester RR (completed 1840) extend its tracks to New London but without success. The New London, Willimantic & Springfield was originally projected towards

Springfield, but even before construction began, the terminus was switched to Palmer. New London residents provided most of the capital for the fledgling line, the rest coming from citizens of other towns along its projected route.

In 1848 a Massachusetts extension was chartered as the New London, Willimantic & Palmer RR and a year later merged with the Connecticut corporation under this name. The route was surveyed by General James Palmer, who greatly underestimated construction costs. Construction began in July 1848. The first segment, New London to Willimantic, opened the following year. The next stretch, Willimantic to Stafford Springs, was completed in March 1850, and rails reached the terminus at Palmer, on the Western RR, in September.

No sooner had the line been completed than attempts were made to extend the route northward. Various towns in and near the Connecticut Valley sought to attract the railroad, Amherst, Mass., being the most eager. The Amherst & Belchertown RR was launched in 1851 to construct a line from Palmer to Amherst. Although the New London, Willimantic & Palmer promised to lease the line when it was completed, the New London had no funds to invest in this project. Amherst interests struggled to build the extension largely on their own. Construction began in April 1852 and the Amherst & Belchertown was completed in May 1853 and leased to the NLW&P. Four years later this line went bankrupt during the aftermath of the financial panic of 1857, and in 1858 it was reorganized as the Amherst, Belchertown & Palmer. Hopes of extending it beyond Amherst could not be realized.

The NLW&P was enjoying no greater success. As early as 1856 it was unable to pay the interest on its bonds and it sought unsuccessfully to sell its Norwich to New London route. The line failed in January 1859, and in April 1861 the New London Northern RR was organized to take over operations from trustees. In 1864 the NLN absorbed the Amherst, Belchertown & Palmer. Under this new management, work was finally begun on extending the tracks north from Amherst, and in 1867 the rails reached Grouts Corners (Millers Falls), where connection was made with the Vermont & Massachusetts RR.

At this time the Vermont Central RR, which was consolidating its control over various short lines in northern New England, was seeking a southern outlet. In 1870 the Rutland RR had leased the Vermont &

A pair of southbound Central Vermont locomotives pass the Palmer, Mass., station after working the Conrail interchange in September 1994.

Massachusetts branch from Brattleboro, Vt., to Millers Falls (completed April 1849). Shortly afterwards the Rutland itself was taken over by the Vermont Central. In December 1871 the VC leased the entire New London Northern. After the VC's empire collapsed in 1873, the NLN remained a part of the new Central Vermont, which took shape out of the VC's remnants. In 1899 a newly reorganized Central Vermont Railway came under the control of the Grand Trunk Railway of Canada. With the nationalization of the entire Grand Trunk system by Canada in 1922, the NLN, as part of the CV, came under the ownership of the Canadian government, where it remained until 1994.

Passenger traffic was never heavy on the NLN. Throughout most of its first century a pair of daily locals served the route. In later years rail cars and mixed trains took over. Passenger service ended September 27, 1947. Steam locomotives held on longer on the CV than on most other southern New England lines, the last regular operation being the Palmer-Brattleboro way freight on April 8, 1957. In the late 1950s, following the disastrous 1955 floods, about three miles of track north of Stafford were relocated to construct a flood control dam.

In recent years freight traffic has been only moderate. Heaviest traffic is found north of Palmer, with through general freights and piggyback trailer trains running north to Canada. South of Palmer only local freights have been operated. On July 9, 1989, passenger service returned to the NLN after an absence of more than forty years when Amtrak rerouted the Washington-New York-Montreal *Montrealer* away from the Hartford & New Haven line. Amherst and Willimantic are currently the only active Amtrak stations on the NLN.

In 1994 the Canadian National, the long-time owner of the CV, put the railroad up for sale. The successful buyer, RailTex, operator of twenty-three short line railroads, took control of the CV in February 1995 and renamed it the New England Central RR.

The NLN had only two short branches. The Fitchville branch was built in 1880 and the Palmerton branch in 1899 to serve local industries. Neither apparently ever had passenger service. The Fitchville branch was abandoned around 1980 and the Palmertown line was given up in 1983.

Sources: Baker, *Formation*, 229; Farnham, *Quickest Route*, 80-89; Harlow, *Steelways*, 275; Kistler, *Rise of Railroads*, 67-69; Jones, *Central Vermont Railway*; Turner and Jacobus, *Connecticut's Railroads*, 68-86.

15. Norwich & Worcester

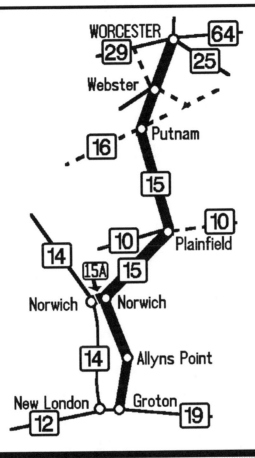

0 Groton, CT	13 River Falls	37 Danielson (Daniel-
2 Submarine Base	(Greeneville)	sonville)
(Navy Yard)	15 Tafts	37.5 North Danielson
5 Gales Ferry	17 Shetucket (Lisbon	39 Dayville (Daysville)
6 Allyns Point	Siding)	45 Putnam (Pomfret)
7 Stoddards Wharf	20 Reades (Reads)	45.5 Klondike (Mechan-
8 Sand Pit	22 Jewett City	icsville) (Thomson)
9 Fort Point	28 Plainfield (Plainfield	48 West Thompson
10 Milk House	Jct.) (Plain)	49 Grosvenordale
11 Crown Hill	31 Central Village	(Grosvenor Dale)
12 Norwich	32 Wauregan	(Masonville)

50	North Gros-venordale (Fisherville)	62	North Oxford	**15A. Norwich Connection**	
		63	Maywood		
		65	Stones Crossing		
52	Wilsonville (Wilsons), CT	66	Auburn	0	Norwich (N&W Sta.), CT
53	Perrys, MA	68	Hope Ave. (Cambridge St.)	0.5	Norwich (NLN Sta.), CT
55	Webster	70	South Worcester (Worcester Jct.) (Grand Jct.) (Jackson)		
56	North Village (North Webster)				
57	Barton	71	Worcester, MA		
60	Oxford				

BUILT: 1835-40, 1843, 1898-99; Norwich Connection, 1854.

OPERATORS: *Norwich & Worcester,* 1839-69; *Boston, Hartford & Erie,* 1869; *New York & New England,* 1869-95; *New England,* 1895-98; *New York, New Haven & Hartford,* 1898-68; *Penn Central,* 1969-1976; *Providence & Worcester,* 1976- ; *Conrail,* 1976-80.

DAILY PASSENGER TRAINS: *1869:* 7 (Norwich-Worcester), *1893:* 9 (Norwich-Worcester), *1919:* 10, *1935:* 2, *1960:* 4, *1971:* 4. Passenger service discontinued 1946, restored 1952, discontinued again, 1971.

ABANDONMENTS: Norwich Connection, 1966.

Norwich businessmen secured a Connecticut charter for the Boston, Norwich & New London RR in May 1832, and an extension into Massachusetts, the Worcester & Norwich, received a Massachusetts charter the following year. The Connecticut and Massachusetts companies were consolidated in 1836 as the Norwich & Worcester RR. Early interest in this route was understandable, for the region it would pass through was densely populated and had industrialized early. Large cotton, woolen, paper, iron, and lumber mills were located on or near the route, as well as quarries. Moreover, grades along the projected path were so easy that the route had once been proposed for a canal.

Capt. William Gibbs McNeill surveyed a route from Norwich to Worcester in 1832, but construction did not begin until November 1835. The route included one of the first American rail tunnels, blasted through ledge at Taftville. The Norwich-Danielsonville section was completed in 1836, and the laying of imported English rail began in 1839. Both the state of Massachusetts and the city of Norwich loaned money for the project.

Freight service between Norwich and Plainfield began in September 1839. Track laying was completed by November, but formal opening of the line from Norwich to Worcester was delayed until March 1840. Although the railroad had been built with an eye to serving heavy local traffic, the N&W also formed part of a through route between Boston and New York. Trains left Boston on the rails of the Boston & Worcester, then used the N&W to reach Norwich, where passengers boarded steamships for New York. Unfortunately, the Thames River regularly froze over at Norwich. In December 1843, the tracks were extended six miles southward from Norwich to Allyns Point on the Thames, where the river was said to remain ice free all winter. Steamships then used the dock at Allyns Point instead of Norwich. In February 1854 the N&W opened a short connection with the New London, Willimantic & Palmer RR at Norwich, over whose rails it operated trains through to New London. New York-bound steamers now departed from New London, although coal ships still used Allyns Point. Through rail service to New London was suspended in November 1855 and not resumed until April 1859.

Despite its promise as both a local and through route, the N&W was not very successful. Without loans from the state of Massachusetts and the city of Norwich in the 1840s, the railroad would not have been able to operate. Conditions improved a bit in the 1850s, but the line was never among the region's more prosperous railroads. The legislature, responding to pressure from the New London, Willimantic & Palmer (and its successor, the New London Northern), thwarted attempts to extend the line from Allyns Point to Groton. In 1869, the N&W was leased by the ambitious Boston, Hartford & Erie system, just before the latter became the New York & New England RR. Here the N&W remained until the entire NY&NE system—which in 1895 had become the New Haven-controlled New England RR—was absorbed by the New Haven in 1898.

Shortly after the New Haven had taken over the N&W, the extension from Allyns Point down the east bank of the Thames to Groton was finally approved. Construction began October 1898 and the extension was completed June 1899, one of the last new railroads to be built in Connecticut. Trackage rights over the New London Northern from Norwich to New London were abandoned. Now that the Thames itself was bridged at Groton, the New Haven could provide direct train service between Worcester and New York via this route.

In the twentieth century the N&W became an active New Haven secondary main line. Long through freights plied the line to and from Worcester, where considerable traffic out of northern New England was interchanged with the Boston & Maine. New York to Maine passenger trains, such as the *State of Maine* and the *Bar Harbor* used the N&W to bypass Boston. Local passenger service on this line was reduced to a gas-electric "doodlebug" car in the 1920s, and finally eliminated in September 1928. Even the Maine trains were rerouted over the Providence & Worcester in April 1946. Passenger service returned to the N&W on June 9, 1952, using a new rail diesel car between Worcester and New London, and making local stops at towns that had not seen passenger service for nearly twenty-five years. This continued until May 1971 when Amtrak took over most intercity passenger trains; the Worcester-New London train had not been included in the Amtrak network.

In 1907 the New Haven strung trolley wire above the N&W's tracks between Tafts and Central Village. The trolley cars originally used were replaced by interurban multiunit cars in 1913. The cars ran from Norwich via street railway tracks to Tafts, then used the N&W to Central Village, and finally back on street railway tracks toward Worcester. This service ended in 1924 and the wires were removed.

The New Haven turned operation of the N&W over to the Penn Central in 1969 along with the rest of the New Haven system. In the early 1970s freight traffic on the southern portion of the N&W, from Groton to Putnam, was moderate, with a daily weekday local working this segment. (Through trains, though, no longer used the N&W to reach Worcester.) Between Putnam and Worcester trains ran only twice weekly, as the line generated only a few carloads of traffic per week. Both the USDOT and the USRA recommended that this segment not be included in Conrail.

Meanwhile, the old Norwich & Worcester RR was still in existence and had plans of resuming independent operation of its railroad that the New Haven had operated under lease since 1898. At the same time, the Providence & Worcester RR, another line long leased to the New Haven and then the Penn Central, actually resumed operation of its own line, and it also expressed interest in acquiring the N&W. In 1976 the USRA transferred the N&W between Worcester and Plainfield to the Providence & Worcester, which has operated it ever since. The remainder of the line, from Plainfield to Groton, was taken over by Conrail at the same time. In 1980 this sector of the N&W was also transferred to the P&W.

In recent years the P&W has operated a daily weekday through freight between Plainfield and Worcester, and local freights run from Plainfield to Groton on weekdays. Plainfield is the operational base of today's N&W.

Sources: Farnham, *Quickest Route*; Harlow, *Steelways*, 220; Kirkland, *Men, Cities, and Transportation*, I: 248-50; Mrazik, "Webster"; Roy, "Providence & Worcester"; Turner and Jacobus, *Connecticut's Railroads*, 36-46; U.S. Railway Association, *Final System Plan*, 2:46-47; U.S. Railway Association, *Preliminary System Plan*, 2:399-400; 320 I.C.C. 466.

16. Southbridge & Blackstone

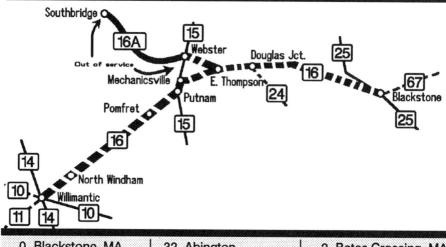

0 Blackstone, MA	32 Abington	2 Bates Crossing, MA
3 Millville Heights (Millville)	34 Elliott	3 Point Pleasant
7 South Uxbridge (Ironstone) (Iron Stone)	38 Hampton	4 Beacon Park
	42 Goshen (Clarks Corner)	6 East Webster
	45 North Windham	7 Webster, MA
10 East Douglas	50 Willimantic, CT	12 Quinebaug, CT
12 Douglas, MA		14 West Dudley, MA
17 East Thompson, CT	**16A. Southbridge Branch**	17 Sandersdale
21 Thompson		18 Southbridge, MA
23 Mechanicsville		
25 Putnam	0 East Thompson, CT	
30 Pomfret		

BUILT: ca. 1849-72; Southbridge Branch, ca. 1866-67.

OPERATORS: *Boston & New York Central, 1854-55; East Thompson, 1857-58; Boston, Hartford & Erie, 1867-75; New York & New England, 1875-95; New England, 1895-98; New York, New Haven & Hartford, 1898-1968; Penn Central, 1969-76; Providence & Worcester, 1976-ca. 1985; Conrail, 1976-82.* Not operated 1858-67.

DAILY PASSENGER TRAINS: *1869:* 6 (Blackstone-East Thompson), *1893:* 11, *1919:* 10, *1935:* 4, *1950:* 6. Passenger service ended August 1955; Southbridge Branch, 1929.

ABANDONMENTS: Putnam-Pomfret, 1959; North Windham-Pomfret, 1963; Blackstone-Putnam, 1969; Wilimantic-North Windham, ca. 1985. Southbridge Branch (East Thompson-Webster, 1937).

The Southbridge & Blackstone RR was chartered in 1849 to build a line between its namesake towns. It was apparently intended as an extension of the Norfolk County RR, which had just been completed from Dedham to Blackstone. In 1853, before it was opened, the S&B was merged with other short lines to form the Boston & New York Central RR. That same year the B&NYC used a charter it obtained for another railroad, the East Thompson RR, to alter the route of the line so that Mechanicsville, Conn., not Southbridge, became the road's destination. One year later the line from Blackstone to Mechanicsville was completed, and B&NYC trains ran from the latter point through to Boston. Plans were laid to extend the tracks to Willimantic and ultimately complete an inland direct route to New York.

Unfortunately the Boston & New York Central could not live up to its grandiose name, and the company soon failed. A series of reorganizations followed, with the S&B operated only intermittently. Plans for extending the line languished for lack of funds. Between 1858 and 1867 the line was not operated for revenue service at all. In 1863 the Boston, Hartford & Erie purchased the S&B as part of its attempt to build a trunk line system in southern New England. Unfortunately, the BH&E was unable to obtain clear title to the Norfolk County RR from the latter's creditors, and could not operate east of Blackstone. Without access to Boston, the Southbridge & Blackstone was scarcely worth operating.

When the BH&E finally obtained control of the Norfolk County in 1866, it revived its plan of extending the Southbridge & Blackstone. The BH&E completed the first extension from East Thompson to Southbridge in February 1867 (at the same time that it began operating the Norfolk County), finally bringing rails to the town that was the original objective of the railroad. The long-awaited extension westward from Mechanicsville to Willimantic opened in August 1872. A year later the Air Line RR reached Willimantic from New Haven and the inland route to Boston was finally a reality. By this time, however, the Boston, Hartford & Erie was bankrupt, and in 1875 the S&B passed to the BH&E's successor, the New York & New England.

During the 1880s and 1890s crack express passenger trains operated over this line between New York and Boston, including the fabled *White Train*. A spectacular wreck involving two passenger and two freight trains occurred at Thompson on December 4, 1891. A dispatcher's error put an express freight on the same track as a local freight. The debris from the resulting head-on crash derailed the *Eastern States Express*, which was passing on another track. A few minutes later the *Express* was rear-ended by the *Norwich Steamboat Express*. Despite widespread damage, there were apparently only three deaths.

In 1895 the New York & New England was renamed the New England RR and became a New Haven subsidiary. Three years later it was incorporated into the New Haven, which downgraded the Air Line route to a secondary route (a fate it shared with most other ex-NY&NE lines). Boston-Hartford passenger trains survived into the 1950s, but freight trains became fewer. On August 18, 1955, floods took out a bridge west of Putnam, and service between Putnam and Pomfret— along with all passenger service between Blackstone and Hartford— was suspended. The New Haven applied for abandonment, arguing that it would not be worth spending the $110,000 it would take to restore the line. The Interstate Commerce Commission agreed, and the 4.3-mile segment was abandoned in 1959, severing the Air Line route. Four years later the New Haven received permission to remove the tracks between Willimantic and Pomfret, although the first five miles out of Wilimantic to North Windham continued in service until around 1985.

During the 1960s, freight traffic on the remaining portion of the S&B continued to dwindle. By 1967 the route was used primarily for through movements of oversized cars; East Douglas was the only active freight station. In March 1968 flood waters caused the collapse of a bridge across the Blackstone River east of Blackstone station on the Norfolk County route, and the New Haven suspended through service (local freights continued to serve Putnam). The financially strapped railroad, which soon would be absorbed by the Penn Central, applied to abandon the S&B from Blackstone to Putnam (and the Norfolk County connection to Franklin Junction, Mass.), claiming it would take $225,000 to repair the bridge and reopen the route. The following year permission was granted to give up the line. The right of way was purchased by the state of Connecticut and is now a scenic bridle path.

Today, the only portion of the S&B that remains intact is the section of the Southbridge branch extending from Webster to Southbridge. Passenger service on the Southbridge branch, provided by a gas-electric car, ended in 1929. The New Haven abandoned the portion of this

Willimantic in the early 1890s was an important rail center served by three railroads. Here two New York & New England locomotives pause at the depot. (Photo courtesy Walker Transportation Collection, Beverly Historical Society & Museum.)

line between East Thompson and Webster in 1937, and henceforth operated it as a branch of the Norwich & Worcester line. The remaining part of the Southbridge branch went to the Penn Central in 1969 when it absorbed the New Haven. Service dwindled to one train a week, and the Penn Central applied for abandonment. The USRA recommended that the Southbridge branch not be included in Conrail. The Providence & Worcester RR assumed operation of the branch in 1976. For a while Southbridge was served by a train out of Plainfield, via Webster, running as needed, but the branch has now been out of service for nearly a decade. The rails, though unused, remain in place.

Sources: Baker, *Formation*, 46, 94; *Chronological History of the New Haven Railroad*; Cornwall and Smith, *Names First*, 16, 36, 69, 114; Kirkland, *Men, Cities, and Transportation*, 2:47-49; Roy, "Providence & Worcester Succeeds on Service"; *Traffic World*, Nov. 23, 1968, 59; Turner and Jacobus, *Connecticut's Railroads*, 176-202; U.S. Railway Association, *Final System Plan*, 2:42-3; U.S. Railway Association, *Preliminary System Plan*, 2:396; 221 I.C.C. 711; 312 I.C.C. 465; 317 I.C.C. 204.

17. Connecticut Western

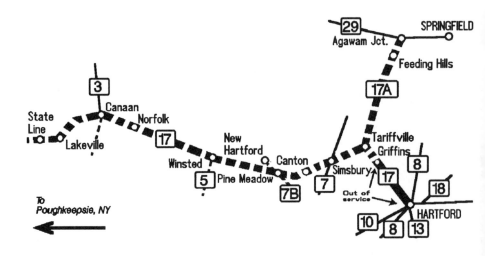

0 Hartford, CT	25 Cherry Brook	60 Taconic (Chapin-
2 Blue Hills	(Cherry)	ville)
4 Cottage Grove	28 Pine Meadow	63 Salisbury
6 Bloomfield	29 New Hartford	65 Lakeville
8 Griffins	35 East Winsted	67 Ore Hill, CT
10 Bernards (North	35.5 Winsted	68 *State Line (State*
Bloomfield) (Scot-	36 West Winsted	*Line Jct.), NY*
land)	38 Colebrook	115 *Poughkeepsie, NY*
12 Tariffville	41 Grants	
13 Hoskins	44 Summit	**17A. Springfield**
15 Simsbury	46 Norfolk	**Branch**
16 West Simsbury	47 West Norfolk	
17 Stratton Brook	51 Canaan Valley	0 Tariffville, CT
(Strattons)	(Whiting River)	3 East Granby
22 Canton	52 East Canaan	8 West Suffield, CT
23 High St. Jct.	55 Canaan	12 Feeding Hills, MA
24 Collinsville	59 Twin Lakes	14 Agawam Jct., MA

BUILT: 1869-71; Springfield Branch, 1899-1904.

OPERATORS: *Connecticut Western, 1871-81; Hartford & Connecticut Western, 1881-89; Central New England & Western, 1889-92; Philadelphia, Reading &*

New England, 1892-98; *Central New England,* 1898-1927; *New York, New Haven & Hartford,* 1927-68; *Penn Central,* 1969-76; *Conrail,* 1976-81; *Boston & Maine,* 1981-ca. 1983; *Housatonic,,* 1984- .

DAILY PASSENGER TRAINS: *1893:* 6, *1919:* 4. Passenger service ended 1927; Springfield Branch (Feeding Hills-Agawam Jct., 1921; Tariffville-Feeding Hills, 1922).

ABANDONMENTS: Simsbury-Tariffville, West Simsbury-High St. Jct., 1937; West Winsted-East Cannan, High St. Jct.-East Winsted, Griffins-Tariffville, Lakeville-State Line, 1938; Cannan [1 mile east of station]-East Canaan, 1940; West Winsted-East Winsted, 1957; Canaan-Lakeville, 1965; Simsbury-West Simsbury, 1968. Springfield Branch, (Agawam Jct.-Feeding Hills, 1921; Feeding Hills-Tariffville, 1938).

Connecticut's rugged topography is broken by river valleys running north and south, and most of its successful rail lines have followed them. Geographic logic, however, never stood in the way of determined railroad promoters. Egbert Butler wanted a railroad in the worst way for his home town, the hill village of Norfolk, Conn. He secured the original charter for the Connecticut Western RR in 1866 to build a line from Collinsville to Canaan, by way of Norfolk. Two years later the railroad was rechartered, this time with authority to build from Hartford all the way to the New York state line. Here the CW would connect with the Dutchess & Columbia RR to extend the route clear to Beacon on the Hudson River. Norfolk would really be on the map.

Construction began in Winsted and Canaan in October 1869, with crews working from both sites in both directions. Frequent curves and steep grades marked the route; at Norfolk Summit the route reached 1333 feet above sea level, the highest point tracks would ever reach in the state. Between Tariffville and Simsbury the line utilized the right of way of a branch of the New Haven & Northampton RR built in 1850 and discontinued in 1869. The Connecticut Western was completed in December 1871. An extension, the Rhinebeck & Connecticut Railway, opned in 1875, giving the CW its own outlet to the Hudson at Rhinecliff.

Traffic on the new railroad was modest, consisting primarily of coal bound for New England from across the Hudson. The CW was unable to stave off bankruptcy, however, in the wake of the great depression of the 1870s. Contributing in no small part to its failure were the legal costs arising from a major rail disaster.

On the evening of January 15, 1878, a westbound train left Hartford crowded with passengers returning from a revival meeting. Two engines hauled the ten-car train. At Tariffville, the tracks crossed the Farmington River on a seven-year old, two-span wooden and iron Howe truss bridge. The lead engine had just reached the far bank when the bridge collapsed. Four of the ten cars, along with both locomotives, were dragged into the ice-covered river. Fortunately, the fall was only ten feet and no fires broke out as was often the case with wooden cars heated by stoves. Even so, thirteen persons, including one of the engineers, were killed, and another seventy injured.

Two years later the Connecticut Western failed, and in 1881 it was reorganized as the Hartford & Connecticut Western RR. The new railroad, including its subsidiaries in New York state, was absorbed in 1889 by the Central New England & Western RR. This company had been created by the owners of the newly opened (December 1888) 6600-foot bridge across the Hudson at Poughkeepsie to give them a direct rail link to southern New England. Coal from Pennsylvania rode the rails eastward, and a smaller volume of manufactured goods flowed westward. Passenger trains also used the route, including the Boston-Harrisburg *Day Express* and the Boston-Washington *Federal*.

The coal traffic of the Central New England & Western attracted the attention of A. A. McLeod, president of the Philadelphia & Reading RR. Having consolidated control over the anthracite coal fields of northeastern Pennsylvania, McLeod was able to raise the price of coal. Much to his chagrin, sales dwindled and his surplus of unsold coal mounted. McLeod moved to capture a market for his anthracite in New England. Moving at lightning speed, he snatched control of the Central New England & Western in 1892 and merged it with the Poughkeepsie Bridge as the Philadelphia, Reading & New England RR. Shortly afterwards he purchased stock sufficient to control both the Boston & Maine and New York & New England. McLeod's empire proved short-lived after he ran afoul of J.P. Morgan's New Haven RR and then encountered the general financial collapse of 1893. By early 1894 McLeod had lost his entire empire.

The Philadelphia, Reading & New England survived and in 1898 became the Central New England Railway. In 1904 the New Haven purchased control in order to obtain the Poughkeepsie Bridge. Although it wanted only the bridge, the New Haven was forced to buy the entire Central New England to get it. The construction of a line between the bridge and the New York & New England's route west from Danbury, Conn. in 1892, however, enabled the New Haven to reach Poughkeepsie without using the CW (see line 10). The CW already was surplus.

Unlike its other purchases in Connecticut, the New Haven operated the CNE as an independent company. Coal and passenger trains continued to operate over the CW. Unfortunately, every town of any consequence on it was also served by a north-south New Haven line. During the First World War much traffic was diverted onto the CW to avoid the New Haven's congested main line to the south. After the war, however, traffic dried up. The New Haven merged with the CNE in 1927 and passenger service over the entire line ended that December. In 1932 the connection between the CW and Poughkeepsie Bridge was abandoned, leaving the CW a long branch line to nowhere. That same year service was suspended on the main line between Tariffville and Simsbury, West Simsbury and Canton, High St. Junction and Pine Meadow, New Hartford and East Winsted, and West Winsted and Norfolk. Formal abandonment of the CW began in 1937 and was largely completed by 1940, leaving what remained of the CW a series of short, disconnected branch lines.

After 1957 only three short segments of the CW main line survived as branch lines: a ten-mile stretch between Canaan and Lakeville (Salisbury), a one-mile spur between Simsbury and West Simsbury, and the initial eight miles out of Hartford to Griffins. The Lakeville branch hung on until 1965 when it was abandoned by the New Haven. The West Simsbury spur was given up in 1968. Presently the Griffins branch is the only significant surviving remnant of the CW. In the early 1970s, after its acquisition by the Penn Central, traffic on this line was fairly light, with trains operating about three days a week, and the USRA recommended that it not be included in Conrail. After local shippers objected strongly, Conrail did assume operation of the branch in 1976. The state of Connecticut bought the Hartford-Griffins segment in October 1981 and hired the B&M to operate it. Operation was short lived and the line has been out of service ever since, although in 1994 the line was repaired with the intention of reopening it in 1995. The only other portion of the CW to survive is a short stretch in Canaan to the east of the railroad station, now operated by the Housatonic RR to access to a limestone quarry. Short sections of abandoned rails remain visible at Lakeville and Salisbury.

The CW had but one branch, Tariffville to Springfield. For many years the CW and the various companies that operated it had dreamed of an extension northward that would enable it to tap the traffic-rich upper Connecticut valley. Construction did not begin until 1899, by which time the New Haven enjoyed a virtual monopoly in southern New England. Many, including the Boston & Albany in Massachusetts, welcomed a connection. Track work was completed in 1900. Suddenly, the New Haven somehow acquired a 313-foot wide strip of land in East Granby, Conn., on which the CNE had already laid tracks. A New Haven crew appeared, ripped up the tracks, and thus prevented the branch from operating. Various court battles followed, and the line was not opened until 1904, a year after control of the CW passed to the New Haven.

The fourteen-mile extension was the last railroad line of any consequence to be built in Connecticut, and it proved to be one of the shortest lived. Trains ran north from Tariffville across the Massachusetts line to Agawam Junction, where a connection was made with the Boston & Albany's main line, and then over the B&A the remaining 3.5 miles into Springfield. Together, the CW main line and the branch formed another Hartford to Springfield route, the third. Tariffville-Springfield service lasted only seventeen years; the tracks between Agawam Junction and Feeding Hills were abandoned in 1921 but remained in place. Passenger service over the remainder of the branch ended the following year, but the branch itself survived until 1938 when it was abandoned with most of the rest of the CW.

Sources: Baker, *Formation*, 96-99; McLaughlin, "Poughkeepsie Gateway"; Milmine, "History of the C.N.E"; Shaw, *History of Railroad Accidents*, 57; Turner and Jacobus, *Connecticut's Railroads*, 130-54; U.S. Railway Association, *Final System Plan*, 2:34-35; U.S. Railway Association, *Preliminary System Plan*, 2:385-86; 70 I.C.C. 441; 187 I.C.C. 361; 221 I.C.C. 570; 224 I.C.C. 323, 435, 654; 228 I.C.C. 4, 193.; 242 I.C.C. 149; 324 I.C.C. 345.

18. Connecticut Central

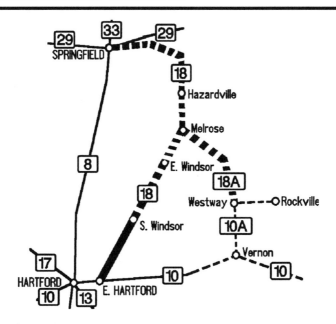

		18A. Westway Branch
0 East Hartford, CT	14 Melrose	
2 Burnhams	17 Hazardville (& Scitico)	0 Melrose, CT
4 Wapping (South Windsor)	19 Shaker Sta., CT	2 Sadds Mills
6 East Windsor Hill (East Windsor)	22 East Longmeadow, MA	4 Ellington
8 Rye St.	26 Water Shops (Water Sta.)	5 Windermere
9 Farnhams	27 Armory	7 West St.
10 Scantic (Osborn) (East Windsor)	29 Springfield, MA	8 Westway (West St.) (Rockville), CT
12 Broad Brook		

BUILT: ca. 1874-76; Westway Branch, 1875-76.

OPERATORS: *Connecticut Valley*, 1876; *Connecticut Central*, 1876-80; *New York & New England*, 1880-95; *New England*, 1895-98; *New York, New Haven & Hartford*, 1898-1968; *Penn Central*, 1969-76; *Conrail*, 1976- ; *Springfield Terminal*, 1982-83; *Guilford*, 1983- .

DAILY PASSENGER TRAINS: *1893:* 4, *1919:* 2. Passenger service ended Springfield-Armory, ca. 1924; Armory-East Longmeadow, ca. 1929; East Longmeadow-Hartford, ca. 1931; Westway Branch, ca. 1929.

ABANDONMENTS: Hazardville-East Windsor, 1976; South Windsor-East Windsor, ca. 1986; Springfield-Hazardville, 1993; Westway Branch (Melrose-Ellington, 1937; Ellington-Westway, 1963).

Nearly thirty years after the Hartford & New Haven RR opened its line from Hartford to Springfield, a group of promoters launched a parallel railroad, several miles to the east. Chartered in 1871, this Connecticut Central RR was originally projected to run from Springfield through East Hartford to a terminus in Portland, Conn. Plans were soon altered to make East Hartford the line's southern terminus; from there, trackage rights over the Hartford, Providence & Fishkill RR were used to reach Hartford proper. A Massachusetts corporation,

Between 1972 and 1990 Hazardville, Conn., represented the endpoint of service on the Armory Branch (as the northern part of the Conncecticut Central was known in recent years). Guilford shut down the line in 1990 and formally abandoned it at the end of 1993 (photo September 1994).

the Springfield & New London RR, was chartered in 1874 to build the portion of the line in the Bay State.

Towns between Hartford and Springfield along the projected route supported the line, and all of the company's directors came from Springfield, East Windsor, South Windsor, East Hartford, Ellington, and Hartford. Coal was the primary traffic the promoters anticipated, with the newly constructed Connecticut Valley RR expected to provide large amounts. The line was completed from East Hartford to Springfield in January 1876, the Connecticut Central taking lease of the Springfield & New London. A few weeks before the lines opened they were leased to the Connecticut Valley.

In 1875 work had begun on a branch from Melrose to Westway, where a connection was made with the Hartford, Providence & Fishkill's Rockville Branch (see line 10). This had the potential of opening another through route from Springfield to New London and Providence. The Westway Branch was completed in 1876, shortly after the rest of the CC.

The Connecticut Valley went bankrupt in 1876, a few months after taking control of the CC, and the lease was cancelled. The CC was thereafter operated independently until 1880, when it was leased to the New York & New England RR. The NY&NE gained access to Springfield, and it had hopes of offering some competition to its arch-rival, the New Haven, on the Hartford-Springfield route. In reality, the NY&NE ended up operating only two round trips between Hartford and Springfield each day over the CC, compared to more than thirty round trip trains on the New Haven. The circuitous CC was thirty-two miles between the two cities, the New Haven's H&NH route only twenty-five.

The New Haven assumed control of the NY&NE system in 1895 and leased it outright three years later. In 1907 the New Haven strung trolley wire above the Westway Branch, and electric cars were operated over this route (and on to Rockville, Vernon, and East Hartford) until the late 1920s. Passenger service on the CC main line dwindled to a single daily Hartford-Springfield round trip and then ended altogether around 1928. Hazardville to Hartford service survived until about 1933. A portion of the Westway Branch between Melrose and Ellington was abandoned in 1937; the remainder of the branch followed in 1963.

By 1969 when the CC was acquired by Penn Central, the line seldom if ever saw through trains. The segment between Hazardville and East Windsor saw its last local freight in 1972, although it was not formally abandoned until four years later. Under the Penn Central, freight service was provided daily on the East Hartford-East Windsor segment, and three times a week on the Springfield-Hazardville portion. In 1976 the two remaining segments were transferred to Conrail; in 1982 the northern part was acquired by the Boston & Maine. Guilford operated the Springfield-Hazardville trackage as its Armory Branch until 1990. Permission to abandon came at the end of 1993; as of the summer of 1994 the tracks remained in place. Conrail abandoned five more miles between South Windsor and East Windsor around 1986, but continues to service the rest of the line out of Hartford.

Sources: Baker, *Formation*, 46, 56; Cornwall and Smith, *Names First*, 31; *Poor's Manual of Railroads*, 1878, 103-4; Turner and Jacobus, *Connecticut's Railroads*, 172-202; U.S. Railway Association, *Final System Plan*, 2:41-43; U.S. Railway Association, *Preliminary System Plan*, 2:394-97; 224 I.C.C. 127.

19. New York, Providence & Boston

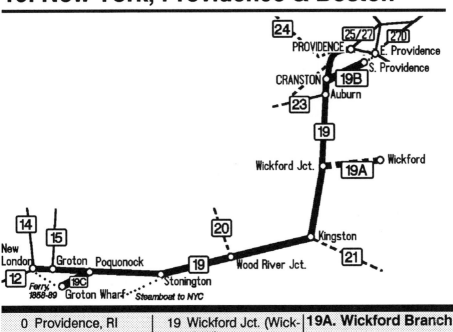

		19A. Wickford Branch
0 Providence, RI	19 Wickford Jct. (Wick-	
1 West Switch	ford)	0 Wickford Jct., RI
(Atwells Ave.)	23 Slocums	1 La Fayette
2 Westminster St.	27 Kingston	2 Belleville
2.5 Cranston St.	31 Kenyons	2.5 Wickford
3 Elmwood	32 Shannock	3.5 Wickford Landing,
4 Cranston (Crans-	33 Carolina	RI
ton Jct.) (Auburn	35 Wood River Jct.	
Jct.)	(Richmond Switch)	**19B. South Provi-**
5 Auburn (Elmville)	39 Bradford (Niantic)	**dence Branch**
6.5 Norwood	(Charleston)	
7.5 Lincoln Park	44 Westerly, RI	0 Cranston Jct., RI
8.5 Hills Grove	49 Stonington, CT	2 South Providence,
9.5 Greenwood	53 Mystic	RI
10.5 Apponaug (War-	54 West Mystic	
wick)	55 Noank	**19C. Groton Wharf**
12 Cowesett	58 Midway	**Branch**
12.5 Chepiwanoxet	59 Poquonnock	
13 East Greenwich	(Poquonnock	0 Poquonnock
(Greenwich)	Switch)	(Poquonnock
17 Davisville	61 Groton	Switch), CT
	62 New London, CT	2 Groton Wharf, CT

BUILT: 1832-37; Providence Extension, 1848; New London & Stonington RR (Groton Extension), 1857-58; Wickford Branch, 1871; Thames River Bridge and connection (Poquonock-New London), 1888-89.

OPERATORS: *New York, Providence & Boston,* 1837-92; *New York, New Haven & Hartford,* 1892-1968; *Penn Central,* 1969-76; *Amtrak (passenger),* 1971- ; *Conrail,* 1976-82; *Providence & Worcester,* 1982- .

DAILY PASSENGER TRAINS: *1869:* 8, *1893:* 28, *1919:* 29, *1935:* 28, *1950:* 34, *1960:* 29, *1971:* 18, *1981:* 20, *1994:* 20.

ABANDONMENTS: Wickford Branch (Wickford Landing-Wickford, 1938; Wickford-Wickford Jct., 1962).

Shortly after the Boston & Providence RR was chartered in 1831 to secure a connection between these two cities, plans were underway to extend tracks toward New York City. In 1832 the Providence & Stonington RR was chartered in Rhode Island and the New York & Stonington in Connecticut, the intention being to build a line from Providence to Stonington, Conn, where steamers would transport passengers to New York. Indeed, New York investors controlled the

Southbound Amtrak 175 The Patriot *approaches Westerly, R.I., in July 1994.*

line. This line had the important advantage of avoiding the frequently rough seas off Port Judith, R.I., that travelers sailing from Providence, Fall River, or Newport were wont to encounter.

The Connecticut and Massachusetts companies merged in 1833 to form the New York, Providence & Boston RR, popularly known as the Stonington Road. The route from Providence to Stonington was surveyed and constructed by William H. Swift, William G. McNeill, and Major George W. Whistler (father of the noted painter), the latter on assignment from the U.S. Army. Construction began in August 1832. The NYP&B was completed in November 1837; the six miles of the route in Connecticut was the first railroad to operate in that state. When first built, the line was did not physically connect with any other rail line. At its northern end the line stopped at the western bank of Providence Harbor at Field's Point, South Providence, where a ferry connection was made with the Boston & Providence across the bay. Not until 1848 was the line extended into downtown Providence and connection made with the Boston & Providence, which had entered the city the previous year. The original NYP&B route to the ferry became the South Providence Branch, part of which remains in use even today.

The NYP&B went bankrupt in 1839, but was restored to fiscal health by 1843. Thousands of passengers rode the railroad to the large steamboats out of Stonington that sailed to New York City via Long Island Sound. The position of the NYP&B improved still further with the building of the New London & Stonington RR. Chartered in 1852 to run from Stonington to Groton, the NL&S was intended as an extension of the newly completed New Haven & New London RR. The NL&S failed before it was completed, and was merged with the NH&NL in 1857 to form the New Haven, New London & Stonington RR. The road was completed in December 1858. A year later, however, the NHNL&S was leased to the NYP&B. In 1864 another New London & Stonington RR was formed out of the old NHNL&S and sold to the NYP&B, where it became known as the Groton extension.

Ferries across the Thames and Connecticut Rivers prevented the NYP&B from enjoying an all-rail connection with New York. The Connecticut was bridged at Old Saybrook in 1870, leaving only the ferry across the Thames between Groton and New London. To forge the last link in the all-rail route to New York, the NYP&B began construction of a massive steel drawbridge over the Thames. The 1400-foot long structure opened October 10, 1889. New track was laid from Poquonock to the bridge at Groton, and the old main line became a branch line to Groton Wharf.

With the completion of the Thames River bridge, the NYP&B found itself part of the primary New York to Boston rail route. Traffic on the various other rail and rail-boat routes dwindled as the shore route gained in popularity. In 1892 the rapidly expanding New Haven RR leased the NYP&B and shortly afterwards the entire New York-Boston line. The NYP&B became an integral part of this, the New Haven's busiest route. Over its rails ran nearly all of the best-known New Haven varnish, including the *Merchants Limited*, the *Yankee Clipper*, the *Federal*, and many others.

Passenger traffic predominated on this line; although used by some through freights bound to and from Boston, the sparsely populated region traversed by the NYP&B generated little local traffic. After the Penn Central assumed control in 1969 through freights out of Boston were rerouted via the Boston & Albany. In 1971 Amtrak began operating passenger service over this road, and as an integral part of the Northeast corridor the NYP&B sees as many daily intercity passenger trains as almost any rail line in the country. Amtrak purchased control of the NYP&B in 1976 and freight operations were taken over by Conrail; in 1982 the Providence & Worcester replaced Conrail. In recent years local P&W freights have operated out of Providence and Plainfield.

In the 1970s Amtrak and the U.S. Department of Transportation announced ambitious plans to upgrade the NYP&B for high-speed passenger transportation, including electrification. Tight budgets forced postponement of these plans for many years, but by 1994 electrification of the entire Northeast Corridor between New Haven and Boston seemed increasingly likely. The NYP&B carries some of the heaviest volume of intercity rail passengers in the country.

Aside from its original entrance into Providence (the South Providence branch) and to the wharf at Groton (the Groton Wharf branch), the NYP&B acquired only one true branch, to Wickford. The Wickford Branch RR was chartered in 1862 and re-chartered two years later as the Wickford RR. It changed its name a third time in 1870 to the Newport & Wickford RR & Steamboat Company, and opened in June

On its way to Boston, Amtrak 170 The Yankee Clipper *speeds past the Westerly, R.I., depot in July 1994. Electrification, slated in the near future, will change this view dramatically.*

1871. This three-mile spur carried passengers from Wickford Junction on the NYP&B to Wickford Landing on Narragansett Bay where they boarded steamers for Newport. Although controlled by the NYP&B the Wickford was operated independently until World War I, when it became another branch of the New Haven. Steamboats and the passenger trains ceased in October 1925, and the half mile of the branch between Wickford station and the wharf was abandoned in 1938. The remainder of the branch survived until 1962.

Sources: Baker, *Formation*, 24, 72, 93; Harlow, *Steelways*, 220-23, 233-34; Kirkland, *Men, Cities, and Transportation*, 1: 245-47; Pierce, "Newport and Wickford Railroad"; Roy, "Providence & Worcester Succeeds on Service"; Turner and Jacobus, *Connecticut Railroads*, 2-16; 224 I.C.C. 241.

20. Wood River Branch

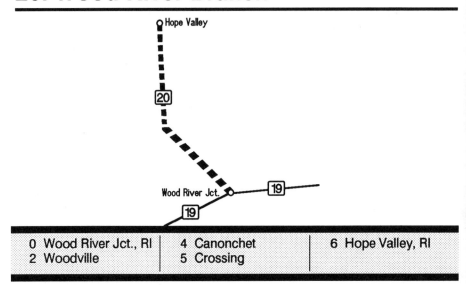

| 0 Wood River Jct., RI | 4 Canonchet | 6 Hope Valley, RI |
| 2 Woodville | 5 Crossing | |

BUILT: 1874.

OPERATORS: *Wood River Branch, 1874-1927; New York, New Haven & Hartford, 1928-37; Wood River Branch, 1937-47.*

DAILY PASSENGER TRAINS: *1893:* 10, *1919:* 6. Passenger service ended 1927.

ABANDONMENTS: Entire line 1947.

Only six miles long, the Wood River Branch RR was chartered in 1872 to provide access for the town of Hope Valley to the New York, Providence & Boston main line. It opened July 1, 1874. Although the NYP&B owned much of its stock, the diminutive short line was operated independently. When the New Haven RR succeeded the NYP&B in 1892 the Wood River continued to be operated separately.

The Wood River was always a very small operation. In 1877 its entire rolling stock consisted of one locomotive (a twenty-ton 4-4-0 named the *Gardner Nichols*), one passenger car, and one other car. In 1900 it had three locomotives, one passenger car, one baggage car, and one combination car. It carried on average only about 50 passengers a day and less than 10,000 tons of freight a year. In 1924 the railroad defaulted on its loan to the New Haven, but the latter, not really wanting the Wood River, did not foreclose.

The Wood River's locomotive Gardner Nichols, *a classic American (4-4-0), in 1903. (Photo courtesy Walker Transportation Collection, Beverly Historical Society & Museum.)*

A flood in November 1927 washed out track and the covered bridge over the Wood River at Woodville. The railroad lacked the cash needed to restore service, and its owners sought abandonment. Local shippers persuaded the New Haven to reopen the line, and traffic resumed in 1928. Although the New Haven was in charge, the line appears to have operated independently. Passenger service was dropped at this time.

The New Haven found the line unprofitable and in 1937 sold it to Roy Rawlings for $301. Rawlings' grain and feed mill in Hope Valley provided 85% of the railroad's traffic. When this mill was destroyed by fire in March 1947 the operation practically ceased. On August 8, 1947, the I.C.C. granted permission to abandon, and the tracks were removed shortly afterwards.

Aside from its first locomotive, the motive power for this short line was leased from the New Haven. In its final years it used a small gasoline-powered engine. At one time its depots had been painted yellow and the line became known locally as the "Yellow Dog Road."

Sources: Brown, "Wood River Branch Railroad"; *Poor's Manual of Railroads, 1878,* 100; *Poor's Manual of Railroads, 1900,* 46; *Railroad Gazette,* November 14, 1874, 449; Smith, "End of the Line."

21. Narragansett Pier

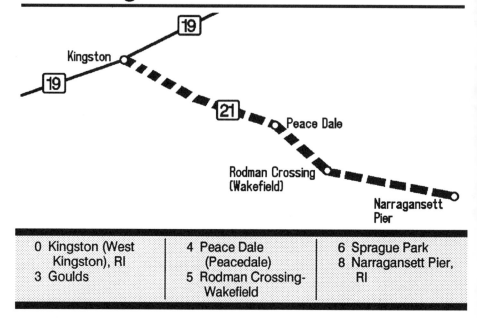

0 Kingston (West Kingston), RI	4 Peace Dale (Peacedale)	6 Sprague Park
3 Goulds	5 Rodman Crossing-Wakefield	8 Narragansett Pier, RI

BUILT: 1876.

OPERATORS: *Narragansett Pier,* 1876-1911; *Rhode Island Co.,* 1911-1920; *Narragansett Pier,* 1920-1981.

DAILY PASSENGER TRAINS: *1893:* 8, *1919:* 12, *1935:* 10, *1950:* 6. Passenger service suspended June 21, 1952; permanently discontinued, Dec. 31, 1952.

ABANDONMENTS: Rodman Crossing-Narragansett Pier, 1953; remainder of line, 1981.

Chartered in 1874, the eight-mile Narragansett Pier RR was completed in July 1876. The New York, Providence & Boston, with which it connected at Kingston, helped with the construction but did not control the line. The line had two objectives: freight service for the textile mills at Peace Dale and Wakefield, and passenger service to the resort community of Narragansett Pier. Peace Dale was dominated by the Peace Dale Manufacturing Company, owned by Rowland G. Hazard & Sons, and it was the Hazard family that built the line.

Before the railroad, Narragansett Pier was an established but isolated resort. The railroad touched off a building boom, with hotels and casinos transforming the sleepy community into a popular middle-class resort. The Hazards even ran a steamer line to Newport for many years. Like most railroads the Narragansett Pier lost money for the Hazards in its early years, but by 1890 it was paying dividends. Passenger traffic (strongest, of course, in the summer) accounted for most of the revenue, with the mills providing some freight. For a time in the 1890s through sleeping cars operated over the line to New York City.

The fortunes of the line began to decline after the burning of the Narragansett Pier casino in September 1900. In August 1902 the track from Narragansett Pier to Peace Dale was electrified for the use of the Sea View Electric RR. Nine years later the Rhode Island Company (a New Haven RR subsidiary) leased the entire Narragansett Pier. After the bankruptcy of the Rhode Island Co. in 1919, the line reverted to the Hazards in 1920. Sea View trolley service ended that same year.

Narragansett Pier locomotive 20, an ex-New Haven RR American (4-4-0) at Kingston in May 1934. (Photo courtesy Walker Transportation Collection, Beverly Historical Society & Museum.)

During the 1920s freight service became increasingly important as the automobile cut into what remained of the traditional summer resort traffic. In 1921 gas-motor rail buses were used, and in 1933 highway buses began to replace rail service. The buses were discontinued in 1938, however, and in 1940 a gas-electric rail car replaced steam passenger trains. In 1946 the Hazards finally sold the railroad. All remaining passenger service ended in 1952 when the gas-electric rail car broke an axle. Since Narragansett Pier generated little freight traffic, the line beyond Rodman Crossing in Wakefield was abandoned the following year so that the state would not have to build an overpass on a highway it was building.

Freight traffic continued to dwindle. During the mid-1960s a new owner briefly and unsuccessfully attempted to operate excursion passenger service. Subsequent owners sought to utilize the line as a locomotive engineer training facility but without success. With no reason to exist, the remaining five miles of the Narragansett Pier were abandoned late in 1981.

Source: Henwood, *Short Haul to the Bay.*.

22. Warwick

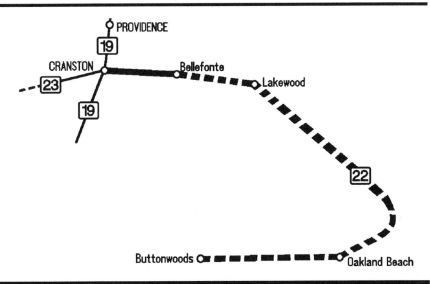

0 Cranston (South Auburn), RI	3 Spring Green	8 Oakland Beach
1 Bellefonte	4 Hoxsie	10 Buttonwoods, RI
2 Lakewood (Warwick)	5 Coiss	
	6 Bayside	
	7 Warwick Sta.	

BUILT: 1875-80.

OPERATORS: *New York, Providence & Boston*, 1875-76; *Warwick*, 1876-79; *New York, Providence & Boston*, 1880-92; *New York, New Haven & Hartford*, 1892-99; *Rhode Island Suburban*, 1899-1921; *United Electric*, 1921-1949; *Warwick*, 1949-82; *Providence & Worcester*, 1982- .

DAILY PASSENGER TRAINS: *1893:* 12. Passenger service ended 1935.

ABANDONMENTS: Buttonwoods-Lakewood, 1936; Lakewood-Bellefonte, 1954.

The Warwick RR received a charter in 1873 to build from South Auburn, on the New York, Providence & Boston RR, eight miles south to Oakland Beach on Narragansett Bay. The primary purpose of the route seems to have been to provide passenger access from Providence to shorefront real estate. The line was opened July 5, 1875. At first the

New York Providence & Boston operated the line, but in 1876 the new railroad went on its own. Troubles overtook the short line, and in 1879 the Warwick shut down, bankrupt. That year the Warwick was re-organized as the Rhode Island Central RR, and on July 1, 1880, service resumed under the auspices of the New York, Providence & Boston. Soon after it acquired control, the NYP&B extended the Rhode Island Central from its terminus at Oakland Beach another two miles to the adjoining waterfront community of Buttonwoods.

In 1892 the New Haven RR in turn acquired control of the New York, Providence & Boston, and hence of the Rhode Island Central. Seven years later the New Haven transferred the Rhode Island Central to the Rhode Island Suburban RY, a New Haven subsidiary which operated trolley lines. The new owners electrified the Rhode Island Central and converted it into a trolley operation. In 1921 the Suburban RY was succeeded by the United Electric RYs. Although passenger trolleys last ran in 1935, electric freight service continued. In 1936 the line was cut back to Lakewood, leaving only two miles of track between there and Cranston.

In 1949 United Electric sold the remaining line to a new Warwick RY. The Warwick converted from electric to diesel operation in 1952 and lopped off another mile of track two years later. Chemicals accounted for the bulk of the railroad's traffic. In 1960 the line was purchased by Oscar Greene, who personally ran the railroad, and in the process became perhaps the best-known short line president in the nation. With only a single-mile route, two small locomotives, and three employees (as of 1967), this diminutive short line continued to operate independently until October 3, 1982, when it was sold to the Providence & Worcester RR. It continues as the P&W's Warwick Industrial Track, serving a plastics plant and a Flex-Flo terminal.

Sources: Ackerman, "Meet Oscar Greene"; Francis, "Oscar Greene's 9/10 of a Mile"; Greene, "The Warwick Railway"; Lewis, *American Short Line Railway Guide*, 96; *Moody's Transportation Manual, 1983*, 871; Roy, "Providence & Worcester Succeeds on Service."

23. Pawtuxet Valley

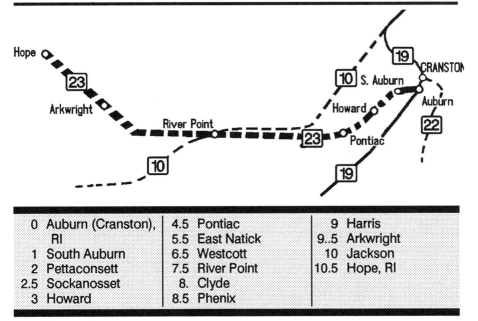

0	Auburn (Cranston), RI	4.5	Pontiac	9	Harris
1	South Auburn	5.5	East Natick	9..5	Arkwright
2	Pettaconsett	6.5	Westcott	10	Jackson
2.5	Sockanosset	7.5	River Point	10.5	Hope, RI
3	Howard	8.	Clyde		
		8.5	Phenix		

BUILT: 1874-80.

OPERATORS: *Hartford, Providence & Fishkill, 1874-78; New York & New England, 1878-79; New York, Providence & Boston, 1880-92; New York, New Haven & Hartford, 1892-1968; Penn Central, 1969-1976; Providence & Worcester, 1976-* .

DAILY PASSENGER TRAINS: *1893:* 12, *1919:* 5. Passenger service ended Auburn-River Point, Jan. 1922; River Point-Hope, ca. 1926.

ABANDONMENTS: Pontiac-River Point, 1924; Arkright-Hope, 1951; River Point-Arkwright, 1965; South Auburn-Pontiac, 1991.

The Hartford, Providence & Fishkill RR received a charter in 1872 to build the Pawtuxet Valley RR from its station at River Point to the village of Hope, three miles away. This line was opened August 1874, and was operated as a branch of the Hartford, Providence & Fishkill. In 1878 it became part of the New York & New England system.

Meanwhile, in 1875 the New York, Providence & Boston RR secured a charter for a Pontiac Branch RR authorized to construct a line from its Auburn station five miles to Pontiac. Around 1879 the NYP&B struck a deal with the New York & New England whereby the

NYP&B would lease the Pawtuxet Valley, which in turn would build an extension to Pontiac, where it would link up with the Pontiac Branch.

On January 1, 1880, the Pontiac Branch and the extension of the Pawtuxet Valley opened simultaneously, forming a through route from Auburn to Hope operated by the New York Providence & Boston. The New Haven took control in 1892 when it absorbed the New York, Providence & Boston. During the 1890s commuter rail service of a sort was operated over this line between Hope and downtown Providence (the schedules, though, did not encourage commuting).

With the end of passenger service in 1922 the New Haven no longer needed the entire line. The two-mile segment between Pontiac and River Point was abandoned, dividing the remaining trackage into two short branches. The abandoned portion had no freight customers. On the western branch the outermost mile from Arkwright to Hope was abandoned in 1951, after revenues the year previous had plunged to $361; the rest of the western segment was let go in 1965.

Freight traffic also dwindled on the eastern segment from Auburn to Pontiac. Under the Penn Central in the early 1970s the track beyond Howard was out of service and Howard, the only active station, averaged but one freight car a week. With the establishment of Conrail in 1976, the line was sold to the Providence & Worcester, who continued to operate it into the 1980s. At the end of 1991 the P&W received permission to abandon all but the initial mile of what remained of the Pawtuxet Valley, and even this final remnant may soon be gone.

Sources: *Chronological History of the New Haven Railroad*; *Poor's Manual of Railroads, 1878*, 98; *Poor's Manual of Railroads, 1888*, 67; *Poor's Manual of Railroads, 1890*, 57; U.S. Railway Association, *Final System Plan*, 2:485-86; U.S. Railway Association, *Preliminary System Plan*, 2:802-03; 86 I.C.C. 473.

24. Providence & Springfield

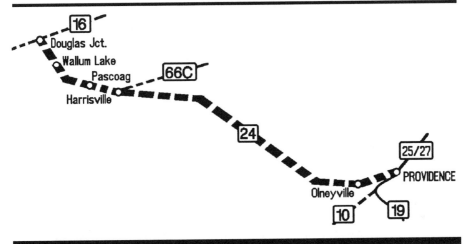

0 Providence, RI	7 Graystone	17 Tarkiln
1.5 Dike St.	8 Esmond (Enfield)	19 Oakland
2 Olneyville	(Allenville)	21 Harrisville
3.5 Dyerville	9 Georgiaville	22.5 Pascoag
4 Manton	10 Stillwater	23 Bridgeton
5 Lymansville	12 Smithfield	27 Wallum Lake
6 Allendale	14 Primrose	28 Clear River, RI
6.5 Centredale	16 Fields Sta.	29 Douglas Jct., MA

BUILT: 1872-73; Douglas Jct. extension, 1893.

OPERATORS: *Providence & Springfield*, 1873-90; *New York & New England*, 1890-95; *New England*, 1895-98; *New York, New Haven & Hartford*, 1898-1965.

DAILY PASSENGER TRAINS: *1893:* 10, *1919:* 6. Passenger service Pascoag-Douglas Jct. discontinued 1895 or 1896 and restored 1904; discontinued Wallum Lake-Douglas Jct., 1921, Pascoag-Wallum Lake, 1924 or 1925; passenger service on rest of line ended ca. 1931.

ABANDONMENTS: Pascoag-Douglas Jct., 1937; Olneyville-Pascoag, 1962; Providence-Olneyville, 1965.

Chartered in 1871 as the Woonasquatuckett RR, this Rhode Island railroad was renamed the Providence & Springfield RR before construction began in 1872. Both the city of Providence and the town of Burrillville assisted the project. The initial portion of the road from

Olneyville to Pascoag opened in August 1873. The P&S used two miles of Hartford, Providence & Fishkill track between Olneyville and Union Station, Providence, until its own line was completed between these points in 1874. In 1880 it opened its own Providence station on Gaspee Street. By 1878 the line had three locomotives, three passenger cars, and seventy-seven freight cars, and it still had hopes of pushing onward toward its goal of providing a direct rail link between Providence and Springfield. Although the P&S never seriously contemplated building its own line as far as Springfield, it at least hoped to secure a connection with the Boston & Albany main line at Palmer.

The P&S was unable to realize its ambition, and for twenty years it was a long branch line to Pascoag, providing commuter service to Providence and freight service to several textile mills along its route. Although revenues exceeded expenses, the P&S never paid a dividend to its stockholders. In 1890 it was leased by the New York & New England RR. In June 1893 that railroad extended the P&S an additional seven miles to Douglas Junction, Mass., on the NY&NE main line. Tracks of the Southbridge & Blackstone branch of the NY&NE brought the route within fifteen miles of a connection with the main line of the Boston & Albany.

But the connection was never built. In 1895 the NY&NE was swallowed by the New England RR, controlled by the New Haven RR, which was not interested in completing the Providence-Springfield route. The New Haven soon discontinued operation of the newly built Pascoag-Douglas Junction extension. Freight and passenger service on this line was not restored until 1904. Passenger service between Wallum Lake and Douglas Junction ended by September 1921, and trains between Pascoag and Wallum Lake vanished between September 1924 and April 1925. Freight service was permanently suspended west of Pascoag in 1926, and eleven years later the track was officially abandoned. Passenger service on the rest of the line continued until the early 1930s. The remaining segment from Providence to Pascoag was operated as a New Haven freight branch until 1962 when all but the first two miles of track out of Providence were abandoned. Three years later the remaining two miles of track met the same fate.

Sources: Ozog, "Another Way to Boston"; 221 I.C.C. 591.

25. Providence & Worcester

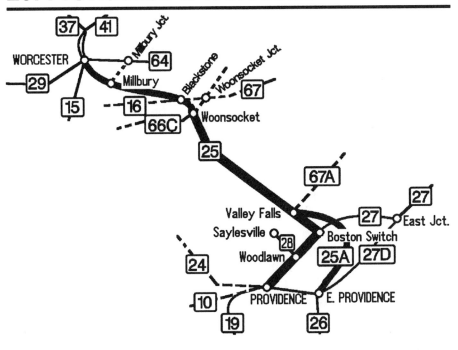

0	Providence, RI	18	Blackstone (Blackstone Jct.)	42	South Worcester (Grand Jct.)

0   Providence, RI
4   Woodlawn
4.5   Pawtucket (Central Falls)
5   Boston Switch
6   Valley Falls
7   Lonsdale
8   Berkeley
9   Ashton
11   Albion
12   Manville
15   Hamlet
16   Woonsocket, RI
17   Waterford, MA

18   Blackstone (Blackstone Jct.)
20   Millville
24   Uxbridge
26   Whitins
29   Riverdale
31   Northbridge
33   Farnumsville (Farnums)
34   Saundersville (Grafton)
35   Wilkinsonville (Sutton)
37   Millbury

42   South Worcester (Grand Jct.)
43   Worcester, MA

25A. East Providence Branch

0   Valley Falls, RI
2   Darlington
5   Phillipsdale
6   East Providence, RI

BUILT: 1846-47; East Providence Branch, 1874.

OPERATORS: *Providence & Worcester,* 1847-89; *New York, Providence & Boston, 1889-92; New York, New Haven & Hartford,* 1892-1968; *Penn Central,* 1969-72; *Providence & Worcester,* 1973- .

DAILY PASSENGER TRAINS: *1869:* 6, *1893:* 16, *1919:* 15, *1935:* 2, *1950:* 4, *1960:* 2. Passenger service discontinued 1960. Passenger service on the East Providence Branch was only operated ca. 1893-1898.

ABANDONMENTS: None.

In 1828 the Blackstone Canal was completed between Providence and Worcester. Never particularly successful, the canal was sold in 1844 to the Providence & Worcester RR. This railroad had been chartered that year as separate corporations in Massachusetts and Rhode Island; the two were merged to form a single company the following year. Providence interests raised funds for the P&W and afterwards controlled the railroad. (Worcester investors were notably leery of purchasing stock).

The Blackstone Canal was abandoned, and construction began in the spring of 1846. The railroad, which generally utilized the canal right of way, opened in October 1847. At that time the Boston & Providence RR obtained rights over the first five miles of the P&W between Providence and Boston Switch to extend its line into downtown Providence. Afterwards both railroads jointly operated this segment, and today it forms part of Amtrak's Northeast Corridor. In 1848 the P&W built a union station in Providence, which it shared with the Boston & Providence and New York, Providence & Boston Railroads.

The line was originally intended as a replacement for the canal, which mostly carried local traffic from the busy textile villages of the Blackstone Valley. Gradually, its potential as a part of through routes between Providence and the West began to be appreciated. Double tracking of the line began in 1853 (but took until 1885 to complete!). By the 1880s both the Boston & Albany and the Boston & Maine coveted it as logical extensions of their systems. But the P&W continued to operate independently until 1889 when it was leased to the New York, Providence & Boston. This lease was assumed by the New Haven RR in 1892.

By the 1930s passenger service on the P&W had been reduced to a single daily round trip between Worcester and Providence. In April 1946 the New York-to-Portland *State of Maine* was rerouted from the Norwich & Worcester to the P&W (this train ran by way of New Haven,

The former P&W depot in Uxbridge, Mass., lives on as a stylish bank.

Providence, Worcester, and Lowell). Local passenger service between Providence and Worcester, which had been reduced to a single daily round trip, was increased to four round trips in 1953, then cut back to one again the following year. The local train was eliminated in 1956 or 1957, and all passenger service came to an end in 1960 when the *State of Maine* made its final run. By 1963 all double tracks had been reduced to single.

Although the P&W was operated as an integral part of the New Haven, that railroad never got around to acquiring more than 28% of its stock. A peculiar form of voting stock shares made it difficult for a single interest to control the line. The Penn Central, when it took over the New Haven in 1969, refused to continue the lease unless rewritten. The majority stockholders of the P&W therefore petitioned the I.C.C. to be allowed to resume independent operation, and in February 1973 the P&W once more became an operating railroad. Since 1973 the new P&W has grown to include several former New Haven and Boston & Maine lines and has acquired trackage rights over Amtrak's shore line west of Providence. Service on the original P&W main line now consists of one daily round trip through freight between Worcester and Valley

Falls and several local weekday freights operating out of Worcester and Valley Falls.

The sole major accident on the P&W occurred only a few years after the line had been completed. On August 12, 1853, an eastbound excursion train crowded with mill workers pulled out of the Valley Falls station and attempted to reach the double track at Boston Switch before the scheduled westbound arrived. It lost the race, and in the resulting head-on collision fourteen persons died.

In 1872 the P&W struck a bargain with the New Jersey Central RR and the Pennsylvania Coal Co. to build a large wharf and coal storage facility near India Point in East Providence. Two years later the P&W opened its only branch line, a six-mile extension from the main line at Valley Falls to the new facility in East Providence. This line appears to have been operated only for freight service until around 1893 when commuter trains began running between Valley Falls and East Providence. These were discontinued between June 1896 and July 1898.

Sources: Armstrong, *Railfan's Guide*, 34-35; Baker, *Formation*, 72, 93; Cady, *Civic and Architectural Development*, 104-5, 115-18; Thomas Humphrey, personal correspondence; Kirkland, *Men, Cities, and Transportation*, 1:250-51; Lewis, *American Short Line Railway Guide*, 96; Lewis, *Blackstone Valley Line*; Poor, *History*, 146; Roy, "Providence & Worcester Succeeds on Service"; Shaw, *History of Railroad Accidents*, 31-33.

26. Providence, Warren & Bristol

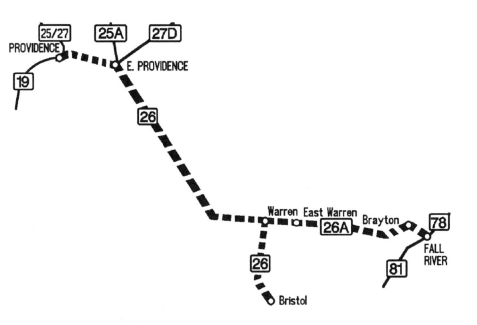

0 Providence, RI	7 Drownville (Cres-	16 Bristol, RI
2 East Providence	cent Park)	
(India Point)	7.5 West Barrington	**26A. Fall River**
3.5 Gulf	8.5 Nayatt	**Branch**
4 Vue de L'Eau	10 Barrington	
(Kettle Point)	10.5 Hampden Meadows	0 Warren, RI
4.5 Squantum	11 North Warren	0.5 East Warren, RI
5 Silver Spring	11.5 Warren	3 Touisset, MA
5.5 Pomham	12 South Warren	3.5 Ocean Grove
6 Riverside	13.5 Beach Terrace	4 South Swansea
6.5 Bullocks Point	14 Bristol Higlands	7 Brayton
	15 Poppasquash Rd.	8 Fall River, MA

BUILT: 1853-55; Fall River Branch, 1865, 1875.

OPERATORS: *Boston & Providence, 1855-1860 Providence, Warren & Bristol, 1860-91; Old Colony, 1891-93; New York, New Haven & Hartford, 1893-1968; Penn Central, 1969-1976; Providence & Worcester, 1976-81.* Fall River Branch operated by *Fall River, Warren & Providence*, 1865-73; *Boston & Providence*, 1873-75; *Old Colony*, 1875-93.

DAILY PASSENGER TRAINS: *1869:* 8, *1893:* 21, *1923:* 64, *1935:* 22. Electric trolleys provided all passenger service, 1901-34. Passenger service ended Warren-Fall River 1932; all remaining service ended 1937.

ABANDONMENTS: Warren-Bristol, 1973; East Providence-Warren, 1976; Providence-East Providence, ca. 1981; Fall River branch (Brayton-Fall River, 1932; East Warren-Brayton, 1937; Warren-East Warren, 1976).

The Providence & Bristol RR received a charter in 1850 to build a rail line from East Providence to Warren and Bristol. Construction began in September 1853 and the line was opened July 12, 1855 under the new name of Providence, Warren & Bristol RR. Passenger cars were hauled by horses to the Providence & Worcester depot until 1857, when the PW&B built its own Providence depot on India Street.

At first the Boston & Providence operated the line, but in 1860 the P&B began running its own equipment. For a time in the late 1860s Bristol became a steamboat port with ships sailing for New York. The Boston & Providence gained control of the railroad in 1873 (though it continued to be operated separately). This interest was transferred to the Old Colony RR in 1888 as part of a settlement of competition between the two lines over traffic in the Taunton area. The Old Colony took over operation in 1891 and the PW&B, along with the rest of the Old Colony, became part of the New Haven system two years later.

In 1856 and 1857 railroads were chartered in Massachusetts and Rhode Island to extend the PW&B from Warren to Fall River, opening a new direct route from Providence to Fall River and ultimately, Newport. This railroad, the Fall River, Warren & Providence opened in April 1865, as the Civil War ended. The new line ran from the connection with the PW&B at Warren to Brayton, Mass., on the Taunton River, where a ferry took passengers to Fall River on the far shore. The Fall River, Warren & Providence was briefly operated by the PW&B before it began to run its own trains. The Boston & Providence bought the line in 1873 but sold it to the Old Colony in 1875, when the ferry at Fall River was replaced by the Slades Ferry Bridge (this double-decker structure featured rail tracks on top and a highway—in later years a trolley line as well—underneath). After the Old Colony absorbed the Providence, Warren & Bristol in 1891 the latter line and the Warren-Fall River branch functioned as a single unit.

In 1900 the New Haven RR, which now operated these lines, strung wires above the tracks and introduced frequent electric car service between Providence, Bristol, and Fall River. A power station was built in Warren. Car service terminated at Fox Point, Providence, since efforts to operate the railroad-sized electric cars through to Union Station over Providence's narrow city streets had proved unsuccessful. The opening of the 5980-foot East Side Tunnel—as well as a 1000-foot viaduct and an 800-foot drawbridge across the Seekonk River—in November 1908 brought the electric trains directly to downtown Providence. The Bristol cars used streetcar trackage to reach stops at Church Street and Constitution Street beyond Bristol station. For a time these lines carried heavy traffic, but first the automobile and later the Great Depression cut into this business. In January 1932, after the Slades Ferry Bridge was damaged, trolley service between Warren and Fall River was replaced by buses, and the bridge was transferred to the state for use by automobiles. The rest of the line, Warren to Brayton, was operated for freight only until its abandonment in 1937, with the first half mile, Warren to East Warren, retained.

Electric service continued to Warren and Bristol until 1934, when gas electric cars took over passenger service. These continued until July 1937 when the line became used exclusively for freight. In 1969 the PW&B passed to the Penn Central, which abandoned the Warren-Bristol segment in 1973. The remaining segment saw only twice weekly freight service involving only three or four cars per train. When Conrail took over most of the Penn Central in 1976 the remainder of the PW&B was transferred to the newly independent Providence & Worcester RR, but the latter never operated the line beyond East Providence. The tracks were removed and converted into a bicycle path. The sole remaining segment of the PW&B, the East Side tunnel, was acquired by the state of Rhode Island in 1981 and freight operations halted shortly after the takeover.

Sources: J. Leonard Bachelder, personal communication; Cady, *Civic and Architectural Development*, 119-21; Harlow, *Steelways*, 229-30; Mitchell, "Providence, Warren, Bristol"; U.S. Railway Association, *Final System Plan*, 2:484-85; U.S. Railway Association, *Preliminary System Plan*, 2:802; 221 I.C.C. 453.

27. Boston & Providence

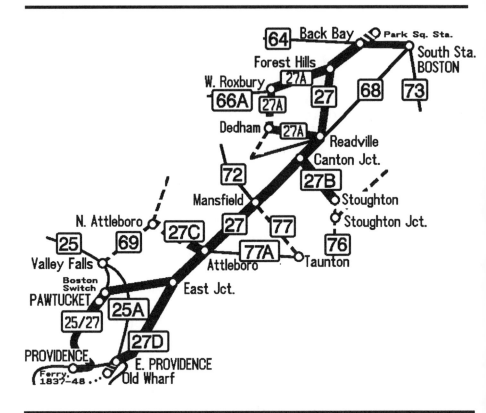

0 Boston (South Sta.), MA	7.5 Hazelwood	25 Mansfield
1 Back Bay	8 Hyde Park (Fairmount)	28 West Mansfield (Tobeys)
2 Ruggles St.	10 Readville	32 Attleboro
3 Roxbury	11 Green Lodge	34 Dodgeville
3.5 Heath St. (Heath)	12 Route 128	35 East Jct.
4 Boylston St. (Boylston)	13 Dedham Rd. (Canton Rd.)	36 Hebronville
4.5 Jamaica Plain	15 Canton Jct. (Canton)	38 South Attleboro, MA
5 Forest Hills (Forest Hill) (Toll Gate)	18 Sharon	39 Boston Switch, RI
6.5 Mt. Hope (Monterey)	19 Sharon Heights	39.5 Pawtucket
7 Clarendon Hills	23 East Foxboro (Foxboro)	40 Woodlawn
		44 Providence, RI

27A. Dedham Branch	27B. Stoughton Branch	
0 Forest Hills (Toll Gate), MA	0 Canton Jct., MA	4 Chestnut St.
1 Roslindale (South St.)	1 Canton (South Canton)	5 North Attleboro (High St.), MA
2 Bellevue (Central)	2 Springdale (Spring Dale)	**27D. East Providence Branch**
2.5 Highland	3 West Stoughton (Birds)	0 East Junction, MA
3 West Roxbury	4 Stoughton (Stoughton Central), MA	2 Perrins
3.5 Spring St.		3.5 Daggetts, MA
5 Dedham	**27C. Attleboro Branch**	4 Slater, RI
5.5 Stonehaven (Stone Haven)		5 Rumford
6 East Dedham (Walnut Hill)	0 Attleboro, MA	7 East Providence (India Point), RI
7 Readville, MA	1 Farmers	7.5 Old Wharf (Providence) (Fox Point), RI
	3 Falls Village	

BUILT: 1832-35, (East Jct.-Providence, 1847); Dedham Branch (Dedham-Readville), 1834, (Forest Hills-Dedham), 1850; Stoughton Branch, 1844-45; Attleboro Branch, 1871.

OPERATORS: *Boston & Providence*, 1834-88; *Old Colony*, 1888-93; *New York, New Haven & Hartford*, 1893-1968; *Penn Central*, 1969-1976; *Amtrak*, 1976- ; *MBTA (Commuter passenger service)*, 1976- ; *Conrail (freight)*, 1976- ; *Providence & Worcester (freight)*,1976- .

DAILY PASSENGER TRAINS: *1869:* 14, *1893:* 42, *1919:* 49, *1935:* 58, *1950:* 54, *1960:* 44, *1971:* 30, *1981:* 18 (Boston-Attleboro, 42), *1994:* 30 (Bosto-Attleboro, 52). Passenger service discontinued on Dedham Branch, West Roxbury-Dedham, 1940; Dedham-Readville, 1967. Regular service ended on East Providence Branch ca. 1914, although used by Narragansett Park racetrack excursions until 1968.

ABANDONMENTS: Dedham Branch (West Roxbury-Dedham, 1965; Dedham-East Dedham, ca. 1980). Attleboro Branch converted to trolley operation, 1903.

Chartered in 1831, the Boston & Providence was one of New England's first three railroads. Captain William Gibbs McNeill surveyed an almost straight line between the two cities, with a maximum grade of thirty-seven feet to the mile. McNeill also supervised the construction of the road itself, including the massive viaduct at Canton, which is still

Outbound from Boston, a passenger train approaches Forest Hills, Mass., in September 1971.

very much in service after nearly 160 years. Raising funds was not easy, since the project attracted little support in Providence, which viewed the railroad as competition for the Blackstone Canal, which linked Providence to Worcester and the West. Providence, it was feared, might become "a mere way station on the road from New York to Boston" (Harlow, 104-5).

Construction commenced at Boston late in 1832. The road began at Park Square, then crossed the Back Bay heading south on an embankment. The first trains were operated between Boston and Dedham in June 1834, and the line was opened to Canton the following September. Service was initiated between Boston and Providence in June 1835, although passengers had to transfer around the still uncompleted Canton Viaduct and had to take a ferry between India Point (East Providence) and Providence. The viaduct opened in July 1835, and the tracks reached Providence by the end of the year, via a wooden drawbridge. A ferry provided a connection across the harbor in South

Providence with the New York, Providence & Boston RR, which opened in 1837.

The new railroad became one of the key routes in New England, a status it has retained ever since. In 1847 it constructed a new, more direct route to Providence. Departing from the old main line at East Junction (in Attleboro) the new line passed through Pawtucket, R.I., where it met the tracks of the Providence & Worcester RR, then under construction. The B&P obtained rights over the the final 5-½ miles of the P&W from Pawtucket to Providence, where it met the New York, Providence & Boston in a union station. The old main line through East Providence was reduced to a branch line.

Almost from the beginning the B&P formed part of the main route between Boston and New York. In the early years most of this traffic continued on the New York, Providence & Boston to steamships on Long Island Sound at Stonington and later, Groton, Conn., to reach Manhattan; but with the completion of the rail bridge across the Thames River at New London in 1889 the P&B—now part of the Old Colony system—became part of the all-rail shore line. Within a few years crack trains like the *Merchants Limited* and the *Federal* rode the P&B each day. The New Haven, which absorbed the Old Colony system in 1893, elevated the B&P tracks into Boston onto a tall embankment and in 1899 abandoned its old Park Square depot for the new South Station, which it shared with trains from the Old Colony lines and the Boston & Albany.

In addition to considerable long-distance traffic the B&P was a prime commuter route. By the mid-1890s the New Haven was operating trains every half hour between Boston and Forest Hills, and after 1897 the frequency was increased to every fifteen minutes. This lasted until 1904 when competition from trolleys and the new elevated railroad to Roxbury (completed 1901 and extended to Forest Hills in 1909) cut into the New Haven's commuter business. Nevertheless, traffic remained heavy enough on the B&P for the New Haven to consider electrifying the route.

The P&B remains an important rail link. The New Haven continued to operate the line until 1969 when the Penn Central absorbed the New Haven. Amtrak took over intercity passenger service in May 1971 and in January 1973 the MBTA bought the portion of the B&P in Massachusetts; Amtrak purchased the Rhode Island main line in 1976.

Intercity passenger trains are operated by Amtrak; Amtrak also provides commuter service, under contract to the MBTA. In February 1981 the MBTA cut back B&P commuter service to Attleboro, and MBTA trains did not return to Providence until February 1988. Freight service is provided by Conrail and the Providence & Worcester (the East Providence Branch from East Providence to the Massachusetts state line. The P&W also has trackage rights between Providence and Attleboro to service the Newport & Fall River line which it no longer uses). Between 1979 and 1987 the line between Forest Hills and Back Bay station was taken out of service and the old embankment demolished. Amtrak and the federal government funded the reconstruction of the line for 100-mph trains.

The Dedham Branch, originally constructed in 1834 and initially operated by horse power, was one of the earliest branch lines in New England. In 1850 it was extended northward and eastward through West Roxbury to Forest Hills. On March 14, 1887, a Boston-bound commuter train was passing over the Bussey Bridge near Forest Hills. Without warning the bridge collapsed, sending cars crashing to the street below. Twenty-four people died and another 125 were injured, many seriously. A subsequent investigation found the iron bridge poorly designed and indifferently maintained.

The entire Forest Hills-Dedham-Readville route eventually was double tracked to accommodate frequent commuter trains to Boston. Between 1926 and 1938 commuter trains used this route to form a loop that enabled New Haven commuter trains to return to Boston without turning the train. Passenger and freight service between Dedham and West Roxbury was discontinued in 1940. For several years part of this track was used to store old locomotives awaiting the scrapper's torch, until finally it was abandoned altogether in 1965. The part of the loop between Forest Hills and West Roxbury, which had been extended to Needham Junction in 1906, remains in service for commuter trains between Forest Hills and Needham Junction.

The Massachusetts legislature chartered the Stoughton Branch RR in 1844 to construct a branch from the B&P main line at Canton to Stoughton, a distance of four miles. Construction began in the summer of 1844 and the line was completed in April 1845. The B&P operated the line as a branch under contract. In 1855 the Easton Branch RR (operated by the B&P) extended the branch another four miles from

Stoughton to North Easton. In 1866 the Old Colony & Newport RR took control of the Easton Branch and incorporated part of it into its Dighton & Somerset extension. After the Old Colony acquired the B&P in 1888 it began rerouting some of its through trains from Boston to Fall River and New Bedford over the Stoughton Branch, including the famous *Fall River Boat Train*. A second track was added on the branch in 1890 (removed in 1941) to accommodate this main line traffic. Through passenger trains to New Bedford were discontinued in 1958, but commuter service from Stoughton to Boston has continued to the present.

The Attleboro Branch RR received a charter in 1867 to build a line between Attleboro and North Attleboro. This railroad was completed in January 1871 and leased to the Boston & Providence. After the Old Colony constructed its Walpole & Wrentham Branch in 1890, the Attleboro Branch became part of a secondary route between Boston and Providence. When the B&P's lease expired in 1901, the New Haven decided to construct its own line from North Attleboro to

A Penn Central commuter train between Roslindale and Forest Hills on the part of the Dedham Branch that now serves Needham (March 1971).

Adamsdale. This line was completed in June 1903, and the Attleboro Branch was returned to its owners, who converted it to a trolley line. After the construction of the direct line to Providence in 1847 the

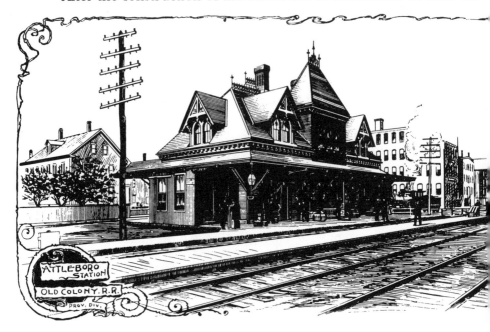

Attleboro station in the 1890s. (History of the Old Colony Railroad, *1893).*

original main line from East Junction to East Providence became the East Providence branch. For most of its history this line has been operated primarily for freight. After 1847 only occasional passenger trains used the line, mostly for connections to steamboats. Regular passenger service resumed about 1880 and lasted until around 1910, summer boat trains continuing for another four years or so. Narragansett Park race trains from both Boston and Providence used the branch during racing season from about 1937 to 1968. Today, the Providence & Worcester serves the Rhode Island portion of the branch, while Massachusetts customers are served by Conrail.

Sources: Galvin, *History of Canton Junction*; Harlow, *Steelways*, 78, 104-12; Humphrey and Clark, *Boston's Commuter Rail*, 29-38; Lee, "Dedham Branch"; Poor, *History*, 102-03; Reed, *Train Wrecks*, 86-87; Shaw, *History of Railroad Accidents*, 60-61.

28. Moshassuck Valley

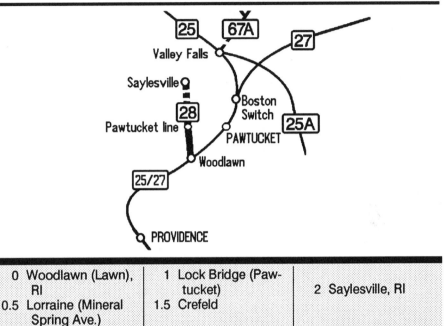

0 Woodlawn (Lawn), RI	1 Lock Bridge (Pawtucket)	2 Saylesville, RI
0.5 Lorraine (Mineral Spring Ave.)	1.5 Crefeld	

BUILT: 1876-77.

OPERATORS: *Moshassuck Valley,* 1877-1982; *Providence & Worcester, 1982-.*

DAILY PASSENGER TRAINS: *1893:* 10, *1903:* 20, *1919:* 6. Passenger service ended 1921.

ABANDONMENTS: Saylesville-Pawtucket city line, 1991.

In 1874 the industrial village of Saylesville, R.I., was two miles from the nearest rail line, the joint Boston & Providence-Boston & Worcester tracks between Pawtucket and Providence. A charter to build a branch line was secured, and in January 1877 the Moshassuck Valley RR opened.

Short branch lines such as these almost inevitably came under the control of the main line railroad with which they connected, but the Moshassuck Valley was different. It remained independent for more than 100 years, one of the few railroads in Rhode Island or Connecticut to escape the monopolistic grasp of the New Haven RR. For most of its existence it owned but two locomotives and limited passenger equipment. Most of its traffic was freight in and out of the Saylesville mills, although until 1921 it also provided a high level of passenger service, with four stations on its less than two miles of track.

The purchase of this line by the Providence & Worcester RR in October 1982 ended its long independence, but the line continued in use as the P&W's Moshassuck Industrial Track. In 1991 the P&W abandoned the outer three-quarters of a mile of track between Saylesville and the Pawtucket city line, leaving little more than a mile in service.

Sources: Cornwall and Smith, *Names First*, 73; Lewis, *American Short Line Railway Guide*, 95; *Moody's Transportation, 1983*, 821; *Poor's Manual of Railroads, 1890*, 42.

Moshassuck Valley locomotive number 3, an 0-6-0 switcher built by the Rhode Island Lomotive Works in 1893, is here shown at Saylesville in April 1932. (Photo courtesy Walker Transportation Collection, Beverly Historical Society & Museum.)

29. Western (Boston & Albany)

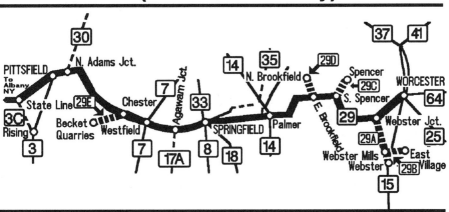

0 Worcester, MA	68 Woronoco	7 West Oxford
1 South Worcester (Hammond St.) (Worcester Jct.)	71 Russell	8 Glenwood
	75 Huntington (Chester Village)	10 Webster Mills
3 Jamesville	82 Chester (Chester Factories)	11 Webster, MA
7 Webster Jct.	86 Middlefield	**29B. East Village Branch**
9 Rochdale (Clappville)	90 Becket	
13 Charlton	93 Washington	0 Webster Mills, MA
18 South Spencer (Spencer)	98 Hinsdale	1 East Village, MA
20 East Brookfield	101 Dalton	**29C. Spencer Branch**
23 Brookfield (South Brookfield)	104 North Adams Jct.	
	106 Pittsfield	0 South Spencer, MA
26 West Brookfield	110 West Pittsfield (Shaker Village)	2 Spencer, MA
29 Warren	112 Richmond Summit	**29D. North Brookfield Branch**
31 West Warren	114 Richmond	
35 West Brimfield	115 Richmond Furnace	0 East Brookfield, MA
40 Palmer	117 State Line, MA	4 North Brookfield, MA
45 North Wilbraham	*156 Albany, NY*	
48 Oak St. (Indian Orchard)		**29E. Chester & Becket Branch**
52 Athol Jct.	**29A. Webster Branch**	
54 Springfield		0 Chester, MA
56 Mittineague	0 Webster Jct., MA	5 Becket Quarries, MA
57 West Springfield	0.5 West Auburn	
58 Agawam Jct.	2.5 Texas	
63 Westfield	3 North Oxford Mills	
	6 Howarths	

BUILT: 1836-41; North Brookfield Branch, 1875; Spencer Branch, 1879; Webster Branch/East Village Branch, 1884; Chester & Becket Branch, 1897.

OPERATORS: *Western*, 1840-67; *Boston & Albany*, 1867-1900; *New York Central (Boston & Albany)*, 1900-68; *Penn Central*, 1968-76; *Amtrak (passenger service)*, 1971- ;*Conrail*, 1976- .

DAILY PASSENGER TRAINS: *1869:* 9, *1893:* 17, *1919:* 19, *1935:* 17, *1950:* 16, *1960:* 7, *1971:* 2, *1981:* 2, *1994:* 2. No passenger service Springfield-Albany, May 1971-October 1975. Passenger service on Webster Branch ended ca. 1919; Spencer Branch, 1932 or 1933; North Brookfield Branch, 1935. Chester & Becket Branch freight only.

ABANDONMENTS: Chester & Becket Branch, 1931; Webster Branch/East Village Branch, 1958; Spencer Branch, 1972; North Brookfield Branch, 1972.

The Western RR formed part of New England's first great through rail route, which more than 150 years later remains the region's most important. It began in 1833 when the directors of the Boston & Worcester RR (then under construction) received a charter to construct a second railroad from Worcester through Springfield to the Massachusetts border. As surveyed by William H. Swift, George W. Whistler, and William G. McNeill the route was a construction challenge of the first magnitude. Only seven miles of the entire route were level, and many expensive deep cuts and embankments would be required. At the summit the tracks would be 1,456 feet above sea level. Funds proved to be more difficult to raise than anticipated, and the business depression in the wake of the Panic of 1837 nearly killed the project. Worcester investors were leery of a scheme that might reduce their city to a way stop between Boston and Albany. The railroad obtained $3 million in loans from the state of Massachusetts . Construction began from Worcester during the winter of 1836-37.

The Western also had trouble securing permission from New York State to extend the railroad from the Massachusetts border to Albany. As a temporary measure the Western obtained the right to use the Hudson & Berkshire RR, which extended from West Stockbridge, Mass., to Hudson, N.Y. Construction of the Hudson & Berkshire commenced in 1838 and was completed by 1840. The Hudson & Berkshire was lightly built, with difficult grades and tight curves. The Western finally secured its own Albany connection in 1840 when it leased the unbuilt Albany & West Stockbridge RR. When completed it

A westbound Conrail freight approaches Washington summit in the heart of the Berkshires in July 1992. The tracks here are more than 1400 feet above sea level.Construction in 1841 removed 100,000 cubic yards of rocks here and lowered the grade 55 feet.

would run from Greenbush, N.Y., (on the east bank of the Hudson opposite Albany) to the Massachusetts border at West Stockbridge.

The initial section of the Western between Worcester and Springfield opened in October 1839. The original Worcester depot was nearly a mile from that of the Boston & Worcester, although the tracks connected. Not until 1876 were these replaced by a single union station at Washington Square (the present unused union station dates from 1911). At Springfield the Western confronted the Connecticut River, which took nearly two years to bridge.

Meanwhile, the Western began building east from the Massachusetts border. Pittsfield was reached by May 1841. Even though the Connecticut River bridge was not completed the Western started construction west from West Springfield and reached Chester by March 1841. The bridge was finally finished in July, and in October the remaining gap between Chester and Pittsfield was closed. By using the Hudson & Berkshire, passengers could now travel from Boston to Hudson, N.Y., entirely by rail. In December the Western (Albany & West Stockbridge) line between Greenbush and Chatham, N.Y., opened, and the Boston to Albany railroad became a reality. (Actually, Boston and Greenbush: the ferry between Greenbush and Albany was not replaced by a bridge until 1866.) "The Western was the longest railroad yet constructed in America by a single corporation, and the most expensive" (Harlow, 134). Boston finally had its link to the west.

In 1842 the Albany & West Stockbridge was completed to the Massachusetts line, enabling the Western to ditch the substandard Hudson & Berkshire. Despite financial constraints the Western had been well built. After a few years of low revenues the Western's high construction standards paid off. Heavy through traffic—flour, grain, and manufactured goods—and growing local traffic kept the road prosperous. Double tracking began in 1847 and was completed twenty-one years later. The steep grades that challenge even modern diesels severely taxed the small locomotives of the day; "as late as the mid-[1860s] the most powerful engines were carrying over the road trains of only eight to ten cars" (Kirkland, 1:137).

In 1849 part of the Western became part of the first all-rail route between Boston and New York City. Trains on the Inland Route, as it would later be known, traveled through Worcester, Springfield, Hartford, and New Haven. For nearly forty years this was the most popular

Led by a GE C30-7A locomotive, an eastbound Conrail freight passes through Charlton, Mass., in July 1991.

route between the two cities until the completion of the shore route along the coast of Long Island Sound in 1889. Even today Amtrak operates four trains a day over this route.

The Western had been built as an extension of the Boston & Worcester, but the two railroads constantly clashed over the division of through freight and passenger revenues. Peace finally came in 1867 when the two lines merged to form the Boston & Albany RR, which in 1900 was leased to the New York Central system. For years the B&A retained its separate identity within the NYC system, but this gradually diminished until the B&A was formally merged into the NYC in 1961. The Western subsequently passed on to the Penn Central in 1968 and Conrail in 1976, where it forms part of one of the only routes in New England that still carries heavy through freight traffic. Most New England rail freight enters and leaves over this route; Amtrak operates daily a pair of Boston-Chicago and two pairs of Boston-Springfield-Hartford-New York passenger trains.

The worst accident on the Western occurred August 31, 1893, when repair crews working for a private contractor dangerously weakened Wilcutt's Bridge over the Westfield River at Chester. The bridge collapsed under the Boston-bound *Chicago Limited*, sending four cars into the river. Fourteen persons died in the wreck.

The Western RR avoided building branch lines. With the exception of the Pittsfield & North Adams (see chapter 30) all of the line's branches were built after the Western became part of the Boston & Albany. The Webster Branch was constructed as the Providence, Webster & Springfield RR by Horatio Slater (son of the famous Samuel), the owner of several mills in Webster. Two rail lines already served Webster, but both were controlled by the New York & New England RR, and neither reached Slater's mills in Webster's East Village . On completion in 1884, the line was operated by the B&A, although owned by Slater. This arrangement continued until 1958 when the line was abandoned to build a flood control project. A short segment of track in Webster remained in service after a connection was built to the New Haven's Norwich & Worcester line, but this was discontinued by 1971.

Local interests secured a charter for the North Brookfield RR in 1875, and this four-mile branch from East Brookfield on the B&A to North Brookfield was completed in January 1876. On completion it was leased to the B&A, which operated it as a branch. Passenger service ended on December 31, 1935, on the expiration of a lease agreement. The B&A, and later the NYC and Penn Central, continued to operate the line under lease until 1972 when the line was abandoned.

Local inhabitants also built the two-mile Spencer Branch between South Spencer on the B&A and Spencer. Built as the Spencer RR, the B&A leased the line on completion in 1879 and operated it as a B&A branch. In 1889 the B&A purchased the line outright. Passenger service ended in late 1932 or 1933. With only one customer remaining, Penn Central abandoned the line in 1972.

The freight-only Chester & Becket branch was chartered as the Chester & Becket RR in 1896 and opened the following year. Until 1930 the B&A operated it to serve several granite quarries. Hampered by steep grades, it ran only during the warmer months, since it was not thought to be worth the effort to keep the tracks clear of snow.

Sources: Baker, *Formation*, 5, 7-18, 21-23; Cornwall and Smith, *Names First*, 27, 91, 114; Farrell, *Railfan's Guide to Conrail*; Harlow, *Steelways*, 116-38; Thomas Humphrey, personal correspondence; Kirkland, *Men, Cities, and Transportation*, 1:125-37, 141-47; Mrazik, "Webster, on the Norwich-Worcester Branch"; Salsbury, *The State, the Investor, and the Railroad*; Shaw, *History of Railroad Accidents*, 311-12; 70 I.C.C. 643; 244 I.C.C. 533.

30. Pittsfield & North Adams

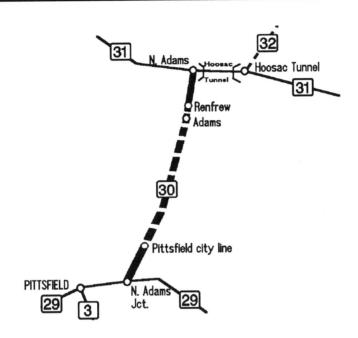

0 North Adams Jct., MA	4 Berkshire (Packards)	12 Maple Grove
0.5 Merrills Crossing	6 Farnams (East Lanesboro)	13 Adams (South Adams)
1 Coltsville	8 Cheshire	14 Renfrew
2.5 Pittsfield city line	11 Cheshire Harbor	15 Zylonite
		18 North Adams, MA

BUILT: 1845-46.

OPERATORS: *Western,* 1846-67; *Boston & Albany* , 1867-1900; *New York Central (Boston & Albany),* 1900-68; *Penn Central,* 1968-76; *Conrail,* 1976- , *Boston & Maine,* 1981-83; *Guilford,* 1983- .

DAILY PASSENGER TRAINS: *1869:* 8, *1893:* 10, *1919:* 8, *1935:* 3, *1950:* 4. Passenger service ended 1953.

ABANDONMENTS: Pittsfield city line-Adams, 1990; Adams-Renfrew, 1994.

The Pittsfield & North Adams RR was chartered in 1845 to extend the Housatonic RR northward from Pittsfield toward Rutland, Vt. The Western RR built the road and leased it before it was completed. It opened in December 1846 and became a branch of the Western and later, the Boston & Albany. It was apparently never particularly profitable, but its owners did not want it in the hands of rival lines. The Boston & Albany's successor, the Penn Central, in 1973 sought unsuccessfully to have the line between North Adams and Zylonite abandoned. In 1976 the line was transferred to Conrail.

Limestone has been the primary traffic on this line in recent years, with Adams, Renfrew, and Zylonite the busiest stations. In 1981 operation of the line north of the Pittsfield city limits at milepost 2.5 was transferred to the Boston & Maine (later Guilford). By the mid-1980s the line was in poor physical condition. In 1988 service between milepost 2.5 and Adams was suspended, and two years later this ten-mile segment was abandoned altogether. The Commonwealth of Massachusetts acquired the abandoned portion in 1993 with the intention of converting it to recreational uses. The rails were removed in 1993 and 1994.

Guilford abandoned another mile of track between Adams and Renfrew at the beginning of 1994, while continuing to provide freight service between Zylonite and North Adams. Later that year, however, it announced that it intended to abandon the remainder of its portion of the line by 1997. Conrail continues to operate part of the branch within the city limits of Pittsfield.

Sources: Bachelder, *Half-Century Limited*, 52-3; Baker, *Formation*, 5, 18; Harlow, *Steelways*, 136; Poor, *History*, 145; U.S. Railway Association, *Final System Plan*, 2:141; U.S. Railway Association, *Preliminary System Plan*, 2:503-04.

31. Vermont & Massachusetts (Fitchburg)

0	Fitchburg, MA	61	West Greenfield
2	West Fitchburg		(West Deerfield)
3	Wachusett	63	South River
5	Westminster	64	Bardwells (Bard-
10	South Ashburnham		dwell)
	(Ashburnham)	64.5	Shelburne Jct.
12	East Gardner	69	Shelburne Falls
15	Gardner	72	Buckland
19	Otter River	78	Charlemont
21	Baldwinville	81	Zoar
26	Royalston	85	Hoosac Tunnel
32	Athol	86	East Portal
36	Orange	91	West Portal
39	Wendell	93	North Adams
41	Erving	94	Braytonville
44	Farley	95	Greylock
47	Millers Falls	96	Blackinton
	(Grouts Corner)	98	Williamstown, MA
49	Lake Pleasant	102	Pownal, VT
51	Montague	105	North Pownal, VT
53	East Deerfield	109	*Petersburgh Jct.,*
54	Turners Falls Jct.		*NY*
55	Greenfield	141	*Troy, NY*

165 *Rotterdam Jct., NY*

31A. Ashburnham Branch

0	South Ashburn-ham, MA
1	Manns Crossing
1.5	Careys Crossing
2	Cashmans Cross-ing
2.5	Ashburnham, MA

31B. Turners Falls Branch

0	Turners Falls Jct., MA
1	Riverbank
1.5	Montague City
3	Turners Falls, MA

BUILT: 1845-76; Turners Falls Branch, 1868; Ashburnham Branch, 1874.

OPERATORS: *Vermont & Massachusetts,* 1849-74; *Southern Vermont,* 1859-60; *Troy & Boston,* 1860-87; *Fitchburg,* 1874-1900; *Boston & Maine,* 1900-83; *Guilford,* 1983- .

DAILY PASSENGER TRAINS: *1869:* 4 (Fitchburg-Hoosac Tunnel); 6 (Troy-North Adams), *1893:* 11, *1919:* 13, *1935:* 10, *1950:* 10, *1960:* Freight only, *1971:* Freight only, *1981:* 4 (Fitchburg-Gardner). Passenger service ended Troy-Greenfield, 1958; Greenfield-Fitchburg, 1960. Restored by MBTA, Fitchburg-Gardner, 1980; discontinued 1986. Passenger service on Ashburnham Branch ended 1924; Turners Falls Branch, 1913.

ABANDONMENTS: Ashburnham Branch, 1937; Turners Falls Branch (River Bank-Turners Falls, 1947).

At the heart of the Vermont & Massachusetts route lies New England's greatest feat of rail engineering, the Hoosac Tunnel. Even before it had completed its Boston to Fitchburg main line, the Fitchburg RR in 1844 secured a charter for the Vermont & Massachusetts RR to continue its line westward and up into Vermont. The V&M was promoted and built by Alvah Crocker of Fitchburg, the force behind the Fitchburg. Heated controversy arose over whether the route should run through Winchendon or Gardner. The latter town prevailed, but the route proved so difficult to construct that the V&M was forced to build a switchback at South Ashburnham. Until 1877 all V&M trains were forced to stop and have the engine switched around the train (in the latter year a horseshoe curve replaced the switchback). The V&M was completed in 1851 from Fitchburg to Miller's Falls (then known as Grout's Corner) and then northward to Brattleboro, Vt. A branch from Miller's Falls to Greenfield was also constructed. The portion of the original V&M between Miller's Falls and Brattleboro was leased to the Rutland RR in 1870 and sold outright to the New London Northern in 1880.

What had started as the V&M's Greenfield Branch soon became a main line, as the railroad changed its destination from Vermont to the West. In 1850 the Troy & Greenfield RR was chartered to continue the V&M westward from Greenfield. Back in 1825 a canal had been proposed to run westward across northern Massachusetts, crossing the Berkshires through a tunnel. The promoters of the Troy & Greenfield

With B&M 360, an EMD GP39-2, in the lead, an eastbound Guilford freight approaches Orange, Mass., in July 1992. Since 1990, trains have become less common on the old Vermont & Massachusetts.

revived this improbable idea, since the only easy grades across the Berkshires lay to the south, on the route already used by the rival Western RR. Construction of the Troy & Greenfield began in 1851. The route followed the Deerfield River up a narrow gorge, until it confronted Hoosac Mountain. Continuation of the line would require a tunnel of no less than four miles!

Promoters grossly underestimated the difficulties and costs of building the Troy & Greenfield. When private funds were exhausted they persuaded the Massachusetts government to loan and ultimately to invest millions of dollars to tunnel through Hoosac Mountain. Construction of the tunnel did not really get under way until engineer Herman Haupt took charge in 1856. The mountain defeated the best tunnel-building technology available. After five years less than half a mile at the east end and a scant 600 feet at the west had been cut. In 1861 the state refused to pay Haupt, who then became a general in the Union Army in charge of military railroading. Work on the tunnel was suspended while the state pondered its next course. The tunnel was now extremely controversial, and some wanted to see it abandoned altogether.

In 1863 the state government decided to build the tunnel by itself. Newer technology resulted in some gains, but political corruption and incompetence dogged the project. By 1869 the tunnel had been extended only a mile from the east portal and less than a mile from the west. More than two miles remained unbuilt. The state abandoned the effort to finish the tunnel itself, and hired Canadian contractors, Walter and Francis Shanly. Using a coordinated approach and the latest power drills, the Shanlys' work crews finished the job. The ends of the tunnel met on November 27, 1873, and the tunnel opened for rail traffic in February 1875, a full twenty-five years after the Troy & Greenfield was begun. The monetary cost was high, but the human toll was staggering: 196 lives were lost in building the tunnel.

While the Hoosac Tunnel was under way, another group of promoters from Troy, New York, had built a line from their city eastward through Vermont to North Adams, at the west end of the tunnel. This railroad, the Troy & Boston (known as the Southern Vermont RR in Vermont) was opened from Troy to the Vermont line in August 1852 and reached the Massachusetts border in April 1859. Meanwhile, the Troy & Greenfield, confident that it would complete the Hoosac

The East Portal of the Hoosac Tunnel as it appeared in 1902, before electrification. Note the trial bore to the left. (Photo courtesy Walker Transportation Collection, Beverly Historical Society & Museum.)

Tunnel, built a line from the west portal of the Tunnel at North Adams to a connection with the Troy & Boston. It leased this line to the Troy & Boston, pending the completion of the tunnel.

In 1874 the Fitchburg had leased the Vermont & Massachusetts and the Troy & Greenfield, and in 1875 could use the tunnel to reach the Troy & Boston at the Vermont-Massachusetts line. In January 1879 a new railroad, the Boston, Hoosac Tunnel & Western RR, was opened from Rotterdam Junction, N.Y., to the Vermont line, where it ran alongside the Troy & Boston. In 1880 it was extended across Vermont paralleling the Troy & Boston-Southern Vermont until it reached the Troy & Greenfield at the Massachusetts line, thus giving that road a choice of two western connections. In 1887 the Fitchburg purchased both the Troy & Boston and the new Boston, Hoosac Tunnel & Western. It operated both single-track lines as one double-tracked main line (railroaders called it the "wide track"). This arrangement lasted until 1980, when all of the second track had been removed.

The Hoosac Tunnel at last gave the Fitchburg the western traffic it long had envied on the rival Boston & Albany. The tunnel was not enough to hold off the Boston & Maine, however, which finally absorbed the Fitchburg in 1900. Under the B&M the tunnel continued to carry large volumes of traffic. In 1910-1911 the B&M electrified the tunnel, solving the long-standing problem of smoke and cinders that hampered tunnel operations. Diesels made it possible to remove the wires in 1946.

Passenger service on the V&M/Fitchburg never matched the varnish that rode the Boston & Albany that paralleled it to the south. Travelers on the B&A after 1900 could ride the rails of a single system as far as Chicago, while taking the Fitchburg route involved changing to other railroads beyond Albany. Passenger service declined in the 1950s, ending west of Greenfield in 1958 and over the rest of the line two years later. In 1980 the MBTA restored commuter rail service to Fitchburg and extended a pair of trains to Gardner. These survived until the end of 1986, when disputes with Guilford forced the MBTA to terminate Boston commuter service at Fitchburg.

An eastbound train unloads at Montague station circa 1900. (Photo courtesy Walker Transportation Collection, Beverly Historical Society & Museum.)

In recent years the tunnel has seen decreasing traffic, as the great majority of rail freight enters and leaves New England via the Boston & Albany. Since 1990 Guilford operating subsidiary Springfield Terminal has been sending few trains through the Hoosac Tunnel, the rest of its western traffic interchanging with Conrail at Worcester. The heaviest used portion of the line is between Fitchburg and West Deerfield (site of what until recently was one of the B&M's major classification yards, now largely abandoned), but even this sees but a few trains daily. Recently there have been attempts to obtain state aid to upgrade the V&M for double stack container traffic, but these have proved unsuccessful.

In 1871 the Ashburnham RR was chartered to connect Ashburnham Center with the V&M main line at South Ashburnham (where the Cheshire RR met the V&M). The two-and-a-half-mile short line opened in January 1874. It owned but one engine and one passenger car. Operated independently, the Ashburnham went bankrupt in 1878, reorganized, and continued in business until 1885 when it was taken over by the Fitchburg. Passenger service on this branch ended September 2, 1924, and the line was abandoned in 1937 after suffering heavy flood damage the year before.

The V&M opened a branch to the factory village of Turners Falls in 1868. When the great floods of March 1936 destroyed its bridge over the Connecticut River, the B&M made use of trackage rights over the New Haven's parallel Turners Falls branch (part of the New Haven & Northampton system) and rerouted its trains over the New Haven line. In 1943, when the New Haven discontinued its own service to Turners Falls, the B&M continued operations, and four years later it bought the line from the New Haven. At the same time the B&M formally abandoned all but the initial mile of the old V&M Turners Falls branch, which had not been used in over a decade.

Sources: Allen, "The Great Bore"; Bachelder, *Half-Century Limited*; Byron, *Pinprick of Light*; Coyne, "Hoosac Tunnel"; Cramer, "Hoosac Tunnel"; Goodwin, "Ashburnham Hill"; Kirkland, *Men, Cities, and Transportation*, 1:387-432; Lee, "North of Northampton"; 117 I.C.C. 679; 217 I.C.C. 475.

32. Hoosac Tunnel & Wilmington

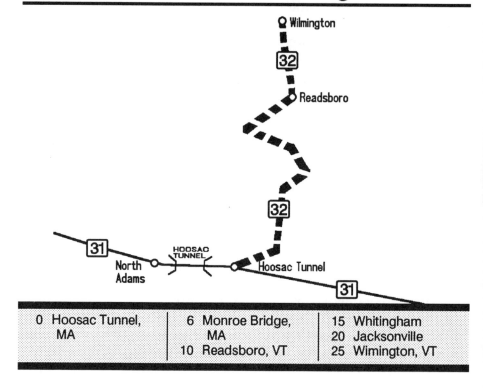

0 Hoosac Tunnel, MA	6 Monroe Bridge, MA	15 Whitingham
	10 Readsboro, VT	20 Jacksonville
		25 Wimington, VT

BUILT: 1884-85; 1891.

OPERATORS: *Deerfield River Co.*, 1885-86; *Hoosac Tunnel & Wilmington*, 1886-1971.

DAILY PASSENGER TRAINS: *1893:* 3, *1919:* 4. Passenger service ended November 1927,

ABANDONMENTS: Readsboro-Wilmington, 1938; Hoosac Tunnel-Readsboro (remainder of line), 1971.

The Deerfield River Co., a venture of the Newton brothers of Holyoke, in July 1885 opened a three-foot narrow gauge logging railroad up the Deerfield River valley from the Hoosac Tunnel station on the Fitchburg RR eleven miles north to Readsboro, Vt. Virgin forests in this relatively isolated area were ripe for cutting, and in 1882 the company built a large pulp mill in Readsboro. In 1886 the line was assigned to a new common carrier, the Hoosac Tunnel & Wilmington

Hoosac Tunnel & Wilmington locomotive number 5, a Mogul (2-6-0), on the Readsboro turntable in July 1941. (Photo by Harold W. Boothroyd, courtesy Walker Transportation Collection, Beverly Historical Society & Museum.)

RR (later affectionately known as the Hoot, Toot & Whistle). A thirteen-mile extension completed in November 1891 with financial support from town governments along the way brought the tracks to Wilmington, Vt. A number of factories were constructed along the right of way, and the line enjoyed a modest prosperity.

In 1904 the Newton family sold its holdings to a New York syndicate. Narrow gauge operation continued until 1913, when the gauge was switched to standard. (The rolling stock ended up on a sugar plantation in Cuba.) In 1922 the HT&W was bought by the New England Power Co., which that same year constructed Lake Whitingham behind a dam on the Deerfield River. This reservoir required extensive rerouting of track on the Readsboro-Wilmington extension. Major floods in November 1927 swept the extension out of service for two years and permanently ended regular passenger service on the HT&W. On August 26, 1934, passenger service returned for a day when the railroad hosted the first American railfan excursion, sponsored by the Massachusetts Bay Railroad Enthusiasts, Inc.

With the end of lumbering, freight traffic to Wilmington dwindled. Severe flooding in March 1936 took out the trestle which carried the rails across the Deerfield River south of Wilmington. Later that year the HT&W became the first railroad acquisition of Samuel Pinsly, who would become New England's short line mogul. In September 1937 Pinsly applied to abandon the Wilmington extension, and the I.C.C. granted permission at the end of the year. During the 1938 hurricane the Deerfield River washed away three bridges and much track. The HT&W recovered from this disaster to become a profitable railroad for many years. New business came during the late 1950s when the Yankee Rowe nuclear power plant was constructed along the HT&W about seven miles north of Hoosac Tunnel near Sherman Dam.

A steam locomotive hauled freight on the HT&W until 1949, when it was replaced by a GE 44-ton industrial diesel. Similar locomotives were used into the 1960s. The railroad's shops and offices were located in Readsboro. Its primary customer was the Deerfield Glassine Corp. at Monroe Bridge, which received shipments of wood pulp and chemicals (but shipped its own products out by truck). Faced with the prospect of relocating its tracks due to the construction of the Bear Swamp hydro-electric project the HT&W in 1970 requested approval to abandon its entire line, and in September 1971 the I.C.C. allowed the railroad to close shop.

Sources: Bachelder, *Half-Century Limited*, 4-9, 50-51; Carman, *Hoot, Toot & Whistle*; Cornwall and Smith, *Rails First*, 35, 50-51; Nelligan, "Short Lines of Samuel Pinsly"; Shaughnessy, "Short Line They Call the Hoot, Toot & Whistle"; 224 I.C.C. 255.

33. Connecticut River

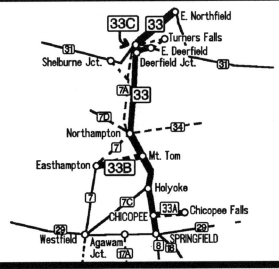

0 Springfield, MA	33 Deerfield	0.5 Chicopee Center
2 Brightwood (Moores)	34.5 Deerfield Jct.	2 Oak St.
	36 Greenfield	2.5 Chicopee Falls , MA
3 Chicopee (Chicopee Jct.) (Cabotville) (Cabot Jct.)	43 Bernardston (Northfield Farms)	**33B. Easthampton Branch**
	46 Mount Hermon (Northfield)	
7 Willimansett	50 East Northfield, MA (South Vernon, VT)(West Northfield, MA)	0 Mount Tom, MA
7.5 Riverside		2 Hampton Mills
8 Holyoke		3 Easthampton, MA
13 Smiths Ferry		
15 Mount Tom		**33C. East Deerfield Branch**
17 Northampton	**33A. Chicopee Falls Branch**	
20 Laurel Park		0 Deerfield Jct., MA
21 Hatfield	0 Chicopee (Chicopee Jct.) (Cabotville) (Cabot Jct.), MA	1 East Deerfield, MA
24 North Hatfield		
26 Whately		
28 South Deerfield		

BUILT: 1844-49; Chicopee Falls Branch, 1845; Easthampton Branch, 1872; East Deerfield Branch, 1906.

OPERATORS: *Connecticut River,* 1845-93; *Boston & Maine,* 1893-1983; *Guilford,* 1983- ; *Amtrak (intercity passenger),* 1972-1987.

DAILY PASSENGER TRAINS: *1869:* 6, *1893:* 12, *1919:* 16, *1935:* 11, *1950:* 14, *1960:* 8, *1971:* Freight only, *1981:* 2. Passenger service not operated 1967-Fall 1972. Amtrak ended service 1987 and line is now freight-only. Passenger service on Easthampton Branch ended ca. 1926; on Chicopee Falls Branch, 1918. East Deerfield Branch freight-only.

ABANDONMENTS: Easthampton Branch, 1983; Chicopee Falls Branch (Chicopee Center-Chicopee Falls, 1984; Chicopee-Chicopee Center, 1994).

Boston investors, joined by businessmen from Hartford, Northampton, and Springfield, secured a charter in 1842 to construct the Northampton & Springfield RR along the Connecticut River valley northward from Springfield. In 1845, shortly before the line began operations, this railroad was merged with the unbuilt Greenfield & Northampton RR to form the Connecticut River RR. The first section, between Springfield and Northampton, was opened in late in 1845; the tracks were extended to Deerfield in August 1846 and to Greenfield by the following November. In January 1849 the line was extended to South Vernon, Vt., on the Massachusetts-Vermont border, where it connected with the Miller's Falls, Mass.-Brattleboro, Vt., line of the Vermont &

B&M freight train 588 approaches NO tower in Northampton in May 1905, on route to the Central Massachusetts branch which began here. (Photo courtesy Walker Transportation Collection, Beverly Historical Society & Museum.)

Massachusetts RR, then under construction. In 1850 the V&M reached Brattleboro, and for many years the Connecticut River RR used this route to provide through service from Springfield to Brattleboro.

The Connecticut River RR operated independently for more than forty years, eventually acquiring a system of lines extending northward along the Connecticut valley to Canada. In 1893 the Boston & Maine leased the Connecticut River, and it has formed an integral part of the B&M system ever since. Until recent years a moderate amount of traffic used this route to reach Vermont and Canada. As early as the 1860s the Connecticut River RR formed part of a through route between Montreal and New York City. Crack express trains, such as the *Montrealer* and the *Washingtonian*, continued to use this route until the fall of 1966; remaining local passenger service was terminated by the end of that year. In the fall of 1972 Amtrak brought back the *Montrealer* and *Washingtonian* (by 1974 the former name was being used for both the north- and south-bound trains). This train continued until 1987, when Amtrak was unable to persuade Guilford, the current operator of the line, to improve poor track conditions. Amtrak therefore discontinued the *Montrealer* altogether. In 1989 the *Montrealer* returned once more, but this time rerouted over the Central Vermont via Amherst.

The two-and-a-half-mile Chicopee Falls Branch was built in 1845 in conjunction with the initial main line from Springfield to Northampton. Intended to serve the industrial village of Chicopee Falls, it saw both freight and passenger trains until the First World War, when passenger service ended. In 1984 Guilford abandoned the outermost two miles beyond Chicopee Center and ten years later abandoned the remainder of the branch.

The Easthampton Branch was built in 1872 to reach Easthampton, which had been served exclusively by the New Haven & Northampton RR since 1856. Passenger service ended around 1926, but the branch survived until 1983.

In 1906 the B&M constructed the mile-long East Deerfield branch to provide a better connection between the Connecticut River RR and its large freight yard in East Deerfield on the Fitchburg main line. It has never been used for regular passenger service.

Sources: Bachelder, *Half-Century Limited*, 46-8; Baker, *Formation*, 146, 172; Cornwall and Smith, *Names First*, 32, 46, 90; Kistler, *Rise of Railroads*, 41, 57-65, 202-04; Poor, *History*, 108; *Poor's Manual of Railroads, 1878*, 67.

34. Central Massachusetts

0 North Cambridge Jct. (North Cambridge), MA	22 Gleason Jct.	62 New Braintree
	23 Hudson	64 Creamery
	25 South Bolton (Bolton)	66 Gilbertville
1 Hill Crossing (Hills Crossing)	27 Berlin	70 Ware
	28 West Berlin Jct. (West Berlin)	75 Forest Lake
2 Belmont		78 Bondsville
3 Waverley	30 South Clinton	81 Canal Jct.
4 Clematis Brook (Blue Hill)	32 Boylston	83 Belchertown (Bondsville)
	35 West Boylston	
5 Waltham North (Waltham)	36 Oakdale	88 Pansy Park
	38 Springdale	90 Norwottuck (South Amherst) (Dwight)
6 Waltham Highlands (Hammond St.) (West Waltham)	41 Quinapoxet (Holden)	
	43.5 Holden Jct.	93 Amherst
9 Weston	44 Jefferson (Jeffersons)	95 East Hadley
10 Cherry Brook		97 Hadley
11 Tower Hill	47 Muschopauge	99 Northampton, MA
12 Wayland	50 Rutland	
14 East Sudbury	52 West Rutland	**34A. Clinton Extension**
16 South Sudbury	56 Coldbrook	
17 Wayside Inn	56.5 Barre	0 West Berlin Jct., MA
19 Ordway (Ordways Crossing)	57 Barre Jct.	4 Clinton Jct., MA
	59 Barre Plains	
21 Gleasondale (Rockbottom) (Rock Bottom)	61 Wheelwright (Hardwick)	

BUILT: 1871-87; Clinton Extension, 1903.

OPERATORS: *Massachusetts Central*, 1881-83; Operation suspended 1883-85; *Boston & Lowell*, 1885-87; *Boston & Maine*, 1887-1983; *Mass Central*, ca. 1980; *Guilford*, 1983-87.

DAILY PASSENGER TRAINS: *1893:* 7, *1919:* 6, *1935:* 6 (Boston-Clinton), *1950:* N/A (Boston-Clinton), *1960:* 2 (Boston-Hudson), *1971:* 2 (Boston-South Sudbury). Passenger service ended Nov. 26, 1971.

ABANDONMENTS: West Berlin-Oakdale, 1903; Oakdale-Wheelwright, 1939; Forest Lake-Creamery, Norwottuck-Canal Jct., 1941 (trackage rights acquired over parallel B&A and CV routes); Hill Crossing-Clematis Brook, 1952; West Berlin-Berlin, Clinton Extension, 1959; Northampton-Norwottuck, Canal Jct.-Bondsville, Berlin-Waltham North, 1980; Creamery-Wheelwright, 1983; Waltham North-Clematis Brook, 1994.

By the end of the Civil War eastern and central Massachusetts could boast one of the densest rail networks anywhere in the country. Two prosperous railroads, the Boston & Albany and the Fitchburg, connected Boston to the West, their tracks at most 40 miles apart. Together with their branches and connections they served every community of any size in the region.

Somehow, the dream of building still a third western railroad from Boston took hold. In 1868 the Wayland & Sudbury Branch RR was authorized to build a seven-mile line from Weston, on the Fitchburg RR main line, to Sudbury. That same year citizens from the central Massachusetts town of Barre petitioned the legislature to charter a Massachusetts Central RR from Boston to Northampton, incorporating the unbuilt Wayland & Sudbury Branch. The legislature responded as requested in 1869, authorizing the new railroad to build from Weston to Northampton.

Surveying began at once and construction started in 1871 westward from Weston. Progress was slow, particularly after the road's contractor failed in the great depression of 1873 and work ceased for five years. Building resumed in 1878 and in October 1881 the first twenty-eight miles from Boston to Hudson opened for business. From Boston to North Cambridge Junction the line used the Boston & Lowell and the latter's Lexington & Arlington branch; from North Cambridge to Waltham a line was built alongside the tracks of rival Fitchburg RR.

By 1882 trains were running to Jeffersons, forty-six miles west of Boston. The following year, however, the Massachusetts Central ran out of cash and operations ceased for two years. The Boston & Lowell

By the time this picture was taken in 1975, the depot at Wayland had not seen a commuter train in more than three years. In 1980 the line was abandoned.

then took control, reorganizing the railroad as the Central Massachusetts RR and resuming operations in September 1885. In 1886 the Central Mass was leased by the B&L, which itself was leased to the Boston & Maine the following year. In December 1887 the B&M finished the line to Northampton. The hundred-mile railroad had taken more than sixteen years to complete.

The first years of the Central Massachusetts were its busiest. The B&M used the line to compete with the Fitchburg and the Boston & Albany for through traffic to and from the West. Passenger trains from points as far distant as Harrisburg, Pa., and Washington, D.C., used the Central Massachusetts to reach Boston by way of the Poughkeepsie Bridge and the Connecticut Western and the New Haven. Long-distance passenger traffic ended in 1893 after the collapse of the Connecticut Western and its connecting lines. The Central Massachusetts lost whatever importance it retained in 1900 when the Fitchburg was absorbed by the B&M, finally giving the B&M its own superior western route.

In 1903 the construction of the Wachusett Reservoir flooded out several miles of track between West Berlin and Oakdale. Rather than replace this segment, the B&M rerouted traffic over a parallel section of its Worcester, Nashua & Portland division (Worcester & Nashua). The B&M constructed a four-mile extension from West Berlin to Clinton Junction on the W&N, including a tunnel and a viaduct.

Boston to Northampton through passenger service was reduced from three to two daily round trips in the 1920s. On April 23, 1932, all passenger service west of Clinton ceased. Freight traffic also dwindled, prompting the B&M between 1931 and 1933 to obtain trackage rights over parallel sections of the Boston & Albany's Winchendon Branch and the Central Vermont and to suspend service on the Central Massachusetts's own line. Trains no longer used the line between Oakdale and Rutland after June 1, 1938.

The torrential rains that accompanied the great hurricane of September 1938 caused extensive flood damage to the Central Massachusetts. Trackage at Barre Plains was washed away and not replaced. In 1939 the B&M abandoned twenty-four miles between Oakdale and Wheelwright, severing the Central Massachusetts into two long branches, Boston-Oakdale and Wheelwright-Northampton. In 1952 Central Mass tracks between Hill Crossing and Clematis Brook were removed and traffic rerouted over the B&M's closely parallel Fitchburg line.

Passenger service remained only on the Boston-Clinton segment. Some of the last regularly scheduled steam locomotives on the B&M ran on this route daily until 1956. On May 11, 1958, passenger service out of Boston was cut back to Hudson, and the trackage between Berlin and Clinton was abandoned. Passenger trains were further cut back to South Sudbury on January 15, 1965. A single round trip daily train consisting of two Budd RDC cars served this route until 1968, when it was reduced to a single car. In the fall of 1971 a final attempt to preserve service increased trains to four daily round trips. Two months later, on November 26, 1971, all passenger service ceased.

The remaining segments of the Central Massachusetts managed to survive into the 1970s. In 1974 the B&M discontinued service between Bondsville and Forest Lake and eliminated trains between Bondsville and Canal Junction in 1979. Freight service between Berlin and Hudson ended in March 1977, and the remaining operations between

Waltham and Hudson dwindled to three times a week and then to as needed. By 1980 speed was restricted to 5 mph. In 1980 the I.C.C. granted the B&M permission to abandon virtually all of what remained of the Central Mass. In 1992 the final six miles of the Central Mass right of way between Amherst and Northampton, including the Connecticut River bridge, became the Five College Bikeway.

After 1980 only three short sections of the Central Mass still existed. Today only one of them is in use. Until around 1987 Guilford operated freight service over about a mile and a half of trackage owned by the MBTA from Clematis Brook westward to Waltham North. In 1994 the I.C.C. permitted Guilford to give up its trackage rights over this line, which in effect permitted the MBTA to abandon the line. About three miles between Forest Lake and Bondsville were operated briefly by the Mass Central RR in 1980, but have been out of service for many years. The one remnant of the Central Mass still in operation is a short stretch of track in Ware that the Mass Central uses to reach a paper mill. This is all that remains of what once was a hundred-mile railroad to nowhere.

Sources: Armstrong, *Railfan's Guide*, 32; *Central Mass.*; Crouch and Conard, "Central Mass. Revisited"; 189 I.C.C. 218; 236 I.C.C. 132; 249 I.C.C. 431, 761, 763, 773.

35. Springfield, Athol & Northeastern

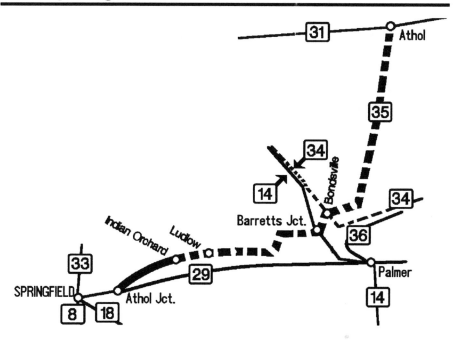

0 Athol Jct., MA	16 Bondsville	32 Morgan Crossing
3 Fiberloid	20 West Ware	(Morgans)
4 Indian Orchard	25 Enfield	33 Soapstone
5 Ludlow	26 Smiths	35 North Dana
8 Collins	27 Greenwich Lake	37 New Salem
10 Red Bridge	28 Greenwich	40 South Athol
13 Three Rivers	29 Greenwich Village	45 Athol, MA
15 Barretts Jct.		

BUILT: 1870-73.

OPERATORS: *Athol & Enfield, 1871-72; Springfield, Athol & Northeastern, 1872-73; Fitchburg, 1873-79; Springfield & Northeastern, 1879-80; Boston & Albany (New York Central), 1880-1968; Penn Central, 1968-76; Conrail, 1976- .*

DAILY PASSENGER TRAINS: *1893:* 4, *1919:* 4. Passenger service ended June 1935.

ABANDONMENTS: Bondsville-Athol, 1935; Ludlow-Bondsville, 1939; Indian Orchard-Ludlow, 1982.

Four Massachusetts towns were drowned when the massive Quabbin Reservoir was built in the 1930s. Four towns—and one railroad. The Athol & Enfield RR was chartered in 1869 to build a line south from Athol. Construction began at Athol in June 1870. Town governments along the route subscribed to its stock. The first segment, Athol to Barretts Junction (Belchertown), opened in October 1871, and was completed to Springfield in December 1873.

The new railroad, renamed the Springfield, Athol & Northeastern in 1872, was burdened with a heavy construction debt compounded by the great business depression of the 1870s. In 1873 the railroad's directors contracted with the Fitchburg RR to operate the line. After several profitless years the railroad failed in May 1879 and was reorganized as the Springfield & Northeastern, which resumed operation as an independent short line. Among the investors wiped out in this bankruptcy were town governments along the route who had invested in the railroad's stock.

The Boston & Albany purchased the Springfield & Northeastern in 1880, mostly to prevent its rivals, the Fitchburg and the Central Massachusetts, from using it to reach Springfield. The line sold for less than a third of its construction cost! As the B&A's Athol Branch the line saw modest freight and passenger service for more than fifty years. Here in the early 1930s could be found the last of the B&A's 4-4-0 American type locomotives.

The railroad ran through the valley of the Swift River, which in the 1920s caught the attention of engineers seeking to enhance Boston's water supply. The damming of the Swift would create a mighty lake, the largest in the state, and would force the rerouting of much of the rail line. But by 1934, when construction of the dam was underway, traffic on the railroad had declined significantly; between 1929 and 1933 freight traffic had fallen 35% and passengers from 6,213 per year to 1,195. The B&A therefore sought permission to abandon the northernmost twenty-nine miles of the line between Bondsville and Athol. Despite protests from Athol, the commission approved the request late in 1934, effective the following spring. Passenger service on the entire railroad ended with the abandonment. By the onset of World War II, most of the line north of Bondsville was under water.

Smith's Village in Enfield in March 1930, five years before abandonment of the railroad. This scene is now under the waters of the Quabbin Reservoir. The sign on the tracks was placed by the photographer. (Photo courtesy Walker Transportation Collection, Beverly Historical Society & Museum.)

Floods in the wake of the great hurricane of September 21, 1938, severely damaged parts of the line between Ludlow and Bondsville. With traffic on this section already in steady decline, the B&A again petitioned and once more received permission to abandon rather than reopen the line. The Massachusetts Turnpike was built over part of the right of way near Ludlow. Since 1939, the remaining eight miles of the Springfield & Northeastern has been operated by the B&A and its successors as a minor branch line. A short segment between Barretts Junction and Bondsville was transferred to the Central Vermont, which operated it until the Bondsville mills closed in the 1950s. In 1982 Conrail lopped off another mile. The surviving seven miles between Springfield and Indian Orchard remain in service for freight as Conrail's Athol Industrial Track.

Sources: Armstrong, *Railfan's Guide*, 15; Baker, *Formation*, 5, 17-18; Cornwall and Smith, *Names First*, 5, 115; Lewis, "Ware and the Railroads"; 202 I.C.C. 555; 233 I.C.C. 231.

36. Ware River

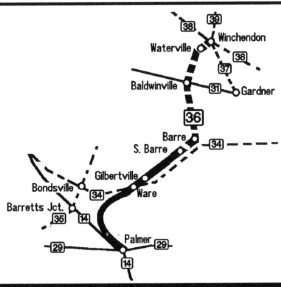

0	Palmer, MA	24	Barre Plains	37	Phillipston
3	Thorndike	25	South Barre	39	Templeton
5	Whipples	26	Barre	43	Baldwinville
12	Ware	26.5	Barre Jct.	48	Waterville
16	Gilbertville	27	Coldbrook	49	Winchendon, MA
18	Creamery	30	Harwoods		
21	Old Furnace	33	Williamsville		

BUILT: 1868-73.

OPERATORS: *New London Northern,* 1870-71; *Vermont Central,* 1871-73; *Boston & Albany (New York Central),* 1873-1968; *Penn Central,* 1968-76; *Conrail,* 1976-79; *Mass Central,* 1979- ; *Boston & Maine,* 1968-84.

DAILY PASSENGER TRAINS: *1893:* 4, *1919:* 4, *1935:* 2 (mixed). Passenger service ended 1948.

ABANDONMENTS: South Barre-Waterville, 1968; Waterville-Winchendon, 1984.

As early as 1850 a railroad had been proposed between Palmer and Winchendon, but construction of the Ware River RR along this route did not begin until 1868. Town governments along the way subscribed to its stock. By the end of 1870 tracks had been laid from Palmer to

Gilbertville. For the next three years first the New London Northern RR and then the Vermont Central operated the line under a short-term lease while construction continued, the rails finally reaching Winchendon in November 1873.

The expiration of the Vermont Central lease in April 1873 put the Ware River up for grabs. Fearing that the line might be dangerous in the hands of a rival railroad, Chester W. Chapin, the president of the Boston & Albany, personally bought control of the Ware River, He then leased the line to the Boston & Albany, turning a tidy profit in the process. The Ware River now became the B&A's Winchendon Branch. The B&A had hoped to operate the Ware River in conjunction with the new Monadnock RR, which would have given it a through route to the popular resort area of Peterborough, N.H. But the B&A was unable to gain control of the Monadnock, and without it the Ware River was not very profitable.

During the 1880s the Central Massachusetts RR was constructed along virtually the same route, the two lines only a short distance apart. In the 1930s sections of the Central Massachusetts (now part of the B&M) were abandoned and trackage rights obtained over the Ware River between Barre Junction and Forest Lake.

Shortly after the New York Central was merged into the Penn Central permission was granted to abandon twenty-five miles between South Barre and Winchendon. The B&M acquired the last mile of the line between Waterville and Winchendon to provide service to a few customers. By the early 1970s the three-times-a-week local freight on this line hauled an average of only five carloads a trip. Service between Gilbertville and South Barre was discontinued in November 1975, and the tracks between Ware and South Barre were slated for abandonment effective with the end of Penn Central operation in 1976.

Conrail continued to operate this line under subsidy, however, until a new short line, the Massachusetts Central, took over the remaining twenty-three miles in 1979. The primary traffic is pulp and paper. Until recently trains seldom operated north of Ware, but the acquisition of a new customer has restored regular freight service to South Barre.

Sources: Armstrong, *Railfan's Guide*, 32; Bachelder, *Half-Century Limited*, 42-43; Baker, *Formation*, 5, 13-17; Jones, *Central Vermont Railway*, 1:79-83; Kirkland, *Men, Cities, and Transportation*, 1:376-78; Lewis, "Ware and the Railroads"; U.S. Railway Association, *Final System Plan*, 2:140-41; U.S. Railway Association, *Preliminary System Plan*, 2:502-03.

37. Boston, Barre & Gardner

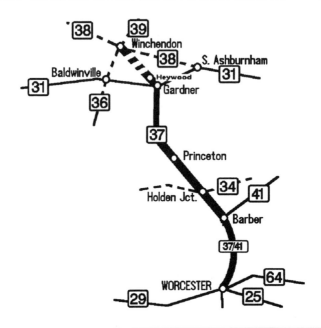

0 *Worcester, MA*	10.5 Holden Jct. (Carr	25 South Gardner
3 Barber (Barbers)	Jct.) (Massa-	26 Gardner
4 North Worcester	chusetts Central	27 Heywood (Hey-
6 Chaffin (Chaffins)	Jct.)	woods)
7 Dawson (Dawsons)	11 North Woods	32 Red School
8 Holden	13 Brooks	36 Winchendon, MA
10 Jefferson (Jeffer-	16 Princeton	
sons)	20 Hubbardston	
	23 Waite	

BUILT: 1869-74.

OPERATORS: *Boston, Barre & Gardner, 1871-85; Fitchburg, 1885-1900; Boston & Maine, 1900-83; Guilford, 1983- ; Providence & Worcester, 1974- .*

DAILY PASSENGER TRAINS: *1893:* 10, *1919:* 6, *1935:* 4, *1950:* 2. Passenger service ended March 1953.

ABANDONMENTS: Heywood-Winchendon, 1959; Barber-Gardner, 1972 (restored by Providence & Worcester, 1974).

In 1847 the Barre & Worcester RR was chartered by Worcester-based promoters to build a rail line west from Worcester toward Palmer to compete with the Western RR. Renamed the Boston, Barre & Gardner in 1849, it remained a railroad in name only for the next two decades. When construction finally got under way in 1869 the destination of the railroad shifted northward toward Gardner and Winchendon; the line never did get to Barre.

In September 1871 the railroad was opened from Worcester to Gardner, and in January 1874 was completed to Winchendon. Later that year it leased the Monadnock RR (finished in 1871), which extended service to the resort town of Peterborough, N.H. It was hoped that with control of the Monadnock a new through route could be opened from Worcester to Concord, N.H. The Boston, Barre & Gardner operated independently for several years, milk and ice accounting for a large part of its traffic. In 1880, however, financial reverses forced it to relinquish control of the Monadnock, and five years later the Boston, Barre & Gardner became part of the Fitchburg RR system. The Boston & Maine absorbed the Fitchburg in 1900, and with it the Boston, Barre & Gardner. In 1959 the line between Heywood station, in downtown Gardner, and Winchendon was abandoned. The B&M and later Guilford continued to operate the remaining mile between Gardner and Heywood.

The Providence & Worcester reopened the route in 1974 and continues to provide freight service, interchanging at Gardner with Guilford, and connecting with the main line of the P&W at Worcester. For a number of years the P&W ran scheduled through freights between Gardner and Worcester, but the branch is now served by local trains out of Worcester on an as needed basis. The Guilford interchange at Gardner generates the most traffic, but other customers include an industrial park in Holden and a lumber yard in Hubbardston.

Sources: Armstrong, *Railfan's Guide*, 34-35; Bachelder, *Half-Century Limited*, 41; Baker, *Formation*, 178, 192; Cornwall and Smith, *Names First*, 12; Morgan, "Boston, Barre & Gardner"; Roy, "Providence & Worcester Succeeds on Service."

38. Cheshire

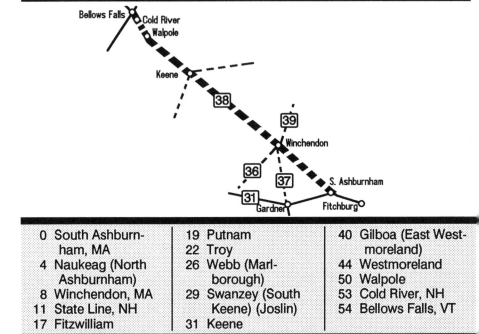

0 South Ashburn- ham, MA	19 Putnam	40 Gilboa (East West- moreland)
4 Naukeag (North Ashburnham)	22 Troy 26 Webb (Marl- borough)	44 Westmoreland 50 Walpole
8 Winchendon, MA	29 Swanzey (South	53 Cold River, NH
11 State Line, NH	Keene) (Joslin)	54 Bellows Falls, VT
17 Fitzwilliam	31 Keene	

BUILT: 1845-49.

OPERATORS: *Cheshire*, 1847-90; *Fitchburg*, 1890-1900; *Boston & Maine*, 1900-83; *Guilford*, 1983-ca. 1990; *Green Mountain*, ca. 1975- .

DAILY PASSENGER TRAINS: *1869:* 6, *1893:* 10, *1919:* 10, *1935:* 8, *1950:* 9. Passenger service ended May 1958.

ABANDONMENTS: Keene-Cold River, Winchendon-Swanzey, 1972; Swanzey-Keene, 1975; South Ashburnham-Winchendon, 1984; at South Ashburnham, 1993.

The completion of the Fitchburg RR from Boston to Fitchburg early in 1845 encouraged extensions, the Cheshire RR among the most successful. A year earlier Keene, N.H., businessmen had received a New Hampshire charter to build a line from the Massachusetts line to Bellows Falls, Vt., via Keene. The following year the same promoters chartered the Winchendon RR in Massachusetts to extend the line to connect with the yet to be built Vermont & Massachusetts RR at Winchendon. According to its charter, the V&M was to pass through

Gardner, but the railroad had chosen a route through Winchendon instead. Construction between South Ashburnham and Winchendon began in October 1845, but when the line was nearly completed, the V&M was unable to change its charter and was forced to return to its original alignment through Gardner. Unable to use this section, the V&M sold it to the Cheshire RR, which completed it in the fall of 1847. The line was extended from Winchendon to Troy, N.H., by December, and reached Keene the following May. The railroad was completed from South Ashburnham to Bellows Falls in June 1849.

For many years the Cheshire was a prosperous independent small railroad. The major link between the Rutland RR of Vermont and the Fitchburg RR, it operated through trains between Boston and Montreal. In 1851 it obtained trackage rights over the Vermont & Massachusetts from South Ashburnham through to Fitchburg. It also for a time leased the Ashuelot RR and later the Monadnock RR.

The Fitchburg RR finally acquired the Cheshire in 1890 to keep it out of the hands of rivals, and it passed with the rest of the Fitchburg system into the Boston & Maine in 1900. Under the B&M this was part of a major through freight and passenger line. Crack express trains like the *Green Mountain Flyer* and the *Mount Royal* used the Cheshire on the Boston-Fitchburg-Bellows Falls-Rutland-Montreal route, until the Rutland discontinued passenger service in 1953. The B&M continued passenger trains on the line another five years.

The demise of the Rutland RR in the early 1960s eliminated what through freight traffic remained, and in 1972 the B&M abandoned more than forty miles of track between Winchendon and Walpole. A short segment of track in Keene, served by the Ashuelot Branch, remained until 1983. Tracks between Winchendon and the Massachusetts boundary were torn up in 1976, but court challenges kept the New Hampshire rails in place until 1979. The remaining Massachusetts segment of the line, from South Ashburnham to Winchendon (except for the initial 0.7 miles at South Ashburnham), was given up in 1984. The trackage at South Ashburnham was no longer used by 1991, and was abandoned in 1993, leaving only the line between Cold River and Bellows Falls, which is operated by the Green Mountain RR. Aside from this the once busy Cheshire is no more.

Sources: Bachelder, *Half-Century Limited*, 40; Baker, *Formation*, 196; Poor, *History*, 52; Valentine, "Brief History of the Cheshire Railroad."

39. Monadnock

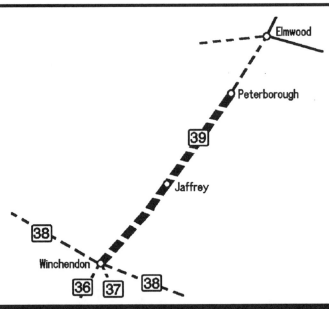

0 Winchendon, MA	7 Woodmere	12 Hadley (Cheshire
4 Rand, NH	10 Jaffrey (East Jaf-	Mills)
5 Thomas	frey)	13 Drury
6 West Rindge	11 Pierces Crossing	15 Noone
(Rindge)		16 Peterborough, NH

BUILT: 1870-71.

OPERATORS: *Monadnock,* 1871-74; *Boston, Barre & Gardner,* 1874-80; *Cheshire,* 1880-90; *Fitchburg,* 1890-1900; *Boston & Maine,* 1900-84.

DAILY PASSENGER TRAINS: *1893:* 6, *1919:* 8, *1935:* 6, *1950:* 2. Passenger service ended 1953.

ABANDONMENTS: Jaffrey-Peterborough, 1972; Winchendon-Jaffrey, 1984.

Peterborough, N.H., near the base of Mount Monadnock, was already a popular resort when the Cheshire RR reached Winchendon, Mass., in 1847. The following year promoters secured a charter to build the Monadnock RR from Winchendon to Peterborough, NH, sixteen miles away. It took more than two decades for the line to materialize. The initial segment, from Winchendon to Jaffrey, opened in December 1870, and the line was completed to Peterborough in June 1871.

The line was operated independently for only three years. The Boston, Barre & Gardner RR leased the road in 1874, in order to secure its own route to Concord, N.H. When the Boston, Barre & Gardner fell on hard times in 1880, the lease passed to the Cheshire RR. The Cheshire took over the Monadnock as protection against further expansion of the Boston & Albany, which had reached Winchendon in 1873 (via its lease of the Ware River RR). The Monadnock in turn was transferred to the Fitchburg, along with the rest of the Cheshire in 1890, and ten years later went to the Boston & Maine. Under the B&M the Monadnock became part of a long through route between Worcester and Concord, N.H., and was known as the Worcester & Hillsboro or Worcester & Contoocook Branch. Through service ended after the 1936 floods, but local passenger trains ran until 1953.

The Monadnock in the 1940s was a picturesque rural Yankee branch line, served by 2-6-0 Mogul locomotives. The line survived intact into the diesel age, the first abandonment, from Jaffrey to Peterborough, not taking place until 1972. The remaining segment of the Monadnock, from Winchendon to Jaffrey, was abandoned by the Boston & Maine in 1984 and the tracks were removed two years later.

Sources: Baker, *Formation*, 17, 178, 192, 196; Cornwall and Smith, *Names First*, 71; Valentine, "Brief History of the Cheshire Railroad."

40. Fitchburg & Worcester

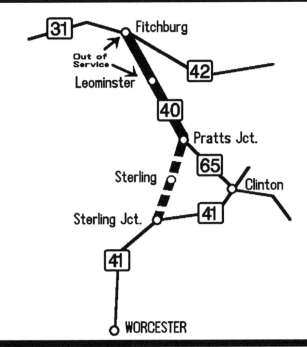

0 Fitchburg, MA	5 Leominster (Leom-	12 Sterling (Sterling
1 South Fitchburg	inster Center)	Center)
3 West Leominster	7 Gates Crossing	13 Washacum
	9 Pratts Jct. (Pratts)	14 Sterling Jct., MA

BUILT: 1848-50.

OPERATORS: *Fitchburg & Worcester, 1850-69; Boston, Clinton & Fitchburg, 1869-76; Boston, Clinton, Fitchburg & New Bedford, 1876-79; Old Colony, 1879-93; New York, New Haven & Hartford, 1893-1969; Penn Central, 1969-76; Conrail, 1976- .*

DAILY PASSENGER TRAINS: *1869:* 6, *1893:* 8, *1919:* 4.   Passenger service ended Sterling Jct.-Pratts Jct., 1926; Pratts Jct.-Fitchburg, 1931.

ABANDONMENTS: Sterling-Sterling Jct., 1937; Pratts Jct.-Sterling, 1962

The Fitchburg & Worcester RR was chartered to connect its namesake cities in April 1846. Construction began in the summer of 1848, and the line was completed in February 1850. At its southern terminus, Sterling Junction, connection was made with the Worcester & Nashua RR (opened in 1848), over whose tracks the F&W operated trains into Worcester, twelve miles to the south. In 1866 the Agricultural Branch RR extended its Framingham-Northboro line to Pratts Junction and obtained trackage rights over the F&W into Fitchburg.

The F&W was independently operated until 1869 when it was consolidated with the Agricultural Branch to form the Boston, Clinton & Fitchburg RR. This latter line in turn absorbed several other lines and became in 1876 the Boston, Clinton, Fitchburg & New Bedford RR. Three years later the latter railroad was itself incorporated into the Old Colony RR system, which in turn became part of the New York, New Haven & Hartford in 1893.

Passenger service between Fitchburg and Worcester ended late in 1925 or early 1926 and between Fitchburg and Pratts Junction (as part of service to Framingham) in 1931. The southernmost two miles of the line, from Sterling to Sterling Junction, were abandoned in 1937, having been out of service since 1934. In 1962 the F&W was cut back to Pratts Junction.

By the time the Penn Central took over the bankrupt New Haven in 1969 only a single daily local freight train operated over the F&W. The route was no longer used as a major interchange between the B&M and the New Haven. Most traffic originated or terminated at Leominster, and in 1974 the U.S. Department of Transportation recommended that the line south of Leominster be considered for abandonment. The USRA, however, found that much of the traffic in and out of Leominster moved southward and the F&W was ordered to be included in Conrail. In 1976 Conrail assumed operation of the line, the outermost part of its Fitchburg Secondary Track.

In recent years service on the surviving nine miles of the F&W has consisted of a Monday-through-Friday local round trip Conrail freight out of Framingham to Leominster via Pratts Junction. The last five miles between Leominster and Fitchburg have been out of service for many years. Trains have not operated to Fitchburg since the mid-1970s nor beyond the Leominster yard since the 1980s.

Sources: Baker, *Formation*, 25, 33; Farrell, *Railfan's Guide to Conrail*, 30; Poor, *History*, 124; U.S. Railway Association, *Final System Plan*, 2:142-43; U.S. Railway Association, *Preliminary System Plan*, 2:505-06; 221 I.C.C. 693.

41. Worcester & Nashua

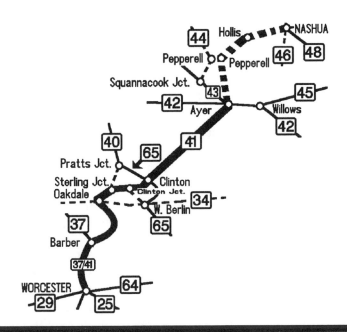

0 Worcester, MA	12 Sterling Jct. (Sterling)	28 Ayer (Groton Jct.) (Ayer Jct.)
1 Lincoln Sq.	15 Clinton Jct.	32 Groton (Groton Centre)
3 Barber (Barbers)	17 Clinton	36 Pepperell, MA
3.5 Greendale	18 Thayer (South Lancaster) (Prescott)	40 Hollis, NH
4 Bradley	19 Lancaster	45 Nashua (Main St.)
5 Summit	23 Still River	46 Nashua (Union Sta.), NH
9 West Boylston	25 Harvard	
10 Oakdale		

BUILT: 1846-48.

OPERATORS: *Worcester & Nashua, 1848-83; Worcester, Nashua & Rochester, 1883-86; Boston & Maine, 1886-1983; Guilford, 1983- ; Providence & Worcester, ca. 1985- .*

Since 1990 the W&N has formed part of the Guilford main line. Heavy freights like southbound NESE, shown here at Oakdale in February 1993, run several times a day. Conrail motive power, such as this GE C36-7, is typical.

DAILY PASSENGER TRAINS: *1869:* 6, *1893:* 12, *1919:* 8, *1935:* 6 (Worcester-Ayer), *1950:* 4 (Worcester-Ayer), *1960:* 2 (Worcester-Ayer). Passenger service ended Ayer-Nashua, 1934; Worcester-Ayer, 1960.

ABANDONMENTS: Hollis-Nashua, 1942; Ayer-Hollis, 1982; at Nashua, 1993

By the mid-1840s Worcester was becoming the most important rail junction in central Massachusetts. Railroads completed or under construction tied this rapidly growing city to Boston, Springfield, Providence, and Norwich, Conn., on Long Island Sound. It seemed logical at this time to project yet another line, northward toward Nashua, N.H. The Worcester & Nashua RR was chartered for this purpose in 1845, and construction got under way the year following. The Worcester Branch RR, a short line a half mile in length which had been built in 1844, was taken over to secure a connection with the Western and Boston & Worcester Railroads. The W&N opened from Worcester to Groton Junction (later, Ayer), in July 1848 and was completed to Nashua in December.

For many years the Worcester & Nashua was a prosperous bridge line between New Hampshire and the various lines that connected at Worcester. The railroad also interchanged traffic at Groton Junction where it met both the Fitchburg RR and the Stony Brook branch of the Nashua & Lowell, which gave it access to the textile towns of the lower Merrimack Valley. At Sterling Junction it connected with the Fitchburg & Worcester RR, which ran to Leominster and Fitchburg.

The fortunes of the Worcester & Nashua declined after it incurred heavy debt in the early 1870s building the Nashua & Rochester RR, which in 1874 extended its reach to Rochester, NH. In 1883 the two lines were consolidated to form the Worcester, Nashua & Rochester RR. Three years later the Boston & Maine absorbed the line. The Worcester, Nashua & Rochester was combined with another B&M acquisition, the Portland & Rochester RR, to form the Worcester, Nashua & Portland division of the B&M. In the 1890s two daily through passenger trains served the route, covering the 147 miles between Worcester and Portland in five and a half hours.

As a result of its expansion through mergers, the B&M at the turn of the century found itself with three parallel routes between Massa-

North of Ayer, the abandoned right of way of the W&N is owned by the state of Massachusetts. Although undeveloped, it already serves as a recreational trail, as this September 1994 view in Pepperell attests.

chusetts and Portland. For a time there was enough traffic between Massachusetts and Maine to keep all three lines busy. In the first decade of this century many passenger and freight trains plied the W&N, despite the fact that it was only single tracked and not signalized. In 1902 the crack *Bar Harbor Express* began using this route. The W&N was double tracked and block signals were installed by 1913. In 1911 the *Bar Harbor Express* was renamed the *State of Maine Express* and rerouted from Ayer to Lowell over the Stony Brook line. After 1911 fewer through freights ran north of Ayer, and these ended altogether in 1930 when the construction of a wye at North Chelmsford allowed freights to reach Nashua via the Stony Brook.

Local through passenger service between Worcester and Portland ended in 1928. In the 1930s the through route was severed when track was abandoned in two places between Nashua and Rochester. Passenger service between Ayer and Nashua, which was now provided by a gas-electric "doodlebug" railcar, was discontinued in April 1934. The second track between Ayer and Nashua had been removed in 1929, and after passenger service north of Ayer ended in 1934, the diamond crossing of the Fitchburg at Ayer was removed, making the W&N two separate lines.

In 1941 the B&M sought to abandon the W&N north of Pepperell, but objections from customers in Hollis, N.H, persuaded the I.C.C. to permit abandonment only from Nashua to Hollis (this segment had been virtually out of service since 1934). Excluded from the abandonment were the first mile and a half in Nashua. The B&M continued to service industrial customers on this track until the late 1980s. Formal abandonment came in 1993.

By the 1970s two paper companies in Pepperell provided nearly all the business on the trackage north of Ayer. (Both had originally been served by the Brookline & Pepperell line before its abandonment in 1940.) Service to Pepperell ceased in November 1981, and the B&M finally received permission in 1982 to abandon the entire line north of Ayer. Five years later the state of Massachusetts acquired the right of way for use as a recreational trail and a future bike path.

The line south of Ayer enjoyed a different fate. As the B&M's sole gateway into Worcester, its importance increased in the 1920s as the line north of Ayer declined. The B&M rebuilt this line in the 1920s to handle even the heaviest trains. Local passenger service between Ayer

Bound for the electric plant at Bow, N.H., a unit coal train passes by the Wachusett Reservoir in Oakdale in August 1992. A junction with the Central Mass branch was located here until 1939.

and Worcester lasted until April 1953, and the *State of Maine* used this route until its demise in October 1960. (The state forced the B&M to operate a single RDC car between Haverhill and Worcester for a few months more.) In the 1970s and 1980s traffic declined on this line, but under Guilford the line has been renovated to serve through freight trains. Since 1990 Guilford has diverted most of its through freights to and from Maine over the W&N to interchange with Conrail at Worcester, instead of the traditional route via the Hoosac Tunnel. Once more the Worcester & Nashua—at least part of it—is the road to Maine.

Sources: Bachelder, *Half-Century Limited*, 36; Baker, *Formation*, 146, 166-67; Crouch, "Worcester, Nashua & Portland"; Poor, *History*, 165; Wilder, "Stony Brook Railroad"; 249 I.C.C. 601.

42. Fitchburg

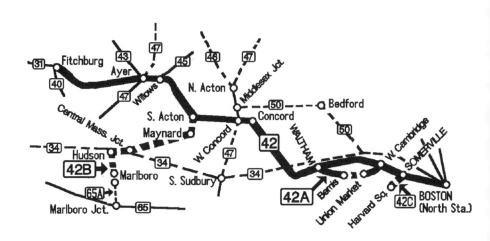

0	Boston (North Sta.), MA	14	Hastings	**42A. Watertown Branch**
1	Charlestown	15	Silver Hill	
2	Union Square (Prospect St.)	17	Lincoln	
3	Somerville	18	Baker Bridge (Bakers Bridge)	0 West Cambridge (Brick Yards), MA
4	Cambridge (Porters)	20	Concord	0.5 Concord Turnpike
5	West Cambridge (Brick Yards)	22	West Concord (Concord Jct.)	1 Fresh Pond
5.5	Hill Crossing (Hills Crossing)	25	South Acton	1.5 Mount Auburn
6	Belmont (Wellington Hill)	27	West Acton	2 East Watertown (Grove St.) (Arsenal)
7	Waverly	29	Boxboro	3 Union Market
8	Clematis Brook	30	Littleton/Route 495	4 Watertown
9	Beaver Brook	31.5	Littleton	4.5 West Watertown
10	Waltham	34	Willows	5 Bemis (& Aetna Mills)
10.5	Riverview	36	Ayer (Ayer Jct.) (Groton Jct.)	6 Bleachery
11	Roberts	39	Shirley	6.5 Newton St. (Chemistry)
12	Stony Brook	42	Lunenburg	7 Waltham, MA
13	Kendal Green (Weston)	45	North Leominster (Leominster)	
		48	East Fitchburg	
		50	Fitchburg, MA	

42B. Marlboro Branch	7 Gleasondale (Rockbottom)	13 Marlboro, MA
0 South Acton, MA	8 Gleason Jct. (Central Massachusetts Jct.)	**42C. Harvard Branch**
3 Maynard		0 Somerville, MA
6 Lake Boone (Whitmans) (Whitmans Crossing)	9 Hudson (Feltonville)	1 Harvard Yard, MA

BUILT: 1839-48; Watertown Branch, 1847-51; Marlboro Branch, 1848-55; Harvard Branch, 1845.

OPERATORS: *Charlestown Branch, 1839-45; Fitchburg, 1843-1900; Boston & Maine, 1900-83; Guilford, 1983- ; MBTA (commuter passenger), 1976-* .

DAILY PASSENGER TRAINS: *1869:* 8, *1893:* 15, *1919:* 19, *1935:* 29, *1950:* 27, *1960:* 16, *1971:* 4 (Boston-Ayer; 38, Boston-S. Acton), *1981:* 10 (32, Boston-S. Acton) *1994:* 20 (32, S. Acton-Boston). Passenger service not operated Ayer-Fitchburg, 1965-75; S. Acton-Fitchburg, 1975-80. Passenger service ended on Watertown Branch, 1938; Marlboro Branch, (Maynard-Central Mass. Jct., 1932; Central Mass. Jct.-Marlboro, 1939 (restored Gleason Jct.-Hudson, ca. 1958-65); Maynard-South Acton, 1958).

ABANDONMENTS: Harvard Branch, 1855; Marlboro Branch (Maynard-Central Massachusetts Jct., 1943; South Acton-Maynard, 1979); Watertown Branch (Union Market-Bemis, 1960; near Bemis, 1991).

Although it eventually grew to encompass a major rail system, the Fitchburg RR began as a short line built to service the docks at Charlestown. The Charlestown Branch RR received its charter in 1836, and in October 1839 opened as a 1.3-mile line from Charlestown to Somerville. Business was disappointing, so in June 1841 construction began on an extension to Fresh Pond in West Cambridge, a major source of ice for both the domestic and foreign trade. The line was completed the following spring. Until this point horses were the sole source of power on this modest road, but now steam locomotives were introduced.

The Charlestown Branch was soon engorged by a much more ambitious project. In 1842 paper mill tycoon Alvah Crocker of Fitchburg had secured a charter to build a rail line from Charlestown to Fitchburg, and via extensions, to New Hampshire, Vermont, and ultimately, Canada. The Fitchburg commenced construction at West Cambridge in May 1843 and opened from that point to Waltham in

With a train of automobile carriers in tow, Guilford local freight AY-3 works the Fitchburg east of Ayer in February 1993.

December. By June 1844 it reached Concord. (A year later Thoreau built his cabin at Walden Pond a quarter-mile away from the rails, where, he wrote in *Walden*, "the whistle of the locomotive penetrates my woods summer and winter." He also noted, "I usually go to the village along its causeway, and am, as it were, related to society by this link.") By October it was in Acton, December in Shirley, and in March 1845 it was completed to Fitchburg. In September the Fitchburg leased the Charlestown Branch, gaining access to the wharfs at Charlestown across the harbor from Boston. In 1848 tracks were extended into the city.

The Fitchburg developed into one of New England's major railroads. As early as 1849 the entire main line had been double tracked. The Fitchburg's owners wasted little time in chartering an extension westward, the Vermont & Massachusetts RR. After the opening of the Hoosac Tunnel in 1875 the Fitchburg came to control lines as far as Schenectady, N.Y., and heavy freight traffic from the west flowed over its rails to Boston. The Fitchburg became highly competitive with the region's other major east-west trunk line, the Boston & Albany, and by 1895 was hauling more western grain and livestock than its rival to the south. By the end of the nineteenth century the Fitchburg had expanded into a 460-mile system that controlled lines in four states. The Boston & Maine finally leased the entire Fitchburg system in 1900, the last major addition to the B&M before the 1980s.

The only major wreck on the Fitchburg took place a few years later, on November 26, 1905. On that foggy evening the crack *Montreal Express*, pulled by two locomotives, had left North Station at 7:45 bound for Canada. Half an hour earlier a local for South Acton and Marlboro had departed, only to become delayed. The *Express*, being driven by an inexperienced crew, began to close on the local, ignoring signals to slow. By the time the local reached Lincoln, the *Express* was only a minute behind; as the local left the next station, Baker Bridge, the *Express* smashed into its rear. Seventeen lives were lost in the collision and the fire that followed.

During the first half of the twentieth century the Fitchburg was one of the most important components of the B&M. In 1927, most through freights in and out of Boston were rerouted off of the Fitchburg between West Cambridge and Boston, but the line beyond West Cambridge continued to carry heavy freight traffic. Through passenger trains ran via this route from Boston west to Troy, N.Y. (utimately Chicago), and northward to Canada via New Hampshire and Vermont. Despite some attempts to improve passenger service with streamline trains, ridership declined rapidly after the Second World War. After 1960 passenger trains did not operate on the main line west of Fitchburg; in 1965 the western terminus of commuter service shifted to Ayer, and ten years later to South Acton.

In the early 1970s the Fitchburg main line remained one of the most important freight routes in New England, although traffic was densest on the segment west of Willows, where connection was made with the B&M's route to Maine. After 1965 passenger service on the Fitchburg main line was provided under contract to the MBTA by the B&M's fleet of rail diesel cars. Most trains terminated at South Acton, and in February 1975 the last remaining trains to Ayer were eliminated. In 1976 the MBTA acquired ownership of the Fitchburg, with the B&M retaining trackage rights for freight trains.

Passenger service returned to the entire Fitchburg main line in January 1980 when the MBTA began operating trains from North Station to Fitchburg (and on to Gardner, until 1986). A few months later the abandonment of the freight cutoff through Somerville, necessitated by subway construction, caused freights between Boston and the West to be rerouted over the Boston & Lowell and Stony Brook lines to the Fitchburg at Willows, two miles east of Ayer. East of Ayer the Fitchburg sees little freight but frequent commuter trains, now consisting of modern push-pull equipment. Between Willows and Fitchburg both passenger and freight traffic remained heavy until 1990, when Guilford began diverting most of its freight trains onto the Worcester & Nashua line at Ayer to interchange with Conrail at Worcester. On the Fitchburg west of Ayer only a few through freights run each day.

The Fitchburg's branches were built shortly after the road was completed. The Watertown Branch was chartered as an independent venture in 1846. A second company, the Waltham & Watertown RR, was chartered to extend the line. Fearing that these lines might come under the control of a rival railroad, the Fitchburg acquired both before they were built. Construction began in 1847, and was completed from West Cambridge to Bemis in 1849. In 1851 the branch was extended from Bemis to Waltham. For many years the Fitchburg ran commuter trains from Boston over the Watertown branch to Waltham and Roberts on the main line. In 1893 it became one of the few branch lines to be double tracked. Passenger service finally ended in 1938 and most of the second track was removed the following year. Abandonment of the line through Watertown Square in 1960 split the branch in two. In 1991 another 0.4 mile was further cut back at Bemis.

The Lancaster & Sterling RR was chartered in 1846. Shortly afterwards the Fitchburg obtained control and had the charter changed to authorize construction of a Fitchburg branch toward Marlboro. Construction commenced in 1848 and was completed to Feltonville in June 1850. Under the charter of a second line, the Marlboro Branch RR, the branch was extended to Marlboro in March 1855. The central part of the Marlboro branch, from Maynard to Central Massachusetts Junction, was abandoned in 1943, dividing the branch into two separate lines. By the 1970s traffic on both had dwindled to an occasional freight. The northern section, from South Acton to Maynard, was finally abandoned in 1979, after not having seen trains for many years (aside from RDC cars that used a small part of the track at South Acton as a layover point); the southern portion, from Hudson just south of Gleason (Central Mass) Junction to Marlboro, followed in 1980.

In 1848 the Massachusetts legislature authorized a number of prominent Cambridge citizens to construct a short branch line from Somerville Junction to Harvard Yard. The Harvard Branch RR was constructed in the summer and fall of 1849 and was opened at the end of 1849. The Fitchburg operated this three-quarters-mile road until 1855 when it was abandoned and the rails were removed. No sign of its existence remains.

Sources: Bachelder, *Half-Century Limited*; Baker, *Formation*, 177-82; Harlow, *Steelways*, 236-38; Humphrey and Clark, *Boston's Commuter Rail*, 87-89; Humphrey and Clark, *Second Section*, 10; Kirkland, *Men, Cities, and Transportation*, 1: 316, 390-92, 430-31; Lovett, "Harvard Branch Railroad"; Poor, *History*, 107, 122, 130; Shaw, *History of Railroad Accidents*, 91-92.

Outbound from North Station, an MBTA commuter train passes through posh suburban Lincoln in August 1991. Note the double deck coach, a recent innovation in Boston commuter service.

43. Peterborough & Shirley

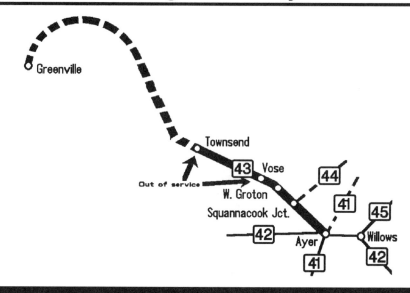

0 Ayer (Groton Jct.) (Ayer Jct.), MA	10 Townsend (Townsend Centre)	19 Pratt (Pratts) (Wilton)
3 Squannacook Jct.	12 West Townsend, MA	24 Greenville (Mason Village), NH
4 West Groton	16 Mason (Mason Centre), NH	
4.5 Vose		
8 Townsend Harbor		

BUILT: 1847-50.

OPERATORS: *Fitchburg,* 1848-1900; *Boston & Maine,* 1900-83; *Guilford,* 1983- .

DAILY PASSENGER TRAINS: *1869:* 4, *1893:* 7, *1919:* 4.   Passenger service ended July 1933.

ABANDONMENTS: Townsend-Greenville, 1979.

No sooner had the Fitchburg RR completed its Boston to Fitchburg line in 1845 than it launched a series of expansions designed to secure it more traffic. Among these projects was a rail line running northwest from the new Groton Junction (Ayer), where the Fitchburg would be crossed by the Worcester & Nashua and Stony Brook Railroads, both in the planning stages. Construction on the Peterborough & Shirley

RR began in 1847 from Groton Junction and was opened to West Townsend in January 1848. The line was completed through to Mason Village (now Greenville, N.H.) in November 1850. It never came any closer to Peterborough, a dozen miles away.

From the beginning the Peterborough & Shirley was a Fitchburg RR project, the Fitchburg having leased the line in 1847 before it was even opened. The Fitchburg bought the line outright in 1860. The Fitchburg's prime motive in building and operating this marginal

Published by F. H. Whiting   New Boston & Maine Steel Bridge, Greenville, N. H.

This trestle across the Souhegan River in Greenville, N.H., was the most scenic feature on the Peterborough &Shirley. It is shown here on a postcard circa 1915 (collection of the author).

branch line was to prevent it from falling into the hands of its rival, the Nashua & Lowell, which might have used it to deprive the Fitchburg of New Hampshire traffic if the line were to be extended further to the northwest.

By the time the Fitchburg became part of the Boston & Maine system in 1900, the Peterborough & Shirley was another of New

England's obscure branch lines, Greenville's textile mills constituting the only significant source of traffic. The closing of these mills in the 1930s left the railroad with only modest local traffic bound for Green-ville, Townsend, and West Groton. In May 1972 a flood washed out several sections of the line in New Hampshire and these portions were never again operated. In 1979 the I.C.C. approved the abandonment of the line beyond the Bates Corrugated Box factory west of Townsend Centre.

In November 1981 the Boston & Maine embargoed service on the P&S beyond a point west of West Groton (Vose), despite previous assurances to shippers that service would continue. Sterilite, a plastics manufacturer who had constructed a factory along the tracks in Townsend only a few years earlier, now found itself forced to switch to trucks. The Massachusetts portion of the P&S has been acquired by the MBTA, although the tracks between Vose and Townsend Centre are no longer in service. (The MBTA permitted the town of Townsend to pave over a grade crossing at Townsend Harbor.) Guilford provides sporadic freight service between Ayer and the line's only remaining customer, the Hollingsworth-Vose paper mill at Vose.

Source: Bachelder, *Half-Century Limited*, 35; Baker, *Formation*, 178, 181.

44. Brookline & Pepperell

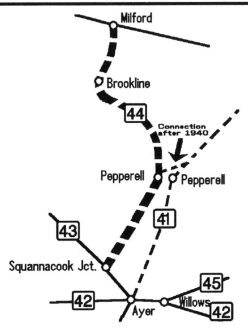

0	Squannacook Jct., MA	6	Pepperell
1	Newell	8	North Pepperell, MA
3	Primus (Hollingsworth)	10	West Hollis, NH
		12	South Brookline

13	Brookline
15	North Brookline
20	South Milford
21	Milford, NH

BUILT: 1891-94.

OPERATORS: *Fitchburg,* 1892-1900; *Boston & Maine,* 1900-42.

DAILY PASSENGER TRAINS: *1893:* 6, *1919:* 4. Passenger service ended September 1931.

ABANDONMENTS: Pepperell-South Milford, 1939; Squannacook Jct.-Pepperell, South Milford-Milford, 1942.

The Fitchburg RR had a number of branches feeding its main line from southern New Hampshire. The last to be built was the Brookline & Pepperell system. The Fitchburg itself could trace its origins to a short line constructed early in the 1840s to haul ice from its source in

Built in 1892 the Brookline & Pepperell depot in Pepperell remains a local landmark, even though passenger trains haven't stopped here since 1931. When this photo was taken in September 1994 the station housed a caterer.

Cambridge's Fresh Pond to Charlestown. For more than forty years the Fitchburg continued to harvest ice until the city of Cambridge appropriated the pond as a reservoir for its water system. The Fitchburg claimed to have found a new ice source at Brookline, N.H. Around 1891 the Fitchburg therefore chartered two railroads: the Brookline & Pepperell, from a point on the Fitchburg's Ayer-Greenville line (the Peterborough & Shirley) through Pepperell to the New Hampshire line; and the Brookline RR, which continued the route to the Brookline ice pond. Both railroads opened simultaneously in September 1892, and from the beginning they were operated as a single branch by the Fitchburg, which formally absorbed them in 1895. In 1893 the Fitchburg chartered still a third line, the Brookline & Milford, which extended the line to Milford, N.H., a year later.

Cynics claimed that Brookline ice was a ruse, and that the line was actually built to enable the Fitchburg to snatch New Hampshire traffic from the Boston & Maine. (Be that as it may, a great deal of us would ultimately be hauled over the line). A few years later, however, the Fitchburg became the last major railroad to be acquired by the B&M, which now had a near monopoly of rail traffic in New Hampshire and northern Massachusetts.

The Brookline & Pepperell was always a marginal operation. Between Ayer and Pepperell it closely paralleled the B&M's Worcester & Nashua line, which ran along the opposite bank of the Nashua River. In Pepperell, the two lines had stations on each side of the river less than a mile apart. North of Pepperell the line ran through sparsely populated territory that even today is mostly rural. During the 1920s the B&M ran passenger trains over this route between Ayer and Manchester. Passenger service ceased in September 1931. Ice made up the bulk of freight traffic until 1935, when a fire destroyed the Brookline ice house. A temporary shortage of ice lead to a final cutting at the Brookline pond in March 1937, with the blocks loaded directly onto freight cars. By 1939 manufactured ice had destroyed what market remained for the natural product.

Freight service between Brookline and South Milford had been suspended in 1932, and after the 1935 fire there was no service north of Pepperell, except for the one shipment in 1937. The I.C.C. permitted the B&M to abandon the line north of Pepperell in 1939, except for the final mile between South Milford and Milford.

This left only the first six miles to Pepperell in operation, with all of the customers located in that town. The B&M proposed building a connection between its Worcester & Nashua line and the shippers on the Brookline & Pepperell across the Nashua River. With this accomplished, the B&M was able to abandon the remainder of the Brookline & Pepperell in 1942. A short segment of track in front of the Pepperell station was used as a wye until the end of all Pepperell rail service in 1982.

Today the Brookline & Pepperell is gone, but its route survives as a hiking trail in Hollis and in northern Pepperell (most of the right of way in Pepperell north of Main Street is owned by the town or by the Massachusetts Division of Fisheries & Wildlife). The century-old Pepperell depot, now beautifully restored and housing a caterer, still stands on Main Street. Depots also remain in Brookline and Milford, N.H.

Sources: Bachelder, *Half-Century Limited*, 36; Baker, *Formation*, 196; 230 I.C.C. 657; 247 I.C.C. 793.

45. Stony Brook

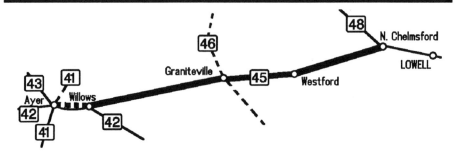

0 North Chelmsford, MA	6 Graniteville	13 Ayer (Ayer Jct.)(Groton Jct.), MA
2 West Chelmsford	7 Forge Village	
3 Brookside	9 North Littleton	
4 Westford	11 Willows (Sandy Pond)	

BUILT: 1847-48.

OPERATORS: *Nashua & Lowell,* 1848-57; *"Boston, Lowell & Nashua" (joint operation, Nashua & Lowell-Boston & Lowell),* 1857-78; *Nashua & Lowell,* 1878-80; *Boston & Lowell,* 1880-87; *Boston & Maine,* 1887-1983; *Guilford,* 1983- .

DAILY PASSENGER TRAINS: *1869:* 6, *1893:* 8, *1919:* 10, *1935:* 6, *1950:* 4, *1960:* 2. Passenger service ended 1960.

ABANDONMENTS: Willows-Ayer, 1946.

The Stony Brook RR was chartered in 1845 by citizens of Lowell seeking direct access between their city and the South and West. The Stony Brook would connect the Nashua & Lowell RR (completed seven years earlier) to the new Fitchburg RR. Construction began in 1847 and the line was opened in July 1848. A few months before its completion its owners contracted with the Nashua & Lowell to operate it for them. It soon became an integral part of the Nashua & Lowell (the Stony Brook never owned its own rolling stock). For many years the Nashua & Lowell was operated jointly with the Boston & Lowell, under the unofficial name of Boston, Lowell & Nashua.

In its early years the Stony Brook was not particularly profitable to the Nashua & Lowell, but was retained to keep it out of the hands of archrival Fitchburg RR. Later, as part of the B&M, the Stony Brook formed part of a through route between Maine and the South and West that avoided Boston. After 1911 many freight and some passenger trains that formerly used the Worcester & Nashua line were rerouted onto the Stony Brook. Despite this increase in traffic the line was not completely double tracked until 1928. The installation of a west wye at North Chelmsford in 1930 made it possible to reroute all remaining through trains between Ayer and Nashua over this route and the Nashua & Lowell to Nashua.

Passenger trains using the Stony Brook included the *Bar Harbor Express*, which passed through without stopping each night on a route from Washington, D.C., to Ellsworth, Me., via New York, New Haven, Providence, Worcester, and Portland. Another overnight train, the *State of Maine* also used this route between New York and Portland starting in 1911. Local passenger service between Lowell and Ayer ended in April 1953, and the *State of Maine* made its final run in October 1960, shortly after the Maine Central exited the passenger business. (The

By the early 1990s Conrail motive power was more common than Guilford equipment on the Stony Brook. Here Conrail 6727, an EMD SD50, leads Guilford freight NESE through Westford in February 1993.

In February 1992 Guilford's westbound NESE crosses School Street in West Chelmsford.

state required the B&M to operate a lone RDC car between Harverhill and Worcester for a few months more.)

In April 1946 the Stony Brook's own tracks between Willows and Ayer were removed and a new junction was constructed at Willows with the Fitchburg line. Trains from the Stony Brook lines henceforth used Fitchburg tracks to reach Ayer station. In 1957 the second track was removed, except near Willows and between Westford and Graniteville.

Today the Stony Brook forms a vital part of Guilford's only major through route from Maine to the West. It probably sees more freight trains each day than any other part of the Guilford system in Massachusetts.

Sources: Baker, *Formation*, 101, 106; Poor, *History*, 152; Wilder, "Stony Brook Railroad."

46. Nashua, Acton & Boston

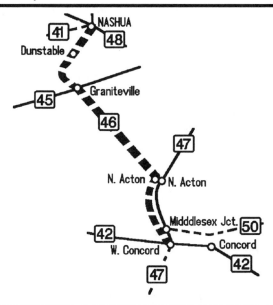

0 Nashua, NH	13 West Graniteville	20 North Acton
1 Otterson St.	(Graniteville)	22 Acton
1.5 Sandy Pond, NH	14 Pine Ridge (West-	23 Middlesex Jct.
6 Dunstable, MA	ford)	24 Concord Jct., MA
9 East Groton	16 East Littleton	

BUILT: 1872-73.

OPERATORS: *Nashua, Acton & Boston,* 1873-76; *Concord,* 1876-81; *Concord-Boston & Lowell (joint operation),* 1881-84; *Concord,* 1884-89; *Concord & Montreal,* 1889-95; *Boston & Maine,* 1895-1925.

DAILY PASSENGER TRAINS: *1893:* 6, *1919:* 4. Passenger service ended 1924.

ABANDONMENTS: Nashua-Concord Jct., 1925; remainder of line (Nashua), ca. 1980.

The Nashua, Acton & Boston RR was chartered in Massachusetts in 1871 and in New Hampshire in 1872 to build a line south from Nashua, N.H., the southern terminus of the Concord RR, to North Acton, Mass., on the Framingham & Lowell RR. This latter railroad connected with routes to Boston and points west. The Nashua, Acton & Boston eventually obtained four miles of trackage rights over the Framingham & Lowell to reach the Fitchburg at Concord Junction; the Old Colony RR, successor to the Framingham & Lowell, later installed a second track for the exclusive use of the NA&B, which in effect extended the line to Concord Junction.

The Concord RR backed the NA&B in order to give it an alternative to its only southern connection, the Nashua & Lowell-Boston & Lowell system. When the line opened in July 1873, the NA&B made a bold bid for Nashua-Boston traffic. Using the Fitchburg RR to reach Boston the new line undercut fares on the existing Nashua & Lowell-Boston & Lowell line by 15%, its trains made the run in as good a time, and the route was six miles shorter.

Despite this strong effort, the Nashua, Acton & Boston never enjoyed success. In 1876 the Concord RR leased the line, extending this major New Hampshire railroad into Massachusetts for the first time. In 1879 the Boston & Lowell built a connection with the NA&B

Although trains last crossed this bridge over Stony Brook in Westford in 1925, it remains an impressive memorial to the Nashua, Acton & Boston.

from its Middlesex Central line at Middlesex Junction, just west of the Concord reformatory. This connection was used for only a few years. It seems to have been out of service as early as 1887, and it was abandoned altogether around 1900.

The Nashua, Acton & Boston remained a part of the Concord system for nearly twenty years, until along with the rest of the Concord it became part of the B&M in 1895. Through freight service ended, and the sparsely populated territory through which the line passed generated little revenue. No station on the Nashua, Acton & Boston was more than four miles from another railroad. Before June 1921 both a daily round trip passenger train and a daily mixed freight were operated between Nashua and North Acton. Passenger receipts averaged only $2.65 per trip! The passenger train made its last run June 27, 1921; the mixed train lasted until June 23, 1924.

By 1924, when the B&M sought permission to abandon the line, freight service was being provided only three days a week, the trains usually running only from Nashua to East Groton. Lumber made up 80% of the road's traffic. The only significant shippers on the line were loggers near East Groton and a coal & ice dealer in Dunstable (population 353). Ignoring objections from these rail customers the I.C.C. approved the abandonment request in April 1925 and operations ended the following month. The tracks—except for the first two miles out of Nashua and a few hundred feet at North Acton—were removed in the summer of 1926. The Nashua trackage remained in use as an industrial spur until around 1980.

Today much of the right of way through Dunstable and Westford remains clearly visible. Older residents refer to the line locally as the "Red Line," supposedly on account of its heavy operating losses. Its most notable surviving artifact is a stone bridge across Stony Brook located some 1200 feet southeast of the intersection of West and Prescott Streets in Westford and accessible by an easy hike. Built of granite blocks without mortar, this has rightfully been called "the most impressive stone arch structure in the lower Merrimack Valley" (Molloy, 105).

Sources: Baker, *Formation*, 114, 124, 141; Crouch and Frye, "Worcester, Nashua & Portland"; Judkins, "I Remember Reformatory Station"; Molloy, *Lower Merrimack Valley*, 105; 94 I.C.C. 737.

47. Framingham & Lowell

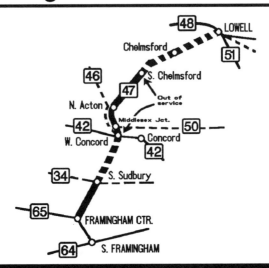

0 Framingham	8 North Sudbury	16 North Acton
Centre, MA	(Raymonds)	(Nagog) (North
(Framingham)	12 West Concord	Acton Jct.)
2 Nobscot (North	(Concord Jct.)	18 Carlisle
Framingham)	13 Middlesex Jct.	20 South Chelmsford
5 South Sudbury	14 Acton	(Byams)
6 Sudbury		23 Chelmsford
		27 Lowell, MA

BUILT: 1870-71.

OPERATORS: *Framingham & Lowell,* 1871-72; *Boston, Clinton & Fitchburg,* 1872-76; *Boston, Clinton, Fitchburg & New Bedford,* 1876-79; *Old Colony,* 1879-93; *New York, New Haven & Hartford,* 1893-1968; *Penn Central,* 1969-76; *Conrail,* 1976- , *Springfield Terminal,* 1982-83; *Guilford,* 1983- ; *Bay Colony,* 1985-. 1993.

DAILY PASSENGER TRAINS: *1893:* 6, *1919:* 4. Passenger service ended 1933.

ABANDONMENTS: Lowell-Chelmsford, 1976; Chelmsford-South Chelmsford and South Sudbury-West Concord, 1982; at Lowell, 1994.

The Framingham & Lowell RR was incorporated in 1870 and opened on October 1, 1871. Shortly afterwards it was leased by the Boston, Clinton & Fitchburg RR, a small carrier serving Fitchburg, Framingham, and Worcester. It eventually became a northern extension of the

Old Colony RR, and later of the Old Colony's successor, the New Haven. Lowell for many years was the northernmost point on the NYNH&H, deep in the territory of the B&M. Although through trains used the line, the F&L never generated much local traffic for the New Haven. Steam-powered passenger trains were replaced first by gas-electric rail cars in the 1920s and then by highway buses in 1933.

The B&M interchange at Lowell was important, since most rail traffic between Maine and southeastern Massachusetts took the F&L. After 1970, however, Penn Central, which had taken over the New Haven, exchanged little traffic with the B&M at Lowell. In the early 1970s trains used the F&L only about twice each week. The USRA, noting that more than 70% of the traffic from this line originated in Lowell, recommended that the F&L not be transferred from Penn Central to Conrail, and when the latter took over in 1976 only the section between Framingham Centre and South Sudbury was included. The tracks between the Lowell city line and Chelmsford Center were abandoned. The state of Massachusetts then paid Conrail to operate the remainder of the line for several years, except for the first few miles within Lowell, which now were served by the B&M (in 1994 Guilford abandoned three-quarters of a mile of this Lowell trackage). In 1982 operation was assigned to Springfield Terminal RR, but service on the line between South Chelmsford and North Acton was discontinued. The line between South Sudbury and West Concord and from Chelmsford to South Chelmsford was abandoned, dividing what remained of the F&L into two branches. In 1985 the Bay Colony RR took over the tracks between West Concord and North Acton.

Today the line between West Concord and South Chelmsford remains intact although out of service. Sporadic train service was provided to a lumber yard in North Acton by the Bay Colony RR (using a Whiting trackmobile) until 1993. Conrail operates the southern section as its South Sudbury Industrial Track. The right of way between Lowell and South Sudbury, now owned by the state, awaits conversion into a bike path. A short stretch of track in Lowell continues to be operated by Guilford.

Sources: Baker, *Formation*, 25, 35; *Chronological History of the New Haven Railroad*; Cornwall and Smith, *Names First*, 42; Patton, "Old Colony Northern Division"; U.S. Railway Association, *Final System Plan*, 2:141-42; U.S. Railway Association, *Preliminary System Plan*, 2:504.

48. Nashua & Lowell

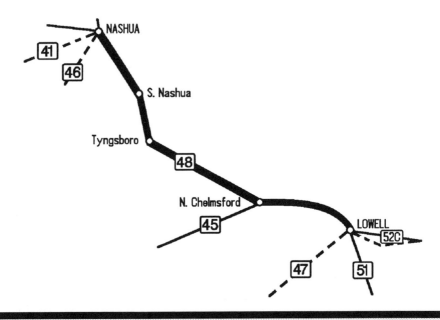

0	Lowell, MA	7	Tyngsboro, MA	13	Concord [RR]
2	Middlesex		(Tyngsboro &		Depot (Nashua
3	North Chelmsford		Dunstable)		Jct.) (Nashua
5	Vesper Club	10	South Nashua (Lit-		Union Sta.)
			tles), NH	14	Nashua (Nashua
					City Sta.), NH

BUILT: 1837-38.

OPERATORS: *Nashua & Lowell,* 1838-57; *Nashua & Lowell-Boston & Lowell (joint operation),* 1857-78; *Nashua & Lowell,* 1878-80; *Boston & Lowell,* 1880-87; *Boston & Maine,* 1887-1983; *Guilford,* 1983- .

DAILY PASSENGER TRAINS: *1869:* 11, *1893:* 19, *1919:* 26, *1935:* 31, *1950:* 18, *1960:* 14. Passenger service ended 1967; restored on trial basis 1980 and discontinued 1981.

ABANDONMENTS: None.

When the Boston & Lowell RR—one of New England's first three railroads—opened in 1835, it seemed logical to extend the line along the banks of the Merrimack River to the growing textile city of Nashua, N.H., only fifteen miles away. The Nashua & Lowell RR was therefore chartered in New Hampshire that year to construct such a line. A Massachusetts charter was obtained the year following. The route of construction seemed particularly easy: "nature seems to have prepared us a bed for our Rail Road already graded," its promoters declared (Kirkland, 1:162).

Construction got under way in 1837, service between Lowell and a point just south of Nashua commenced October 8, 1838, and the road was completed in December 1838, giving Nashua a direct rail link to Boston. This was the first railroad to operate in the Granite State. Business was brisk and a second track was added by 1848. The Nashua & Lowell constructed extensions that brought it west to Greenfield, N.H., while the Concord RR (completed 1842) continued the route northward up the Merrimack Valley to Manchester and Concord. In 1857 the Nashua & Lowell entered into an agreement with its connection to the south, the Boston & Lowell, whereby the two roads would

On a cold winter day in January 1994 along the banks of the Merrimack, a westbound freight approaches the interlocking at North Chelmsford.

be operated as a single company, an arrangement that continued for more than two decades. The Boston & Lowell eventually leased the Nashua & Lowell in 1880, before itself passing to the Boston & Maine in 1887.

Under the B&M the Nashua & Lowell formed part of the New Hampshire division and saw a fair amount of passenger and through freight traffic. The second track was removed and a centralized traffic control signal system installed. Passenger service ended June 30, 1967. Using federal transportation funds, Boston to Concord, N.H., passenger service was restored on January 28, 1980, but low ridership and the end of funding once more left the Nashua & Lowell freight-only on February 28, 1981.

In recent years the Nashua & Lowell has had a split personality. The initial three miles between Lowell and North Chelmsford form part of the busy Guilford main line between Maine and the West, with most traffic going to or coming from the Stony Brook line. Beyond the wye at North Chelmsford to Nashua the line sees less activity, typically a daily freight or two in and out of Nashua and a several-times-each-month unit coal train to Bow, N.H.

In recent years there have been proposals to restore Nashua-Lowell-Boston commuter service (during 1980-81 many of the passengers who used the service boarded at Nashua), and at least one group in Nashua has been scouting a site for a new passenger station. The MBTA has shown little interest, since it believes that most potential riders already board trains at Lowell and that New Hampshire will not help fund the service.

Sources: Baker, *Formation*, 105-07; Bradlee, *Boston & Lowell*; Harlow, *Steelways*, 285-87; Humphrey and Clark, *Boston's Commuter Rail*, 55-58; Kirkland, *Men, Cities and Transportation*, 1:162-63; Poor, *History*, 60, 64, 135.

49. Billerica & Bedford

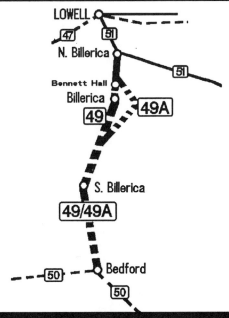

0	Bedford, MA	8.5	North Billerica, MA	2.5	Bedford Springs
1	Spring Rd. Crossing			3	Cliffs
2.5	Bedford Springs		**49A. B&B Narrow Gauge**	3.5	South Billerica
3.5	South Billerica			5	Nuttings Pond
5	Turnpike			5.5	Boston Rd.
6	Billerica	0	Bedford, MA	6.5	Billerica
6.5	Bennett Hall (Main St.)	0.5	Main St.	7.5	Salem Rd.
		1	Spring St.	8	Nasons
		2	Oak Hill	9	North Billerica, MA

BUILT: 1877 (narrow gauge); 1885 (standard gauge, new route).

OPERATORS: *Billerica & Bedford*, 1877-78; *Boston & Lowell*, 1886-87; *Boston & Maine*, 1887-1983; *Guilford*, 1983- .

DAILY PASSENGER TRAINS: *1893:* 8, *1919:* 5. Passenger service ended 1933.

ABANDONMENTS: Narrow gauge line, 1878; Bedford-Billerica, 1962; Bennett Hall-Billerica, ca. 1975.

Most American railroads by the 1870s had settled on a standard track gauge of 4 feet, 8½ inches between the rails. Some, however, believed that a narrower gauge, perhaps three feet, would allow lines to be constructed and operated cheaper. A few found even three feet too wide. George Mansfield, of Hazelwood, Mass., passionately believed that two-foot gauge railroads were the wave of the future. After viewing and riding such a system in Wales, he constructed a miniature railroad on his own property. When he heard in 1875 that the citizens of Billerica were seeking to build a branch line to connect their village to the main line of the Boston & Lowell RR, he rushed to the scene.

Mansfield's considerable powers of persuasion rallied support for a narrow gauge line, and in May 1876 the Billerica & Bedford RR received its charter, the first two-foot gauge common carrier railroad in America. Rolling stock was ordered and construction soon began. The line appears to have begun operating from Bedford to South Billerica in October 1877 and in its entirety a month later.

The new railroad proved to be among the shortest lived of any in New England. Six months after opening, the Billerica & Bedford was out of business. The tracks were removed and the rolling stock was carted off to Maine, where it formed the nucleus of the two-foot gauge railroads of that state.

In 1885 the Boston & Lowell RR rebuilt the branch, this time using standard gauge. The path of the narrow gauge was followed, except for two miles at Billerica Center, where the new line ran about three-quarters of a mile west of the original route. The new line formed an extension of the Boston & Lowell's Lexington & Arlington branch. Passenger trains were run from Lowell to Boston and back via this branch, and this was continued after the Boston & Maine absorbed the line along with the rest of the Boston & Lowell in 1887.

The branch never saw heavy traffic. Passenger service ended in 1933, but freight remained for many years. Finally, in 1962, the B&M received permission to abandon—for the second time—the Billerica & Bedford. A short stretch of track at North Billerica has been retained to provide access to the B&M/Guilford shops.

Sources: Adams, "Born and Buried in Six Months"; Harlow, *Steelways*, 339-40; Moody, *Maine Two-Footers*, 49-54.

The Billerica & Bedford remains in place from North Billerica to just north of Bennett Hall, but as this July 1994 view at Floyd Street, Billerica, shows, it is seldom used.

50. Lexington & Arlington

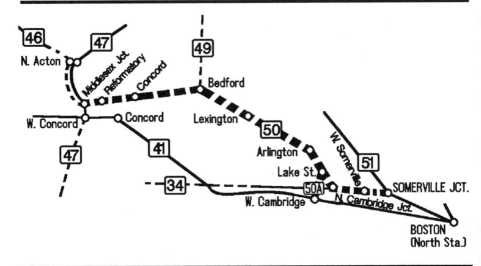

0 Somerville Jct., MA	5 Arlington Heights	19 Reformatory
0.5 Somerville High-	6 East Lexington	(Prison Sta.)
lands	6.5 Pierces Bridge	19.5 Middlesex Jct., MA
1 West Somerville	7 Munroe (Monroes)	
(Willow Ave.)	8 Lexington	**50A. West Cam-**
1.5 North Cambridge	9 North Lexington	**bridge Connection**
Jct. (North Cam-	12 Bedford	
bridge)	13 Shady Hill (Mur-	0 Lake St., MA
2.5 Lake St.	rays Crossing)	1 West Cambridge,
3.5 Arlington	14 West Bedford	MA
4 Brattle (Brattles)	16 Concord	

BUILT: 1845-79

OPERATORS: *Fitchburg*, 1846-58; *Lexington & West Cambridge*, 1858-70; *Boston & Lowell*, 1870-87; *Boston & Maine*, 1887-1981.

DAILY PASSENGER TRAINS: *1869:* 11 (Lexington-W. Cambridge), *1893:* 16 (Reformatory-Somerville Jct.); 44 (Lexington-Somerville Jct.), *1919:* 16 (Bedford-Somerville Jct.), *1935:* 10 (Bedford-W. Cambridge), *1950:* 6 (Bedford-W. Cambridge), *1960:* 2 (Bedford-W. Cambridge), *1971:* 2 (Bedford-W. Cambridge). Passenger service ended Middlesex Jct.-Prison Sta., ca. 1887; Reformatory-Bedford, 1926; remainder of line, 1977.

ABANDONMENTS: Middlesex Jct.-Reformatory, ca. 1900; Reformatory-Concord, 1927; Concord-Bedford, 1962; West Somerville-North Cambridge,

1980; Bedford-West Cambridge, 1991; near Somerville Jct.-West Somerville, 1992; West Cambridge Connection, ca. 1870 (rebuilt 1927, abandoned 1991).

The opening of the Fitchburg RR between Boston and Fitchburg in 1845 inspired a number of short branch line railroads designed to connect towns left off the line, among them Lexington. In 1845 the Lexington & West Cambridge RR received a charter to construct a line from West Cambridge on the Fitchburg to Lexington seven miles away. Construction started in August of that year and was completed in September 1846. Upon completion, the Fitchburg RR operated the line, an arrangement that continued until 1858, when the Fitchburg cancelled the operating contract and the Lexington & West Cambridge began operating the line itself.

The Boston & Lowell RR, which opened in 1835, had been granted a thirty year monopoly on rail service between Boston & Lowell. By the end of the Civil War this monopoly had expired, and speculators hoping to construct another Lowell-Boston route had gained control of the Lexington & West Cambridge, now renamed the Lexington & Arlington RR. The charter of the Lexington & Arlington was changed to allow it to construct an extension to Bedford and ultimately to Lowell. To thwart this challenge the Boston & Lowell obtained control of the Lexington & Arlington in 1869 and bought it outright the following year.

Since the Lexington & Arlington did not physically connect with the Boston & Lowell, the latter in 1870 extended the Lexington & Arlington from West Cambridge through northern Cambridge to Davis Square in Somerville and to the Boston & Lowell main line at Somerville Junction. In 1872 the B&L obtained a charter for the Middlesex Central RR to continue the tracks from Lexington to Concord, and in August 1873 the line was completed. In 1879 the line was extended from Concord Center past Prison Station (Reformatory Station after 1888), where a few hundred yards further west a connection was made with the Nashua, Acton & Boston (Middlesex Junction). The connection, which enabled through service to be operated over this route between Boston and Nashua, was only in use for a few years. Regular passenger service appears to have been operated only in 1885. Railroad mergers rendered it obsolete and it appears not to have been used to any extent after 1887; the tracks were abandoned around the turn of the century.

When the Boston & Maine absorbed the B&L in 1887 the Lexington & Arlington continued as a major commuting route. At Bedford the Billerica & Bedford branch joined, with trains to and from Lowell continuing down the Lexington & Arlington to Boston. Most of the traffic on the line, however, originated between Bedford and Boston. Passenger service beyond Bedford ended in 1926 and the tracks between Concord and Reformatory were abandoned the following year. In 1927 all passenger trains on the Lexington & Arlington were rerouted back onto the Fitchburg RR at West Cambridge (Fens), as they had been from 1846 to 1870. The tracks from North Cambridge Junction to Somerville Junction became the freight cutoff for the Fitchburg line and no longer saw passenger service.

Despite the growth of Boston's suburbs following World War II the Lexington & Arlington branch did not enjoy increased traffic. In 1958 the B&M cut service back to a single daily round trip between Boston and Bedford, and by 1965 the B&M was on the verge of discontinuing service altogether. Subsidies by the MBTA retained the trains until January 1977, when a blizzard halted rail service. Passenger service never resumed.

In 1962 the B&M had received permission to abandon the line between Bedford and Concord, operated only for freight service since 1926. It was noted at the time that this line had seen nineteen cars in nineteen years! The construction of the Alewife Extension of the MBTA's Red Line through Davis Square in Somerville necessitated the abandonment of the Fitchburg freight cutoff between West Somerville and North Cambridge in March 1980. The line between West Cambridge and Bedford was last used in January 1981, but was not formally abandoned until 1991. It has now been converted into the Minuteman Bikeway (Bedford to the MBTA Alewife Station). Until recently a stretch of track in Somerville between Somerville Junction and a point just east of Davis Square remained in place, but in 1992 most of this final remaining segment of the L&A was removed, except for the initial thousand feet or so at Somerville Junction.

Sources: Baker, *Formation*, 114, 180; Cornwall and Smith, *Names First*, 60, 68-69; Crouch, "Two Branch Lines"; Humphrey and Clark, *Boston's Commuter Rail*, 55-57; Judkins, "I Remember Reformatory Station."

51. Boston & Lowell

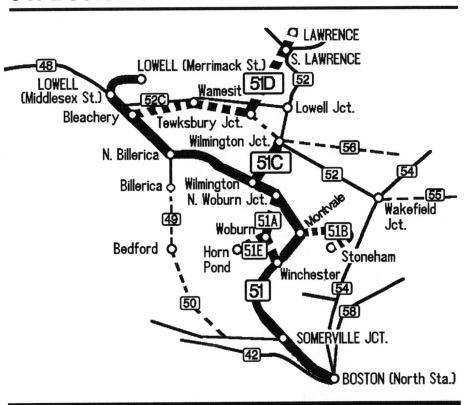

0	Boston (North Sta.), MA	
1	East Cambridge	
1.5	Milk Row	
2	Prospect Hill (Walnut St.)	
2.5	Winter Hill (Somerville Center) (Taylors Ledge)	
3	Somerville Jct. (Somerville)	
3.5	North Somerville (Cambridge Rd.) (Willow Bridge)	
4	Tufts College (College Hill) (Stearns Steps)	
4.5	Medford Hillside (Medford) (Medford Steps)	
5.5	West Medford (Medford Gates)	
7.5	Wedgemere (Mystic) (Bacons Bridge) (Symmes Bridge)	
8	Winchester (South Woburn)	
9	Winchester Heights (Winchester Highlands)	
10	Montvale (East Woburn)	
10.5	Walnut Hill (Woburn) (Water Place)	
11	Lechmere	
12	Mishawum (North Woburn)	
13	South Wilmington	

14 North Woburn Jct. (Woburn Jct.)	1.5 Woburn Highlands (Horn Pond)	2.5 Salem St.
15 Wilmington	2 Woburn (Woburn Center)	3 Wilmington Jct., MA
17 Silver Lake	3 Central Sq.	
19 East Billerica (Billerica & Tewksbury)	4 North Woburn	**51D. Lowell & Lawrence Branch**
22 North Billerica (Billerica Mills)	7 North Woburn Jct., MA	0 Bleachery, MA
23 South Lowell		2 Wamesit (Wamesit-on-Mace)
25 Bleachery	**51B. Stoneham Branch**	3 Tewksbury Centre
26 Lowell (Middlesex St.)		4 Tewksbury Jct. (Lawrence Jct.)
27 Lowell (Merrimack St.), MA	0 Montvale, MA	6 Hagget (Haggets Point) (Haggets)
	0.1 Grape St.	8 West Andover
51A. Woburn Loop	0.5 Oakland	9 Pikes Siding
	1 Lindenwood	10 South Lawrence
0 Winchester (South Woburn), MA	1.5 Farm Hill	11 Lawrence, MA
0.5 Cutters (Symms)	2 Pleasant St.	
1 Cross St. (Richardson) (Richardson Row)	2.5 Stoneham, MA	**51E. Horn Pond Branch**
	51C. Wilmington (Wildcat) Branch	0 Woburn, MA
		0.5 Horn Pond, MA
	0 Wilmington, MA	

BUILT: 1830-35; Woburn Loop (Winchester-Woburn, 1844; Woburn-Wilmington, 1885); Lowell & Lawrence Branch, 1846-48; Horn Pond Branch, 1854; Stoneham Branch, 1862; Wilmington Jct. Branch, 1874.

OPERATORS: *Boston & Lowell*, 1835-87; *Boston & Maine*, 1887-1983 ; *MBTA (passenger)*, 1976- ; *Guilford*, 1983- .

DAILY PASSENGER TRAINS: *1869:* 14, *1893:* 53, *1919:* 14, *1935:* 30, *1950:* 39, *1960:* 26, *1971:* 32, *1980:* 34, *1994:* 42. Passenger service ended on Lowell & Lawrence Branch (Bleachery-Wamesit, 1895; Wamesit-Lawrence, 1924); Stoneham Branch, 1958; Woburn Loop (Woburn-North Woburn Jct., 1959; Winchester-Woburn, 1981); Wilmington Branch, 1979. Horn Pond Branch freight only.

ABANDONMENTS: Horn Pond Branch, 1919; Lowell & Lawrence Branch (Tewksbury Centre-Pikes Siding, 1926; S. Lawrence-Lawrence, ca. 1926; Bleachery-Wamesit, 1936; Wamesit-Tewksbury, ca. 1983); Woburn Loop (Woburn-North Woburn Jct., 1961; Winchester-Woburn, 1982); Stoneham Branch (Stoneham-Lindenwood, ca. 1982; remainder of line, 1994).

One of the original trio of New England railroads, the Boston & Lowell RR received its charter on June 5, 1830, a year ahead of the Boston & Worcester and Boston & Providence Railroads. It was the first common carrier railroad chartered in New England. Lowell, the destination of the new road, was itself of recent origin, having been founded in 1822. By 1830 this burgeoning industrial center already could claim more than 6,000 inhabitants. Behind the new railroad were the Boston Associates, a small group of capitalists headed by Patrick Tracy Jackson who had planned the city, built the mills, and controlled the water power. Lowell already had a connection to Boston via the Middlesex Canal (opened in 1803), but this water route was of little use during the long New England winters. The path, surveyed by James F. Baldwin, was an easy one, with no grade exceeding ten feet to the mile. The line avoided most existing town centers, partly because the promoters did not anticipate local traffic and partly because villagers disdained railroads (a sentiment that soon would change). The original line had only three grade crossings.

The Boston & Lowell opened June 24, 1835, and from the beginning carried heavy traffic between its namesake cities. By the terms of its charter it had a thirty-year monopoly over the Boston to Lowell route. (Early rail lines customarily received these monopolies to encourage investment in what seemed a risky venture.) Extensions, some controlled by the B&L, brought rails northward to Nashua and ultimately to Manchester, Concord, and beyond. By 1841 it was double tracked. Commuter service began in the 1840s, and by 1860 villages of railroad commuters had grown up around most of the line's stations (including branches) within about fifteen miles of Boston.

By the time the Boston & Lowell's thirty-year monopoly on Boston-Lowell traffic expired in the 1860s the railroad had embarked on a program of expansion and vigorous competition with its rivals, particularly the Fitchburg to its west and the Boston & Maine to its east. In 1858 it acquired the Lowell & Lawrence RR (along with the Salem & Lowell RR, which the former controlled). The L&L had been chartered in 1846 and opened in 1848, connecting the two premier industrial cities of the Merrimack Valley. Between 1852 and 1855 the B&M defied the B&L monopoly by operating Lowell to Boston passenger service via the Lowell & Lawrence and Salem & Lowell to Wilmington Junction. The B&L bought the Lowell & Lawrence to keep it out of the hands of the B&M and also to reach Lawrence, on the B&M main line. The B&M eventually retaliated in 1874 by building its own branch into Lowell.

Throughout the 1870s and 1880s the rivalry with the B&M intensified as both railroads expanded. In 1880 the B&L built its own bridge across the Merrimack to give it direct access to downtown Lawrence (this remained in operation until 1926). Ultimately the B&L was unable to gain control over its northern connection, the Concord, which put it at a competitive disadvantage with the B&M, and in 1887 the B&L was leased to its stronger rival. The B&L became first, the Southern Division and then in 1930, the New Hampshire Division of the B&M, and it remained a major route. Commuter rail traffic continued to be heavy.

By the 1920s the B&M could no longer afford the luxury of the numerous parallel branch lines it had inherited from its predecessors, among which were two lines between Lowell and Lawrence. The B&M branch was retained, and the Lawrence & Lowell Branch was abandoned between Tewksbury Junction and South Lawrence in 1926. (The one mile of track between Tewksbury Centre and Tewksbury Junction also seems to have been abandoned about this time.) Passenger trains last used the portion between Lowell and Wamesit in 1895 and freight service appears to have ended around the same time, all trains being rerouted over the parallel B&M line. It was not officially abandoned, however, until 1936. The short segment of track remaining between Wamesit and Tewksbury Centre continued to see local freight service until about 1979, and it was abandoned around 1983.

A major track reconstruction project on the B&L was carried out in Winchester center between 1955 and 1957. At this time a mile of track was elevated, eliminating a grade crossing, and new stations were erected at Winchester and Wedgemere. In 1976 the MBTA purchased the entire B&L system, including branches, from the B&M, with the latter retaining trackage rights for freight. Frequent daily commuter service between Gallagher Terminal in Lowell and North Station is provided over the main line.

From the 1920s to the 1970s most B&M through freight trains in and out of Boston used the Fitchburg cutoff route via North Cambridge

On its way to Lowell, an MBTA commuter train approaches Brown Street in East Billerica in July 1994.

In October 1971 RDCs, such as this car shown running single through West Medford, provided commuter rail service on the Boston & Lowell.

and Somerville Junction. When subway construction caused the abandonment of this line in 1979, freight trains were re-routed over the B&L to Lowell and thence via the Nashua & Lowell and Stony Brook to Ayer.

In December 1844 the B&L opened its first branch, from Winchester (then South Woburn) to Woburn Center, which now regretted having been left off the main line. This had been chartered as the Woburn Branch RR earlier that year, but was always operated as a B&L branch. The B&L extended the line northward from Woburn to make another connection with the main line at Woburn Junction in November 1885, forming the Woburn Loop. This now enabled some Boston-Lowell trains to serve Woburn. Passenger service on the loop was cut back to Woburn Center in June 1959, and the rails between there and North Woburn Junction were abandoned and removed two years later. Woburn commuter trains lasted until January 1981 when poor track brought them to a halt. The line was abandoned the following year.

Another village bypassed by the B&L, Stoneham, was the object of the Stoneham Branch RR. Organized in 1853, this two-and-a-quarter mile line from East Woburn (later Montvale) did not open until 1862. The B&L took control of the line before it was completed. Passenger service ended in May 1958, and all but the first half mile (to a point near its crossing of Interstate 93) was abandoned around 1982. Service had ended on the remainder of the branch by 1992 and the line was abandoned (technically, discontinued) in 1994.

The first railroad to connect with the B&L, the Andover & Wilmington RR, which later became the Boston & Maine, opened in 1836. In 1845 the B&M (described in the following chapter) opened its own line to Boston, reducing the connection with the B&L to a branch. This line was operated by the B&L for three few years and then abandoned around 1850. In 1874 the B&L rebuilt this connection, using part of the original right of way and partly following a parallel route. Today known as the Wildcat Branch, it primarily serves as a freight cutoff, although Boston-Haverhill passenger trains used it between 1959 and 1979.

In 1854 the Boston Ice Company built a half-mile branch from Woburn to Horn Pond. The Horn Pond Branch RR was operated by the B&L during ice cutting season for more than half a century. It was finally abandoned in 1919.

Sources: Bradlee, *Boston & Lowell Railroad*; Cornwall and Smith, *Names First,* 52, 116, 129; Harlow, *Steelways,* 75-88; Humphrey and Clark, *Boston's Commuter Rail,* 7-17, 55-58; Kennedy, "Commuter Services"; Kirkland, *Men, Cities and Transportation,* 1:111-12, 120, 123, 434; 212 I.C.C. 369.

52. Boston & Maine (original system)

0	Boston (North Sta.), MA	
1	Charlestown	
1.5	East Somerville (Somerville)	
2	Reading Jct.	
3	Wellington	
3.5	Medford Jct.	
4	Edgeworth	
4.5	Malden	
5	Oak Grove	
5.5	Fells	
6	Wyoming Hill (Wyoming) (Boardmans)	
6.5	Melrose-Cedar Park (Melrose)	
7.5	Melrose Highlands (Stoneham)	
8.5	Greenwood	
9.5	Wakefield Jct. (South Reading Jct.)	
10	Wakefield (South Reading)	
12	Reading	
13	Reading Highlands	
16	North Wilmington (Wilmington)	
18	Wilmington Jct.	
19.5	Lowell Jct.	
20.5	Ballardvale	
23	Andover	
24	Shawsheen	
25.5	South Lawrence	
26	Lawrence	
27	North Andover	
31	Ward Hill	
32.5	Bradford	
33	Haverhill	
35	Rosemont, MA	
36	Atkinson, NH	
37	Westville	
38	Plaistow	
41	Newton Jct. (Newton)	
42	Russ Crossing	
45	Powwow River	
46	East Kingston	
50	Exeter	
54	Newfields (South Newmarket)	
55	Rockingham (South New Market Jct.) (Rockingham Jct.)	
57	Newmarket	
59	Bennett Rd.	
61	Durham	
64	Madbury	
67	Dover	
70	Rollinsford	
71	Salmon Falls, NH	
72	South Berwick (Cummings), ME	
77	North Berwick, ME	

52A. Medford Branch

0	Medford Jct., MA
1	Glenwood
1.5	Park St.
2	Medford, MA

52B. Wilmington Branch

0	Wilmington, MA
3	Wilmington Jct., MA

52C. Lowell Branch

0	Lowell Jct., MA
3	Baldwin
3.5	Almont
5.5	Wamesit
6	Atherton
7	Wigginville
8	Rogers St.
9	Lowell (Central St.)
7.5	Bleachery, MA

52D. Merrimac Branch

0	Newton Jct. (Newton), NH
2	Newton, NH
5	Merrimac, MA

BUILT: 1834-45; Medford Branch, 1845-47; Merrimac Branch, 1872-73; Lowell Branch, 1874.

OPERATORS: *Andover & Wilmington,* 1836-37; *Andover & Haverhill,* 1837-39; *Boston & Portland,* 1839-42; *Boston & Maine,* 1842-1983 ; *MBTA (passenger),* 1976- ; *Guilford,* 1983- .

DAILY PASSENGER TRAINS: *1869:* 10, *1893:* 12, (Boston-Melrose, 26), *1919:* 14, *1935:* 15 (Boston-Melrose, 46), *1950:* 17, *1960:* 10 (Boston-Melrose, 66), *1971:* (Boston-Reading, 56; Lowell Jct.-Haverhill, 2), *1981:* 12 (Boston-

Haverhill; Boston-Reading, 38), *1994:* 16 (Boston-Haverhill; Boston-Reading, 40).   Passenger service ended Reading-Wilmington Jct., 1959; Dover-North Berwick, 1965; Haverhill-Dover, 1967; Wilmington Jct.-Haverhill, 1976. Passenger service restored by MBTA Reading-Haverhill, 1979. Passenger service ended Merrimac Branch, 1926 or 1927; Medford Branch, 1957; Lowell Branch, 1960.

ABANDONMENTS: Wilmington Jct.-North Andover (original line), Wilmington Branch, 1848; Lowell Branch (Lowell-Rogers St., ca. 1950; Rogers St.-Wigginville, 1982); Merrimac Branch, 1972; Medford Branch (Medford-Park St., 1959; Park St.-Glenwood, ca. 1961).

Central New England's most celebrated railroad began in 1833 when the Andover & Wilmington RR was chartered to construct an eight-mile branch line from Wilmington, on the Boston & Lowell RR (then under construction) north to Andover. It was completed in August 1836, only a year after the Boston & Lowell, by which it reached Boston. Surveyed by James Hayward, it was a well-built road with ambitious plans

Even before the Andover & Wilmington opened, the Boston & Maine RR had been chartered in New Hampshire in 1835 to build a line across the southeastern end of that state. From the onset, the backers of the Andover & Wilmington intended to expand their short rail line northward to connect with the New Hampshire railroad, should it be built. To this end permission to expand was obtained, and the name of the railroad was changed to the Andover & Haverhill RR. The state of Massachusetts provided funds that helped construction continue despite the Panic of 1837. The rails reached Bradford (now part of Haverhill) in October 1837 and by April 1840, Exeter, N.H. By this time the Andover & Haverhill had been renamed the Boston & Portland RR and was being operated in conjunction with the Boston & Maine, which extended the line into New Hampshire. On January 1, 1842, the entire line was merged into the B&M.

By the end of 1842 the B&M had been extended another twenty-five miles to South Berwick, Me., and in February 1843 it secured a connection with the newly completed Portland, Saco & Portsmouth RR which enabled it to reach Portland. (In 1847 the PS&P was jointly leased by the B&M and its rival, the Eastern RR.) The B&M had completed its evolution from a branch line to a major intercity carrier.

There remained, however, the problem of reaching Boston. The B&M, dependent for access on the Boston & Lowell, sought its own

In February 1992 a southbound Guilford freight roars through Andover station. Conrail locomotives, like this GE C40-8W, are commonly seen on the old B&M. This freight will turn onto the Lowell Branch at Lowell Junction.

entry to the city, and in 1844 obtained permission to build a railroad from a point on its line north of Wilmington, through Reading and Malden, to Haymarket Square in Boston. The new route opened in July 1845. When first opened the city of Boston forbid steam locomotives to cross Canal Street, so passenger cars were hauled the final few hundred yards into the depot by oxen. The old connection between Wilmington and the new Boston cutoff was operated by the Boston & Lowell for three years and then abandoned, the B&M pulling up the rails a year or two later. (The Boston & Lowell rebuilt this line in 1874, using a somewhat different allignment.) In 1848 the B&M relocated its line between Ballardvale and North Andover to the west, so as to reach the new factory city of Lawrence. The route of the old main line is still visible in Wilmington and Andover; in North Andover, Waverly Road (formerly Railroad Avenue) follows its path.

The early history of the B&M was marred by a poignant tragedy. On January 6, 1853, a northbound express train out of Boston derailed two miles north of Andover station, sending a passenger car crashing down an embankment. Only one person died in the wreck (althoughtwo others later succumbed to injuries). The victim, a twelve-year-old boy, was the only child of Franklin Pierce, the President-elect of the United States. His horrified parents, who had been seated beside him in the car, escaped injury. The loss cast a pall over Pierce's administration, and the President never recovered from the loss.

By the 1850s the B&M was already one of New England's busiest railroads. The route between Boston and North Andover was double tracked. Commuter rail service was already changing neighborhoods near its stations into railroad suburbs. The B&M competed vigorously with its rival to the west, the Boston & Lowell, and even more so with the Eastern RR on its other flank. The latter road was a direct rival for the Boston to Maine traffic. About 80% of freight and passenger traffic between Maine and Boston used the B&M instead of the Eastern.

The B&M and its competitors built numerous branch lines, frequently over closely parallel routes, until Essex and Middlesex Counties in Massachusetts were crisscrossed with rail lines. For example, the B&M opened its Lowell branch in December 1874, which not only allowed it to compete with the Boston & Lowell for traffic between

At Haverhill the B&M spans the Merrimack on this massive bridge. Here, in September 1992, a Boston-bound MBTA commuter train crosses the river, with a locomotive pushing at the rear of the train.

Lowell and Boston, but also gave it a Lowell to Lawrence route that closely paralleled the B&L's Lowell & Lawrence branch. When first built, this line entered downtown Lowell on its own right of way following the Concord River to a station (still standing) on Central Street. In 1895 a short connection was laid between Wigginville and Bleachery and all passenger trains using the branch were rerouted via the Boston & Lowell. Around 1950 the tracks were cut back from the old depot to Rogers Street, and the rest of the line from Wigginville was abandoned in 1982. The remainder of the Lowell Branch became part of the through freight route between Maine and the West.

One by one the B&M absorbed its competitors—the Eastern in 1884, the Boston & Lowell in 1887, and the Fitchburg in 1900—until at the beginning of the twentieth century it was the dominant railroad in northern Massachusetts, all of New Hampshire, and southern Maine. The original main line retained heavy passenger (particularly near Boston) and freight traffic, at least into the 1950s. In 1958 passenger service ended at all local stations between Boston and Wyoming except Malden. The following year the tracks between Reading and Wilmington Junction became freight only, as passenger trains for Haverhill and beyond were rerouted over the Boston & Lowell via Wilmington. In January 1965 the B&M abandoned intercity passenger service out of Boston, and the only passenger train remaining north of Wilmington was a daily round trip to Dover, N.H. The Dover trains last ran on June 30, 1967, leaving Haverhill as the last passenger stop. For several years four communities at the end of the line subsidized a single daily trip to Haverhill, but this train was discontinued in June 1976, leaving passenger service only on the Boston-Reading segment.

In 1966 the MBTA began construction of the Orange Line rapid transit extension from North Station in Boston to Oak Grove, on the Malden-Melrose line. The line followed the B&M for most of the way, with the railroad sharing the right of way with the transit line. Around 1972 construction between Wellington and Oak Grove stations restricted the remaining railroad track to passenger trains only, and freight trains were diverted to other routes. The new Orange Line was opened between Boston and Sullivan Square on April 7, 1975. Wellington was reached in September, Malden in December, and the line was completed to Oak Grove March 21, 1977.

Energy crises and increased federal aid for mass transit inspired plans to revive commuter rail service, and in December 1979 trains once more ran to Haverhill, using the B&M from Reading, including the tracks between Reading and Wilmington Junction, which hadn't seen scheduled passenger trains for twenty years. Today Amtrak, under contract to the MBTA, operates frequent commuter service between North Station and Haverhill, while the line from South Berwick to Lowell Junction and the Lowell Branch forms part of the second-busiest freight line in New England.

During the early 1990s serious efforts were made to have Amtrak restore Boston to Portland rail passenger service using the B&M, with the aid of the Maine Department of Transportation and other groups. The trains were slated to begin running in 1995, but cutbacks in Amtrak's budget announced late in 1994 have made this uncertain.

The B&M had two short branch lines. A two-mile branch from Medford Junction to Medford was completed in 1847, shortly after the railroad extended its line to Boston. Passenger service lasted until 1957. In 1959 the tracks were cut back a half mile from Medford to Park Street and then another half mile to Glenwood a few years later.

The West Amesbury Branch RR was chartered in 1868 to connect that Massachusetts village with the B&M main line across the border in New Hampshire five miles to the north. The B&M agreed to lease the new railroad on completion, which took place at the beginning of 1873. West Amesbury became the town of Merrimac in 1876, although it was still known as the West Amesbury Branch for many years. Plans to extend the line to connect with the Eastern's Amesbury Branch, which ended only three miles from Merrimac, were never realized. Passenger service declined to a single weekday mixed train before ending altogether by 1927. Carriage, and later automobile, bodies were the major freight product until 1930. Freight trains continued to operate until August 1971. The line was formally abandoned early in 1972 and the rails removed that summer, except for the initial half mile which continued as a private industrial spur to a steel company.

Sources: Baker, *Formation*, 145-48; Bradlee, *Boston & Maine Railroad*; Harlow, *Steelways*, 143-48; Hoisington and Hornsby, "And Never the Trains Shall Meet: Part 2"; Humphrey and Clark, *Boston's Commuter Rail*, 7-17, 67-70; Shaw, *History of Railroad Accidents*, 42-43.

53. Manchester & Lawrence

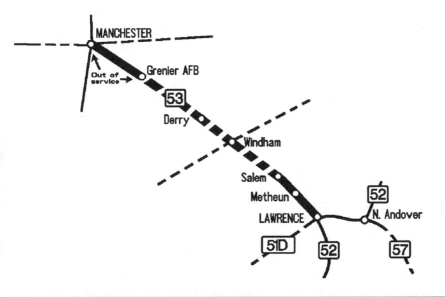

0 Lawrence, MA	6 Rockingham Park	21 Londonderry
1 North Lawrence (Lawrence Essex St.)	7 Salem	24 Grenier AFB (Willey)
2 Methuen, MA	9 Canobie Lake	25 Nutts Pond
3 Hampshire Rd. (Messers), NH	13 Windham (Windham Jct.)	27 Manchester, NH
	16 Derry	
	18 Wilson (Wilsons)	

BUILT: 1848-49.

OPERATORS: *Manchester & Lawrence,* 1849-50; *Concord,* 1850-70; *Northern,* 1870-87; *Boston & Maine,* 1887-1983; *Guilford,* 1983- .

DAILY PASSENGER TRAINS: *1869:* 6, *1893:* 8, *1919:* 10, *1935:* 6, *1950:* 2. Passenger service ended 1953.

ABANDONMENTS: Salem-Derry, 1983; Derry-Grenier Air Force Base, ca. 1986.

In 1847 the Manchester & Lawrence RR was chartered in New Hampshire by Manchester businessmen to build a line from their city to the Massachusetts border. Shortly after the Manchester & Lawrence opened in November 1849 it leased the newly-built Methuen Branch from the B&M. The Methuen Branch had been opened by the B&M that August, from the B&M main line at South Lawrence northward three miles to the state line at Methuen, where it met the tracks of the Manchester & Lawrence. With the Methuen branch the Manchester & Lawrence gained access to Lawrence and opened a second route between Manchester and Boston, independent of the existing Concord RR-Nashua & Lowell-Boston & Lowell line. The B&M had hoped to acquire the entire Manchester & Lawrence, but over the next several decades the line was operated by the Concord RR. Even under Concord control, the line benefited the B&M by diverting Concord-Boston traffic away from the Nashua & Lowell-Boston & Lowell.

The B&M finally took control of the Manchester & Lawrence away from the Concord in 1887. In the twentieth century the line was largely relegated to local traffic. Passenger service declined to a single daily round trip gas-electric railcar, until even this service ended in July 1953. During summers special trains were operated over the M&L from Lawrence to the Rockingham Park race track, but these ended in 1960. By the early 1970s traffic had declined to a few local freights, despite rapid growth in the part of New Hampshire through which the line passed. In 1983 the nine miles between Salem and Derry were abandoned, dividing the Manchester & Lawrence into two branches. Recently, another eight miles of the M&L between Derry and the site of the Grenier Air Force Base have been abandoned and the track removed, leaving only a short remnant out of Manchester. Even this is no longer in service. Freight trains still operate regularly between Lawrence and Salem.

Sources: Baker, *Formation*, 105-06, 123-27; *Boston & Maine Bulletin*, Summer 1977, 5; Harlow, *Steelways*, 148; Kirkland, *Men, Cities, and Transportation*, 1:183-84; Poor, *History*, 57.

54. Newburyport

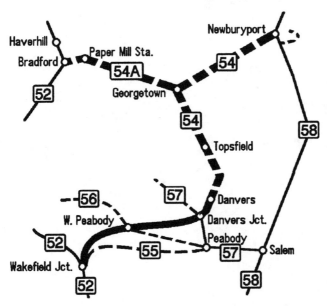

		54A. Haverhill Branch
0	Wakefield Jct. (South Reading Jct.)	
0.5	Wakefield Centre	
1.5	Lowell St.	
3	Lynnfield Centre (Lynnfield)	
6	West Peabody (West Danvers)	
8	Collins St.	
8.5	Tapleyville	
9	Danvers Jct.	
9.5	Danvers	
11	Putnamville	
12	Wenham Rd.	
15	Topsfield	
18	East Boxford (Boxford)	
20	Baldpate (South Georgetown)	
21	Georgetown	
25	Byfield (Pearsons Mills)	
30	Newburyport, MA	
0		Georgetown, MA
3		Groveland
4		Island Park
4.5		Paper Mill Sta. (Haverhill Paper Mills)
5.5		Haverhill Bridge
6		Bradford, MA

BUILT: 1849-54.

OPERATORS: *Newburyport*, 1850-60; *Boston & Maine*, 1855-1983; *Guilford*, 1983- .

DAILY PASSENGER TRAINS: *1869:* 8, *1893:* 10, *1919:* 10, *1935:* 4, *1950:* 2 (Wakefield Jct.-Danvers). Passenger service ended Newburyport-Topsfield, 1941; Danvers-Topsfield, 1950; Wakefield Jct.-Danvers, 1959; Haverhill branch, 1933.

When the Boston & Maine took over the Eastern in 1884 it found itself with two Newburyport stations. In 1890 trains on the ex-Newburyport RR began using the Eastern depot on High Street. Here B&M locomotive number 37, the Hobart Clark, is shown about to pull the final train out of the old Pond Street station. (Photo courtesy Walker Transportation Collection, Beverly Historical Society & Museum.)

ABANDONMENTS: Newburyport-Topsfield, 1941; Danvers-Topsfield, 1981; Haverhill Branch (Georgetown-Paper Mill Sta., 1942; Paper Mill Sta.-Bradford, 1982).

In the mid-1840s Newburyport residents sought an alternative to the monopoly of the Eastern RR. The railroad that resulted, the Newburyport, was built as three separate lines. The first, the Newburyport RR, received a charter in 1846 to build a railroad westward to the shoemaking town of Georgetown. Construction began in February 1849. The initial eight-and-a-half-mile section from Newburyport to Georgetown was completed in May 1850. An extension toward Haverhill was started in January 1851 and completed to Bradford, on the B&M just south of Haverhill, in September of that year.

In 1851 a second company, the Danvers & Georgetown RR, was chartered to extend the line another twelve miles south to Danvers. Construction on this line began in April 1853, and the line was opened to Danvers in the fall of 1854. The Newburyport contracted to operate the Danvers & Georgetown even before it opened, and in 1855 merged the line with itself.

At the same time that the Danvers & Georgetown was completed a third line also began to operate. This was the Danvers RR, chartered in 1852. Construction started in August 1853. The route from Danvers was extended south to South Reading Junction on the Boston & Maine, which took a lease on this road before it was in operation (over the objections of the rival Eastern RR). The long-sought goal of a second route between Newburyport and Boston was realized in 1854 when the Newburyport and the B&M began operating through service. The B&M now obtained control of the Newburyport, although it continued to operate independently. In 1860 the B&M took a formal lease.

For many years the B&M continued Boston to Newburyport passenger service over this route, although not at the level of the parallel

B&M engine number 939, a veteran 4-4-0, at Danvers in August 1939. (Photo by Harold W. Boothroyd, courtesy Walker Transportation Collection, Beverely Historical Society & Museum.)

Eastern RR. Service did not diminish significantly after the B&M absorbed the Eastern RR in 1885, although the B&M closed its own passenger station in Newburyport in favor of the Eastern depot. (The segment between the crossing of the Eastern RR main line and the original Newburyport RR station on Pond Street became a freight-only spur which survived into the 1960s.)

The declining fortunes of the B&M led the railroad to propose total abandonment of the Newburyport in 1924. Faced with opposition from passengers and shippers, the B&M withdrew its application and cut service to two daily round trip Boston-Newburyport trains. A lack of business ended passenger trains on the Haverhill Branch in 1933, and three years later flood damage to a deteriorating railroad bridge east of the Haverhill Boxboard factory (Paper Mill Station) caused the suspension of freight service between there and Groveland. In 1940 the B&M petitioned to abandon this section, along with the rest of the Newburyport north of Topsfield (except west of Paper Mill Station). Despite spirited opposition from shippers and passengers (two Boston-Newburyport trains still ran each way daily), the I.C.C. approved the request and the line was abandoned in December 1941. Passenger service continued to Topsfield until 1950, when it was cut back to Danvers. A single daily round trip was operated until 1959.

The northernmost five miles of the Newburyport between Danvers and Topsfield remained one of the most marginal branches on the B&M. Topsfield was a residential suburb with little rail freight. By 1971 traffic had declined to only sixty carloads of freight for the entire year. In 1977 what service remained was suspended, and by 1981, when the line was formally abandoned, the tracks were overgrown with weeds and had been paved over in several places.

Today only the tracks between Wakefield Junction and Danvers remain in service. (A short segment of the Haverhill Branch at Bradford to Paper Mill Station lasted until 1982.) The MBTA has owned what remains of the Newburyport since 1976, as well as the abandoned right of way from Danvers to Topsfield. Guilford provides occasional freight service on the remaining portion.

Sources: Day, "Georgetown, Mass."; Harlow, *Steelways*, 157-59; Humphrey and Clark, *Boston's Commuter Rail*, 67-68; Kennedy, "Railroads in Essex County"; Long, "Newburyport and Danvers Railroads"; Merriam, "Early Danvers Railroads"; Poor, *History*, 112-13, 137; 105 I.C.C. 68; 249 I.C.C. 507.

55. South Reading Branch

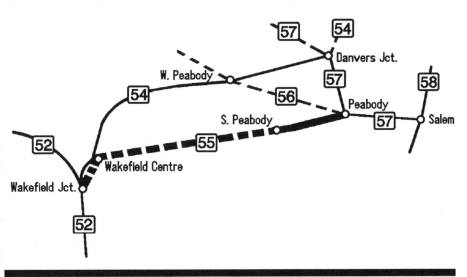

0 Wakefield Jct.	0.5 Wakefield Centre	6.5 Hunt-Rankin Co.
(South Reading)	2 Montrose	8 Peabody (South
(South Reading	4 Lynnfield	Danvers), MA
Jct.), MA	6 South Peabody	

BUILT: 1849-50.

OPERATORS: *South Reading Branch*, 1850-51; *Eastern*, 1851-84; *Boston & Maine*, 1884-1926, ca.1965-83; *Guilford*, 1983- .

DAILY PASSENGER TRAINS: *1869:* 8, *1893:* 7, *1919:* 9. Passenger service ended January 2, 1926.

ABANDONMENTS: Wakefield Centre-South Peabody, 1926; Wakefield Jct.-Wakefield Centre, ca. 1935.

In 1848 a group of promoters from Salem and Danvers secured a charter for the South Reading Branch RR, with authority to build a line from South Reading (as Wakefield was called before 1868) to Peabody (then South Danvers) and from there use two miles of trackage rights over the new Essex RR to reach Salem. Wakefield happened to be on the Boston & Maine, which thus would open another Boston-Salem route, hitherto a monopoly of the Eastern RR.

When the line opened in the summer of 1850 it quickly began to draw traffic away from the Eastern. Fares were lower, and although the route was less direct, it brought passengers directly into downtown Boston, unlike the Eastern, whose passengers had to take a ferry from East Boston. Alarmed by this threat and concerned that the line might be even more dangerous in the hands of the B&M, the Eastern acquired control—at a steep cost—of the South Reading Branch in 1851 and began operating it as an Eastern branch that October.

The legislature forced the Eastern to continue operating Salem-Boston through service over the South Reading Branch for many years. When the B&M acquired the Eastern in 1885 and the Boston & Lowell in 1887, however, the South Reading Branch made even less sense, since it not only duplicated Salem-Boston service but also closely paralleled another Wakefield Junction-Peabody route using the New-buryport and Salem & Lowell lines. After 1900 trolleys and then automobiles took away what passengers remained.

Finally, in 1925 the B&M petitioned to abandon the entire line, noting that at Lynnfield, the only freight station of consequence, traffic had declined from 3,393 tons in 1921 to 466 tons in 1924. Only about sixty passengers a day used the trains, mostly boarding at Lynnfield and Montrose for Boston, for which the railroad promised to substitute highway buses. Another 225 factory hands rode the trains each day from Peabody about two miles to South Peabody; these could take a parallel trolley line instead. Permission to abandon was granted by the I.C.C. in November 1925 and the tracks were removed in 1927. (The first half mile between Wakefield Junction and Wakefield Centre, which closely parallelled the Newburyport line, was retained for another decade.) In the 1950s a short portion of the long abandoned right of way near Montrose became part of the new Route 128. In the 1960s two miles at the Peabody end of the branch were rebuilt to service a new industrial park. Today, nearly seventy years after abandonment, part of the right of way in Lynnfield can still be traced.

Sources: Baker, *Formation*, 146, 150; Bradlee, *Eastern Railroad*, 54-55; Harlow, *Steelways*, 156; 105 I.C.C. 68.

56. Salem & Lowell

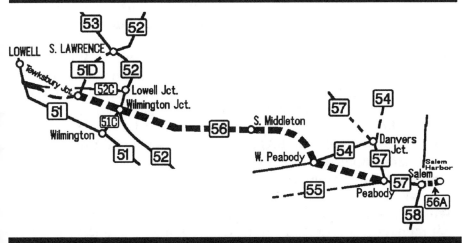

0	Peabody (South Danvers), MA	9	North Reading	**56A. Salem Harbor Branch**
2	Proctor (Proctors) (Proctors Corner)	10	Meadowview	
4	West Peabody (West Danvers)	12	Park St. (Brown) (Wilmington)	0 Salem, MA
5	Phelps Mills	13	Wilmington Jct.	1 Salem Harbor (Phillips Wharf), MA
7	South Middleton (Paper Mills) (Middleton) (Oak Dale)	14	Burtt (Burtts) (Burts Mill)	
		17	Tewksbury Jct. (Salem Jct.) (Lawrence Jct.), MA	

BUILT: 1849-50.

OPERATORS: *Lowell & Lawrence,* 1850-58; *Boston & Lowell,* 1858-87; *Boston & Maine,* 1887-1980.

DAILY PASSENGER TRAINS: *1869:* 6, *1893:* 6, *1919:* 4.   Passenger service ended Tewksbury Jct.-Wilmington Jct, 1924; Peabody-Wilmington Jct., 1932.

ABANDONMENTS: Tewksbury Jct.-Wilmington Jct., 1925; Wilmington Jct.-South Middleton, 1939; Peabody-West Peabody, 1962; South Middleton-West Peabody, 1987; Salem Harbor Branch, ca. 1970.

In 1848 the Salem & Lowell RR was chartered to build a line from South Danvers (Peabody) to Tewksbury, where it would connect with the newly completed Lowell & Lawrence RR to reach Lowell. Stephen C. Philips of Salem was the primary backer of the project. Like the South Reading Branch RR (Peabody-Wakefield Jct.) it secured two miles of trackage rights over the Essex RR to reach downtown Salem. Construction began in August 1849 and the line was completed in the summer of 1850 (including tracks from Salem to Phillips Wharf). The Lowell & Lawrence RR operated the new railroad under contract.

The tracks of the Salem & Lowell crossed the Boston & Maine at Wilmington Junction, where the B&M already had a station. Using the Salem & Lowell to Tewksbury Junction and the Lowell & Lawrence from there to Lowell, the B&M now opened a new Boston to Lowell route that competed for the first time with the Boston & Lowell. The Boston & Lowell promptly sued to protect its monopoly between its namesake cities, and with the help of its eminent attorney, Daniel Webster, it secured an injunction. Realizing, however, that its thirty-year monopoly would soon expire, the Boston & Lowell felt it prudent to lease both the Salem & Lowell and the Lowell & Lawrence in 1858. The S&L remained a branch of the B&L for nearly thirty years until the latter passed under the control of the B&M. In the 1870s the B&L sought to develop Salem as a major coal port, and for a time many a coal train used the S&L to reach Lowell and beyond.

Traffic on the line declined significantly after 1900. The B&M suspended both passenger and freight service on the segment between Wilmington Junction and Tewksbury Junction in August 1924 and abandoned it at the end of 1925. There had been virtually no passengers and no freight on this section. Passenger service over the remainder of the line ended in September 1932. The tracks between North Reading and Wilmington Junction were last used for freight in May 1935, and shipments to North Reading virtually ceased. In early 1939 the B&M abandoned the line beyond South Middleton, although nearly half a mile of track west of South Middleton station was retained as industrial track.

In 1962 about two and a half miles between Peabody and West Peabody were abandoned. The remaining portion of the S&L continued as a lightly used branch to South Middleton until about 1980 when service finally ceased. The line was not formally abandoned until 1987.

Sources: Baker, *Formation*, 101-03, 115; Bradlee, *Boston & Lowell*, 26-29, 38-43; Harlow, *Steelways*, 155-56; 105 I.C.C. 68; 230 I.C.C. 599.

57. Essex

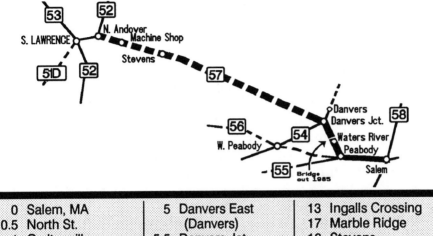

0	Salem, MA	5	Danvers East (Danvers)	13	Ingalls Crossing
0.5	North St.			17	Marble Ridge
1	Carltonville	5.5	Danvers Jct.	18	Stevens
1.5	Grove St.	6	Ferncroft	19	Machine Shop (Suttons Mills)
2	Peabody (South Danvers)	7	Hathorne	19.5	North Andover, MA
		8	Swans Crossing (Howes)		
3	Waters River				
4	Danversport	10	Middleton		

BUILT: 1846-48.

OPERATORS: *Eastern*, 1847-85 (not operated during part of 1849, 1850, and 1851); *Boston & Maine*, 1885-1983; *Guilford*, 1983- .

DAILY PASSENGER TRAINS: *1869:* 6, *1893:* 8, *1919:* 6, *1935:* 16 (Salem-Danvers), *1950:* 7 (Salem-Danvers). Passenger service ended Danvers-North Andover, 1926; Salem-Danvers, 1958.

ABANDONMENTS: Danvers Jct.-Stevens, 1926; Stevens-Machine Shop, ca. 1955;; Machine Shop-North Andover, 1981.

With the help of the Eastern RR the Essex RR obtained a charter in March 1846 to build from Salem to what soon would be Lawrence. The new line lost no time in building its line to North Andover, where it met the rails of the Boston & Maine. It secured trackage rights over the B&M to enable its trains to run through to South Lawrence station.

The first section of the new railroad, Salem-South Danvers (Peabody) opened in January 1847, under the operation of the Eastern RR. (Two other railroads, which opened in 1850, the Salem & Lowell and the South Reading Branch, used trackage rights over this two-mile section of the Essex to reach Salem.) The Essex was completed to North Andover in September 1848, with trackage rights over the B&M to Lawrence. From the start the underfunded line tottered on the brink of bankruptcy. In April 1849 freight service was suspended, and the entire line closed down shortly afterwards. Operations resumed for a time in 1850 but once more ceased. Finally, the Eastern reopened the line in October 1851 under an informal arrangement with the Essex, which became a lease the following year. For more than thirty-five years the Eastern operated the Essex as its Lawrence branch.

When the Boston & Maine absorbed the Eastern in 1885 and the Boston & Lowell two years later it inherited a dense network of rail lines traversing thinly inhabited portions of Essex County, including the Essex. In the twentieth century trolleys and then motor vehicles eliminated any remaining need for the line. (A trolley line paralleled the railroad between Danvers and Middleton.) In 1925 the B&M petitioned to abandon the line between Stevens station in North Andover and Danvers, noting that freight shipments had declined on this segment from 33,821 tons in 1920 to 22,000 tons in 1924 and that passengers carried plunged from 38,568 a year to 16,836 over the same period. Unlike most rail commuters, riders on the northern end of the line were said to be mostly factory workers traveling between Stevens, Machine Shop, Marble Ridge, North Andover, and Lawrence.

Permission to abandon this fifteen-mile section of track was granted late in 1925, although the rails were not removed until 1927. The northern portion of the line was trimmed back from Stevens to Machine Shop in the 1950s, when the Stevens Mill closed. The remaining half-mile of this line was abandoned in 1981. The five miles of track east of Danvers Junction saw relatively heavy commuter traffic until May 1958 when all passenger service was discontinued.

A 1985 fire took the Waters River bridge out of service, severing the line. Customers south of the bridge are served from Salem, while those to the north in Danversport still receive occasional shipments via Danvers Junction and the Newburyport line from Wakefield Junction.

Sources: Baker, *Formation*, 146, 149-50; Bradlee, *Eastern Railroad*, 39; Harlow, *Steelways*, 156; Northey, "Brief History of the Essex Railroad"; Poor, *History*, 118; 105 I.C.C. 68.

58. Eastern

0 Boston (North Sta.), MA	43 Seabrook	0.5 Loring Ave.
1.5 East Somerville (Somerville)	44 Hampton Falls	1 Forest River
3 Everett (South Malden) (Everett Jct.)	47 Hampton	3 Marblehead, MA
4 East Everett	49 North Hampton	**58E. Asbury Grove Branch**
4.5 Chelsea	51 Breakfast Hill (Greenland)	
5.5 Forbes (Highland)	57 Portsmouth, NH	0 Hamilton & Wenham, MA
6 Revere (North Chelsea)	**58A. East Boston Branch**	1 Asbury Grove, MA
8 Oak Island Grove		**58F. Essex Branch**
9.5 Saugus River Jct.	0 Revere, MA	
10 River Works	3 East Boston, MA	0 Hamilton & Wenham, MA
10.5 West Lynn	**58B. Chelsea Beach Branch**	1 Miles River
11 Market St.		2.5 Woodbury (Woodburys)
11.5 Lynn	0 Revere, MA	4.5 Essex Falls
11.7 Green St.	0.5 Crescent Beach	5.5 Essex
12 East Lynn	2 Oak Island	6 Conomo, MA
13 Swampscott	3 Point of Pines	**58G. Amesbury Branch**
15 Pickman Park	4.5 Saugus River Jct., MA	
15.5 Castle Hill		0 Salisbury, MA
16 Salem	**58C. Swampscott Branch**	3 Salisbury Point
18 Beverly		4 Amesbury, MA
18.5 Beverly Jct.	0 Swampscott, MA	**58H. Newburyport City Branch**
19 United Shoe Machinery Co.	1.5 Phillips Beach	
21 North Beverly	2 Beach Bluff	0 Newburyport, MA
23 Hamilton & Wenham (Wenham)	2.5 Clifton	2 Newburyport Wharf, MA
28 Ipswich	3.5 Devereux	
31 Rowley	4.5 Marblehead, MA	
34 Newbury (Knights Crossing)	**58D. Marblehead Branch**	
37 Newburyport		
39 Salisbury, MA	0 Castle Hill, MA	
41 Atlantic, NH		

BUILT: 1836-40 (Boston Extension, 1852-54); East Boston Branch, 1836-38 (partially rebuilt ca. 1918); Marblehead Branch, 1839; Amesbury Branch, 1847-48; Essex Branch, 1872; Swampscott Branch, 1873; Asbury Grove Branch, 1871; Newburyport City Branch, 1872; Chelsea Beach Branch, 1881.

OPERATORS: *Eastern*, 1838-84; *Boston & Maine*, 1884-83; *Guilford*, 1983- ; *MBTA (commuter passenger)*, 1976- .

DAILY PASSENGER TRAINS: *1869:* 10 (Boston-Salem, 35), *1893:* 14 (Boston-Salem, 60), *1919:* 21 (Boston-Salem, 88), *1935:* 16 (Boston-Salem, 64), *1950:* 22 (Boston-Salem, 59), *1960:* 12, *1971:* 2 (Boston-Newburyport; Boston-Ipswich, 25; Boston-Salem, 52), *1981:* 22 (Boston-Ipswich, Boston-Salem, 48), *1994:* 26 (Boston-Ipswich, Boston-Salem, 62). Passenger service ended Newburyport-Portsmouth, 1965; Ipswich-Newburyport, 1976; East Boston Branch, 1905 (partially rebuilt, ca. 1918); Chelsea Beach Branch, 1891; Swampscott Branch, 1959; Marblehead Branch, 1959; Asbury Grove Branch, ca. 1900; Essex Branch, 1942; Amesbury Branch, 1936. Newburyport City Branch freight only.

ABANDONMENTS: Seabrook-Salisbury, 1982, Ipswich-Newburyport, 1994; Chelsea Beach Branch, 1891 (some of track not removed until 1926); Asbury Grove Branch, 1901; East Boston Branch, 1905 (restored in part ca. 1918); Essex Branch (Essex-Conomo, 1927; remainder, 1942); Swampscott Branch, 1961; Marblehead Branch (Forest River-Marblehead, 1962; Loring Ave.-Forest River, ca. 1968, Castle Hill-Loring Ave., 1993); Newburyport City Branch, 1971; Amesbury Branch, 1982; .

Soon after the initial trio of Massachusetts railroads (the Boston & Lowell, Boston & Worcester and Boston & Providence) were chartered in 1830 and 1831, land speculators proposed a fourth rail line from Boston to the port city of Salem. Existing turnpike-based stagecoach and freight wagon and packet boat service between these two cities was the best in Massachusetts and the proposal ran into stiff opposition; an attempt to obtain a charter was rejected in 1833. Backers of the railroad attempted to broaden support by proposing a line from Boston through Salem to Newburyport, Portsmouth, and ultimately, Maine. John M. Fessenden, who surveyed the Boston & Worcester, laid out a route with gentle grades. The state accepted this plan, chartering the Eastern RR in 1836, and even loaning it money. Construction began in August of that year, but slowed when the financial panic of 1837 hampered efforts to raise funds. The line was finally opened from Noddles Island (East Boston) to Salem in August 1838. A ferry in East Boston conveyed passengers across Boston Harbor to Lewis Wharf in downtown Boston. Freight service did not begin until the following year.

In December 1839 the Eastern reached Ipswich and in August 1840, Newburyport. Three months later the line was opened to the New Hampshire line, where it met up with another Eastern RR, this one chartered in the Granite State to extend the road. The latter had by this time built from the outskirts of Portsmouth to the Massachusetts state line. On the last day of 1840 the Eastern opened the entire line to its depot on Vaughan Street in Portsmouth. The ultimate objective of the Eastern was finally obtained in November 1842 when the Portland, Saco & Portsmouth RR was completed, enabling the Eastern to introduce Boston to Portland service. The Eastern's monopoly on Maine traffic ended when the Boston & Maine RR opened its own route to the PS&P in February 1843. The Eastern and the B&M at this time jointly leased the PS&P, to avoid having to construct their own Portland routes if the road fell into the hands of the other.

Thus began one of the greatest of the many rail rivalries in New England. At first, neither line possessed outstanding advantages. Neither route enjoyed a direct connection with Boston (the B&M used the

Until 1912 Eastern trains ran through Lynn at grade. Here B&M locomotive number 116, an American type (4-4-0) leads a commuter train through Central Square a few years before grade separation. (Photo courtesy Walker Transportation Collection, Beverly Historical Society & Museum.)

Boston & Lowell). This changed in the late 1840s when the B&M built its own Boston entrance and rebuilt its main line, putting the Eastern, which ferried its passengers across Boston Harbor from East Boston, at a competitive disadvantage. The Eastern responded by constructing its own line from Revere to Boston utilizing in part trackage rights over the freight-only Grand Junction RR. The Eastern opened its own Boston terminal on Causeway Street in April 1854. Eastern passenger trains used this station until 1894, when it was replaced by North Station.

Over the next several decades the intense competition between the Eastern and the B&M resulted in each line constructing branch lines to raid the other's markets. The Eastern sponsored a line to Lawrence (the Essex RR), and the B&M responded by acquiring its own line to Newburyport (the Newburyport RR). Both railroads evolved into rail systems as they gained control of other railroads. The Eastern fell behind its arch-rival, the B&M eventually capturing about 80% of Maine traffic. In desperation, the Eastern in 1871 bought control of the Maine Central, which soon began sending it the majority of the traffic from Down East. But the price paid for the Maine Central was high, putting increased strain on a financially strapped road. Unlike the more inland B&M the Eastern also faced stiff competition from coastal ships. The long rivalry ended in 1875 when the Eastern effectively went bankrupt. The state-appointed trustees who assumed control were sympathetic to the B&M, and after years of negotiations, court battles, and political maneuvering, the B&M leased the entire Eastern system in December 1884.

Under the B&M the Eastern was operated for many years with little change, despite the considerable duplication of services in eastern Massachusetts and New Hampshire. Although most Boston-to-Portland passenger trains used the old B&M route, some of these took the Eastern until 1952, when Portsmouth became the terminus. Portsmouth remained an active passenger station until January 4, 1965, when the B&M pulled out of the interstate passenger business. Newburyport then became the end of the line for another eleven years until lack of local subsidies cut passenger service back to Ipswich, where it remains today.

After passenger service ended north of Newburyport in 1965 the Eastern RR drawbridge across the Merrimack River in that city was taken out of service, making the northern section of the Eastern main line a long branch line from Portsmouth. In 1982 the old main line north of Newburyport to Seabrook, along with the Amesbury Branch (last used in January 1972), was abandoned. The rest of the Eastern, from Boston to Ipswich, remains an important rail commuter route, although freight service is not provided north of Salem. Since the completion of the Seabrook nuclear power plant the track between Seabrook and Hampton no longer is used. A bridge fire at Beverly in November 1984 ended all service north of that point. Passenger service was restored to Ipswich by the end of 1985, but freight service was not. The track between Ipswich and Newburyport, unused for nearly a decade, was removed in 1994. Plans are currently underway, however, to restore MBTA service to Newburyport as early as 1996 or 1997.

Several major accidents occurred on the Eastern. On August 26, 1871, heavy Saturday night traffic had produced long delays, a direct result of the refusal of the Eastern's ultra-conservative management to use the telegraph to dispatch trains. The engineer of a northbound express train mistakenly believed he had a clear track ahead. By the time he saw the marker lights of a local train ahead, stopped at Revere station, it was too late. Although the engineer of the express managed to reduce his speed to 10 mph, he could not avoid a collision. The resulting wreck and fire caused twenty-nine deaths and many injuries. To this day it remains the second-worst New England railroad accident of all time and the most deadly in Massachusetts.

Two other deadly wrecks took place in the middle of this century. A heavy damp snowstorm on February 28, 1956, made it nearly impossible to read trackside signals. A southbound commuter train halted at Swampscott to try to clear the signals and call for instructions. Three minutes later a second train of four RDC cars slammed into the rear of the stopped train at an estimated speed of 50 mph. Eleven passengers and two crew members perished, and 260 were injured. Ten years later, on December 27, 1966, an RDC car crashed into an oil tanker truck which had stalled on a grade crossing in Everett. Although none of the passengers or crew were seriously injured by the collision, a number of people were unable to escape the resulting fire. Thirteen died of smoke inhalation or burns.

The Eastern built a number of branches, several of which are described separately in this guide. The East Boston Branch was actually

Salem station was the most distinctive in New England and possibly the nation. Built by the Eastern RR in 1847 it was torn down in 1954. A tunnel brought trains into the station. This was lengthened in the 1950s when the depot was razed to eliminate downtown grade crossings. (Photo courtesy Walker Transportation Collection, Beverly Historical Society & Museum.)

the original main line of the Eastern from Revere to East Boston. Passenger service ended when the new line to Boston opened in 1854, but it was restored in 1872 as an unsuccessful attempt to prevent the construction of the Boston, Revere Beach & Lynn narrow gauge railroad, which opened in 1875. This service continued until 1905 when the B&M decided to abandon the line rather than install the costly grade separation the state was demanding. During the First World War the B&M reopened a portion of the branch between Revere and a connection with the Boston & Albany at Curtis Street in East Boston and it has continued in use as a freight-only branch. Between 1935 and 1950 (except for some years during World War II) the B&M ran special passenger trains to Suffolk Downs racetrack via the East Boston Branch.

The Chelsea Beach Branch, which opened in 1881, was operated only during the summer for beach-bound passengers. Originally it formed a loop route paralleling the main line, with the northern junction at the Revere-Saugus (Saugus River Junction) line and the southern at Oak Island Grove. A few years later the southern end was extended another mile to a junction north of Revere. It was discontinued in 1891, but most of the tracks remained in place unused for another thirty-five years.

The seaside town of Marblehead was served by no less than two Eastern branches. The first, the original Marblehead Branch, from Castle Hill in Salem, was constructed in 1839 at the same time as the original Eastern main line. A second connection, from Swampscott, was added in 1873, just before the Eastern collapsed in financial ruin. Providing access to seashore real estate was apparently the motive behind this new branch. Service continued on both branches until the end of passenger service in 1959. The Swampscott Branch was abandoned in 1961 and all but the first mile of the Marblehead Branch to Forest River station the year following. A second abandonment around 1968 further curtailed the line to Loring Avenue, and the last remnant was abandoned in 1993.

The mile-long Asbury Grove Branch was opened in August 1871 to serve a Methodist Church camp meeting ground at Asbury Grove. It only operated summers and only for special campgrounds trains. After 1894 a parallel trolley route also served the site. The branch line continued in use until 1901 when it was abandoned. The Essex Branch was opened between Hamilton-Wenham station and Essex Center in July 1872. In September 1887 the line was extended another half mile to Conomo. For many years the line transported lumber to Essex shipyards and brought out clams, shoes, and other local products. Centennial Grove on Chebacco Lake, established in 1876, was a popular destination for picnickers. After more than half a century of operation the B&M requested permission to abandon the line in 1926. The I.C.C. denied the request the year following, although it allowed abandonment of the final half mile between Essex and Conomo. In the 1920s and early 1930s the branch carried some commuters and the chief freight was ice from Chebacco Lake and wood for the shipyards. The Great Depression destroyed shipbuilding, and the spread of mechanical refrigeration all but eliminated the demand for natural ice. When the B&M once more sought abandonment of the Essex Branch in August 1942, the I.C.C. was convinced by the railroad's argument that the rails were needed for the war effort. Despite objections from residents and the state, the request was approved in November and a week later the tracks were torn up for scrap metal.

In the early 1840s the Merrimack Valley town of Amesbury found itself with mills but without railroads. Several proposed railroads were chartered to remedy the situation but none were built. In 1844 the Eastern secured a charter for the Salisbury Branch RR, but construction did not begin until 1847. The four-mile line opened as the Eastern's Amesbury Branch on January 1, 1848. Until the early twentieth century the primary freight traffic was carriages (and later Essex, Hudson, and Franklin automobile bodies) manufactured in Amesbury. Scheduled passenger service lasted until March 1936. Freight trains continued to run until January 1972, but the unused line was not abandoned until ten years later. The MBTA owns the right of way.

The two-mile Newburyport City Branch, which connected wharfs on the Merrimack River with the Eastern main line, was built in 1872 and leased by the Eastern to keep it out of the hands of the B&M. It apparently never had scheduled passenger service. After it was completed a connection was made with the B&M's Newburyport line, and for a while it supplied the B&M with Lawrence-bound coal traffic, much to the chagrin of the the Eastern. The B&M abandoned the branch in 1971.

Sources: Baker, *Formation*, 147-48; Bradlee, *Eastern Railroad*; Eastern Railroad, *Annual Report, 1875*, 11-12; Eastern Railroad, *Annual Report, 1883-84*, 43-52; Harlow, *Steelways*, 148-59, 166; Hoisington and Hornsby, "Amesbury and Merrimac Branches"; Humphrey and Clark, *Boston's Commuter Rail*, 75-86; Humphrey and Clark, *Second Section*, 9-10; Kirkland, *Men, City, and Transportation*, 1:195-99, 2:2-12; Poor, *History*, 115-16; Shaw, *History of Railroad Accidents*, 77-81, 253-55, 284; Story, "Recollection of the Essex Branch"; Symmes and Munroe, "Great Salem Tunnel Relocation Project"; 117 I.C.C. 679; 254 I.C.C. 121.

59. Gloucester & Rockport Branch

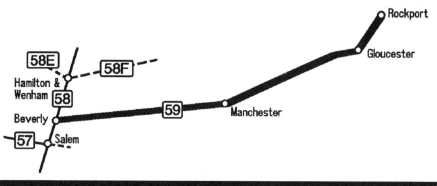

0	Beverly Jct., MA	4.5	Beverly Farms	11	West Gloucester
1.5	Montserrat		(West Farms)	12	Harbor
4	Prides (Prides	6	West Manchester	13	Gloucester
	Crossing)	7	Manchester	16	Bass Rocks
		9	Magnolia	17	Rockport, MA

BUILT: 1847, 1861.

OPERATORS: *Eastern, 1847-84; Boston & Maine, 1885-1983; Guilford, 1983-84; MBTA (passenger), 1976-84, 1985- .*

DAILY PASSENGER TRAINS: *1869:* 8, *1893:* 18, *1919:* 31, *1935:* 32, *1950:* 30, *1960:* 24, *1971:* 26, *1981:* 22, *1994.* 26.

ABANDONMENTS: None.

When the Eastern RR built its line from Boston through Essex County in 1839 it brought rails close to Cape Ann for the first time. In March 1845 the Eastern RR received permission to build a branch line east from Beverly to Gloucester. The line was opened from Beverly to Manchester in August 1847 and completed to Gloucester in December. Although the route follows the shore, it runs some distance from the water and the ocean is seldom in view.

Rockport residents were disappointed that the tracks did not reach their town, but the Eastern was not interested in building an extension. Residents therefore secured a charter in 1853 to construct the Rockport RR to extend the Eastern's branch from Gloucester to Rockport. Unable to interest investors, the line remained unbuilt until a second Rockport RR was chartered in 1860. The line was finally completed in

November 1861 and operated by the Eastern, which bought it outright in 1868. At Rockport trains were turned by an unusual loop track instead of a wye or a turntable. Built early in the twentieth century, the loop was in use until around 1962 when double-ended rail diesel cars rendered it obsolete.

The Gloucester & Rockport Branch became a busy commuter route in its own right, with trains running directly to Boston from Beverly over the Eastern main line. By 1911 the line had been double tracked to Gloucester. Denizens of fashionable North Shore estates rode it each day to their offices in Boston. Between 1892 and 1920 the line featured the *Flying Fisherman* (known locally as the "Dude Train"), for the exclusive use of well-heeled season pass holders. For a time there was even weekend sleeping car service to New York City.

By 1953 diesels had replaced steam-powered Pacific locomotives, although steam could occasionally be seen on the branch as late as 1954. Budd RDC cars took over service in 1955. By the early 1980s the line was being used almost exclusively for passengers. In November 1984 the destruction of the Beverly bridge by fire ended all freight and passenger service. Passenger service resumed in 1985, but freight service is now abandoned. (In 1994 the city of Gloucester was negotiating with the MBTA and Guilford to restore rail freight to Cape Ann.)

Sources: Bradlee, *Eastern Railroad*, 41, 64; Brown, "Gloucester Branch"; Humphrey and Clark, *Boston's Commuter Rail,* 75.

Bound for Rockport, an MBTA commuter train approaches Manchester station in July 1994.

60. Saugus Branch

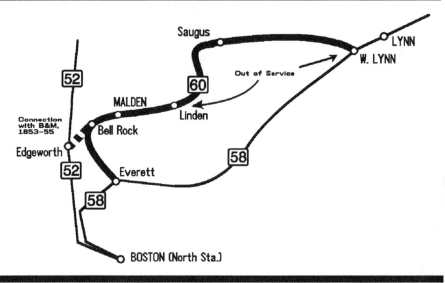

0	Everett (Everett Jct.), MA	2.5	Faulkner	7	Saugus
0.5	West St.	3	Maplewood	8	East Saugus
1	West Everett	3.5	Broadway	8.5	Raddin
1.5	Bell Rock	4	Linden	9	Lynn Common
2	Malden (Malden East)	5	Franklin Park	9.5	West Lynn, MA
		5.5	Cliftondale		
		6	Pleasant Hill		

BUILT: 1850-55.

OPERATORS: *Saugus Branch, 1853-55; Eastern, 1855-84; Boston & Maine, 1885-1983; Guilford, 1983-* .

DAILY PASSENGER TRAINS: *1869: 14, 1893: 36, 1919: 16, 1935: 8, 1950: 5.* Passenger service ended 1958.

ABANDONMENTS: None.

The Saugus Branch was yet another result of the intense competition between the Boston & Maine and Eastern Railroads in the mid-nineteenth century. Unlike most of the other lines that developed from that rivalry, however, the Saugus Branch was a modest success that has survived to the present. The line was chartered in 1848 as the Saugus Branch RR, an independent company with hopes of building a road from Lynn through Saugus to Malden. The Saugus Branch was completed in February 1853 from the Eastern RR at West Lynn to Edgeworth in Malden, where it connected with the Boston & Maine.

The opening of the Saugus Branch posed an immediate threat to the Eastern, since it allowed the B&M to offer its own Boston-Lynn service, heretofore an Eastern monopoly. Moreover, until April 1854 the Saugus route had the advantage of direct access to Boston, while the Eastern until that date reached only East Boston. The Eastern therefore bought control of the line in 1855. The connection with the Boston & Maine was removed, and in October the line was extended another mile and a half south to meet the newly built Eastern RR Boston extension at Everett.

The Eastern developed the Saugus Branch into an important commuter route that helped build the eastern portion of Malden and Saugus. The entire branch was double tracked in 1891-92. It is said to have been the only one of the Eastern's many branches to have been profitable. Service was at its peak around the end of the nineteenth century, before competition from trolleys and then automobiles took away most passengers. In the twentieth century its ancient coaches (some lit by gas light) were pulled by one of the last American-type (4-4-0) locomotives in New England. By the 1930s only a few trains still used the branch, and these were gradually reduced until passenger service ended altogether in May 1958. At about this time the second track was removed.

The Saugus Branch continued to serve a number of industrial customers along its route. Occasionally commuter trains or wide loads for the GE plant in Lynn were diverted onto it when the Eastern main line was blocked or lacked the necessary clearance. Around 1984 General Electric paid to have the branch rebuilt so it could handle heavy transformers from its West Lynn plant that were too heavy to go by the Eastern route. Soon afterwards, however, GE stopped building them in Lynn. By 1993 the line was no longer in service east of Linden, and the rails have been removed in some places. In 1994 Guilford announced its intention to abandon operations over the line.

Sources: J.Leonard Bachelder, personal communication; Baker, *Formation*, 146, 150-51; Bradlee, *Eastern Railroad*, 57-58; Humphrey and Clark, *Boston's Commuter Rail*, 75-86; Humphrey and Clark, *Second Section*, 9-10; "Saugus Branch."

61. Boston, Revere Beach & Lynn

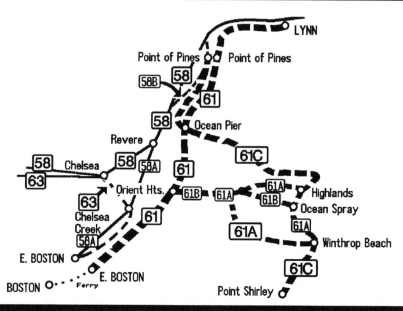

0	East Boston, MA	
1	Wood Island	
1.5	Harbor View	
2	Orient Heights	
	(Winthrop Jct.)	
	(Winthrop)	
2.5	Suffolk Downs	
3	Beachmont	
3.5	Ocean View	
4	Crescent Beach	
	(Pavilion) (Revere)	
4.3	Bath House	
4.5	Atlantic (Revere St.)	
5	Oak Island	
6.5	Point of Pines	
8	West Lynn	
8.5	Lynn, MA	

61A. Winthrop Circuit

0	Orient Heights, MA
0.5	Pleasant St.
1	Battery
1.5	Highlands
2	Ocean Spray
2.3	Playstead
2.5	Winthrop Beach
3	Thornton
3.5	Winthrop Centre
4	Ingalls, MA

61B. BW&S RR (Narrow Gauge)

0	Winthrop Jct., MA
0.5	Pleasant St.
1.5	Winthrop
1.7	Ocean Spray
2	Shirley
2.5	Great Head
2.7	Cottage Hill
3	Short Beach
3.5	Point Shirley, MA

61C. BW&S RR (Standard Gauge)

0	Point of Pines, MA
1.5	Oak Island
2.5	Crescent Beach
3	Ocean Pier
3.3	Ridgeway
3.7	Beachmont
4.2	Winthrop Highlands
4.7	Locust St.
5	Ocean Spray
5.2	Shirley
5.5	Great Head
5.7	Cottage Hill
6	Short Beach
6.5	Point Shirley, MA

BUILT: 1875; Winthrop Branch (Boston, Winthrop & Point Shirley) 1877-83; Eastern Junction route, 1881-84; Winthrop loop, 1886-88.

OPERATORS: *Boston, Revere Beach & Lynn,* 1875-1940; *Boston, Winthrop & Point Shirley,* 1877-83; *Boston, Winthrop & Shore,* 1883-86.

DAILY PASSENGER TRAINS: *1893:* ca. 64, *1919:* N/A, *1936:* 145 (electric). Passenger service ended 1940.

ABANDONMENTS: Crescent Beach-Ocean Spray, Cottage Hill-Point Shirley, 1885; Shirley-Cottage Hill, 1888; Crescent Beach-Point of Pines, 1892; Boston, Revere Beach & Lynn (entire line), 1940.

After the Civil War citizens of the rapidly growing city of Lynn chafed at the monopoly that the Eastern RR enjoyed over travel between their city and Boston. Land speculators who had acquired large parcels of vacant land cheaply in Revere were ready to exploit these sentiments. The result was the Boston, Revere Beach & Lynn RR, chartered in 1874 with authority to construct a line from East Boston along the shore line to Lynn.

Residents of Lynn and other communities along the proposed route supplied most of the funds, and construction commenced in May 1875. To keep costs low, the line was built narrow gauge (three feet). Construction along the flat shore line was easy, and the line opened for business only three months after construction started (although the railroad was not yet entirely finished).

The narrow gauge line was a success. The speculators' dream materialized as the city of Revere took shape on hitherto worthless sand flats. Thousands of passengers rode the line each day to and from their homes or to the amusement complex that developed along Revere Beach. By the turn of the century the passenger-only Boston, Revere Beach & Lynn had taken on many of the characteristics of a rapid transit line. This was taken to its logical conclusion in 1928 when the railroad strung catenary wire and introduced electric operation. Rather than purchase new rolling stock, the management installed motors, controllers, and trolley poles in the old steam cars.

The last steam locomotives were retired in December 1928. Unfortunately, the BRB&L had chosen a poor time to undertake the costly conversion to electric traction. Only a year after electrification the nation was plunged into its worst depression, and the railroad saw its ridership decline at a time when it especially needed cash. Despite measures such as deferred maintenance, the railroad slid into bankruptcy in 1937. The line was unable to stem its losses, and in 1939 petitioned for permission to quit. This was granted, and the trains ran for the final time January 27, 1940.

The BRB&L also operated a loop branch to Winthrop, with a rather complicated history. The original route of the BRB&L had bypassed the small beachfront town of Winthrop, and plans were soon made to connect this town to the railroad. The Boston, Winthrop & Point Shirley RR was incorporated in 1876 to build a second narrow gauge line from the BRB&L to the ocean at Winthrop. Construction began that year, and the initial two-mile segment of the line, from Winthrop Junction in East Boston to Buchanan Street in Winthrop Center, opened June 1877. Construction toward Point Shirley, at the southern end of Winthrop, continued. In 1881 the line through Winthrop Center was realigned to serve a subdivision called Ocean Spray being developed by a promoter with close ties to the railroad.

Except during 1878-79 the Boston, Winthrop & Point Shirley was not operated in the winter. The tracks reached Short Beach, just south of Great Head, in 1882. Meanwhile, in 1880 a second railroad, the Eastern Junction, Broad Sound Pier & Point Shirley RR had been chartered to build a second line to Winthrop. The building of the Eastern Junction line got underway in 1881. Unlike the BRB&L and the Boston, Winthrop & Point Shirley this was to be a standard gauge railroad. The route of the Eastern Junction began at Crescent Beach

BRB&L narrow gauge locomotive number 1 (a Manchester-built 2-4-4T) pulls a train across the Winthrop trestle in October 1909. (Photo courtesy Walker Transportation Collection, Beverly Historical Society & Museum.)

on the Eastern RR (which supported it) and proceeded along the shore line to Ocean Spray. By July 1882 the line was completed to Ocean Spray, but not operated. At the same time a line from Crescent Beach north to the Eastern's Chelsea Beach branch at Point of Pines was also being constructed.

In December 1883 the still incomplete Eastern Junction was consolidated with the Boston, Winthrop & Point Shirley and another unbuilt road to form the Boston, Winthrop & Shore RR. The new railroad consisted of two separate divisions, one narrow gauge and the other standard, the latter still yet to operate. Operation of the narrow gauge portion resumed for the season in March 1884, and the standard gauge finally was put in service from Point of Pines all the way to Point Shirley in June. The two lines shared a right of way between Ocean Spray and Point Shirley, where a ferry provided connections to Boston.

The Boston, Winthrop & Point Shirley was short lived. A severe storm on Thanksgiving Day, 1885, caused major damage, especially to the standard gauge line which hugged the coast. It never operated again. The narrow gauge line was barely kept open. In 1886 the Boston, Revere Beach & Lynn leased what was left of the Boston, Winthrop & Point Shirley. That fall it began to rebuild the narrow gauge line, relocating most of the track along a new route to form a large loop. The new Winthrop line opened in 1888 as a branch of the BRB&L. The extension to Point Shirley and the entire standard gauge line were abandoned.

After the complete abandonment of the BRB&L in 1940 portions of the right of way were acquired by the MTA. A connection was made with the transit line that already connected East Boston to Boston via the harbor tunnel and the new transit line opened to Wonderland station in Revere in 1951. The right of way of the BRB&L is followed from Orient Heights to Wonderland. The right of way between Wonderland and West Lynn, long overgrown, can still be traced. Development has removed most other signs of the narrow gauge, although portions of the right of way are visible in Winthrop along the route of the loop. Over the years proposals have been made to expand the Blue Line northward along the old BRB&L right of way to Point of Pines or even to Lynn, but nothing so far has come of these suggestions.

Sources: Bradlee, "Boston, Revere Beach and Lynn Narrow Gauge Railroad"; Stanley, *Narrow Gauge*.

62. Union Freight

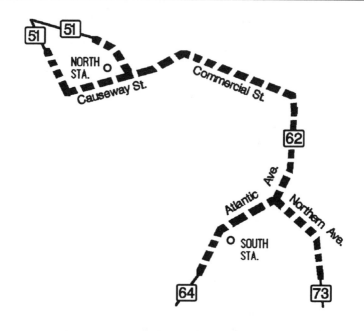

0 Boston (North Sta.), MA	2 Boston (South Sta.), MA	

BUILT: ca. 1867-1872.

OPERATORS: *Union Freight,* 1872-1873; *Old Colony,* 1874-83; *Union Freight,* 1884-1970.

DAILY PASSENGER TRAINS: Freight only.

ABANDONMENTS: Connection with New Haven RR, 1969; remainder of line, 1970.

By the end of the Civil War downtown Boston was served by many independent rail lines approaching the city from the North, the West, and the East. Each line had its own depot and freight yards, but no rail connection existed between them. Boston's waterfront also lacked rail service.

One solution to these problems would be connecting the downtown facilities using tracks laid on city streets. Two companies were chartered in the late 1860s to do just that, but by 1872 only one mile of track was actually in place. In June of that year the Union Freight RR was chartered to finish the project. Construction resumed in September and the line was completed in December 1872. As constructed, the line stretched two miles from the Boston & Lowell freight yards (Lowell and Minot Streets, near the present site of North Station), down busy Commercial Street and Atlantic Avenue along the waterfront to the Boston & Albany freight yards (near today's South Station).

Horses were used briefly on this short line until heavy snows ended operation. When the line reopened in April 1873 four-wheel geared locomotives provided power. Independent operation continued for only another eight months until the Old Colony RR leased the Union Freight and operated it as its own branch. When the lease expired ten years later the line returned to independent operation, although the

Behind an Alco switcher leased from the New Haven, a Union Freight train makes its way down Atlantic Avenue in Boston in 1960. (Photo courtesy Walker Transportation Collection, Beverly Historical Society & Museum.)

Old Colony retained control. The New Haven RR continued this arrangement after it absorbed the Old Colony in 1893.

In the twentieth century the Union Freight remained a busy and convenient connection between the downtown freight yards of the Boston & Maine and the New Haven. Around 1910 a connection was built to the New Haven freight yards in South Boston via tracks in Northern Avenue. The railroad owned its own small fleet of switcher locomotives. Diesels replaced steam in 1946, and after 1953 motive power was leased from the parent New Haven. Operations, almost entirely on city streets, were between midnight and 8:00 a.m. After the mid-1950s the original route between Northern Avenue and the Boston & Albany yards was no longer used but the tracks remained intact.

For years the city of Boston longed to do away with the nuisance of trains running on busy city streets, but the convenience of the Union Freight to the B&M and the New Haven kept the line in operation. The end came after the New Haven was absorbed by the Penn Central at the beginning of 1969. The PC consolidated most of its Boston freight operations at Beacon Park in the city's Allston neighborhood, which already enjoyed a good connection with the B&M via the Grand Junction branch. Service was suspended on the line south of State Street in September 1969. Deprived of its reason for existence, the remainder of the Union Freight ceased operation in March 1970.

Sources: Kyper, "Diminutive High Iron"; Kyper, *Railroad That Came Out at Night*.

63. Grand Junction

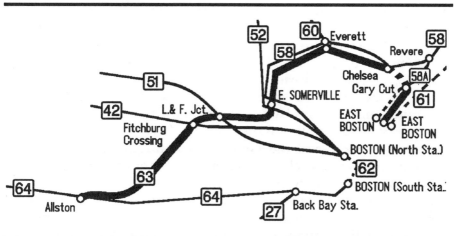

0 Allston, MA	2.5 Fitchburg Crossing	5 Everett
1 Massachusetts	3 Lowell & Fitchburg	6 Chelsea
Ave.	Jct.	6.5 Cary Cut
2 East Cambridge	3.5 East Somerville	9 East Boston, MA

BUILT: 1849-56.
OPERATORS: *Grand Junction,* ca. 1849-1857; *Boston & Albany,* 1869-1900; *New York Central (Boston & Albany) 1900-68; Penn Central,* 1968-76; *Conrail,* 1976- .
DAILY PASSENGER TRAINS: Freight only.
ABANDONMENTS: Chelsea-Cary Cut, ca. 1972.

Unlike many cities, Boston lacks a belt railroad connecting the various lines that enter the city. The line that comes closest to this function is the Grand Junction. Chartered as the Grand Junction RR & Depot Company in 1847, this railroad had opened its initial six-mile line from East Boston to Somerville by 1852. As originally built its primary purpose was to link the busy docks of East Boston, where the clipper ships were built, to the Somerville freight yards of the Boston & Maine. No passenger service was provided.

In 1853 the Grand Junction secured a charter for another freight-only short line, the Union RR, to extend the Grand Junction three miles from Somerville west through Cambridge to a connection with the Boston & Worcester at Allston across the Charles River. The Union RR extension caught the interest of the Boston & Worcester, who invested in Grand Junction bonds. When the B&W was completed in 1835 it had enjoyed direct access to the wharfs of South Cove, but by the 1850s enough land had been filled in to render these docks unusable, and the railroad hoped to substitute the wharfs at East Boston via the Grand Junction. This line was completed in 1855, but the Grand Junction went bankrupt the following year, and service on the line west of Somerville was suspended in 1857. Prolonged litigation between the B&W and the Grand Junction kept the line out of operation until 1869. Freight trains operated over the original Grand Junction between Somerville and East Boston under various operators.

By 1869 the B&W had merged with the Western to form the Boston & Albany RR, and the new railroad soon made the Grand Junction a major freight link. Although hampered by more than forty grade crossings it became one of the Boston area's most important industrial railroads, lined with numerous factories, shops, and warehouses. It connected the Boston & Albany with all of the lines that entered Boston from the west, north, and northeast—the Fitchburg, the Boston & Lowell, the Boston & Maine, and the Eastern. For several years the Eastern used its tracks through Chelsea and Everett until it built its own parallel route to Boston. Although scheduled passenger service was not operated on the Grand Junction, special trains used the line in the 1870s and 1880s to take European immigrants from the East Boston docks to the West.

Under the New York Central, Penn Central, and Conrail the Grand Junction has remained an important urban belt route. Around 1955 the New York Central drawbridge over Chelsea Creek was taken out of service and never replaced (although legal abandonment did not take place until more than a decade later), and its remaining traffic between Chelsea and East Boston was rerouted via the Boston & Maine's East Boston Branch to Cary Cut (Curtis Street). In 1994 Conrail still served one East Boston customer.

Sources: Baker, *Formation*, 5-7; Cornwall and Smith, *Names First*, 45, 119-20; Humphrey and Clark, *Second Section*, 8-9; Kirkland, *Men, Cities, and Transportation*, 1:153-54, 434; Poor, *History*, 125.

64. Boston & Worcester (Boston & Albany)

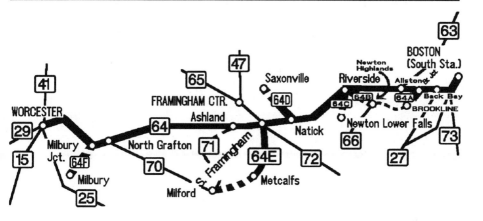

					64A. Brookline Branch
0	Boston (South Sta.), MA	12.5	Wellesley Farms (Rice Crossing)		
1	Back Bay (Trinity Place/Huntington Ave.) (Columbus Ave.)	13.5	Wellesley Hills (Needham) (Grantville)	0	Brookline Jct. (Milldam) (Beacon St.), MA
		15	Wellesley (West Needham)	0.5	Chapel
2	Brookline Jct. (Milldam) (Beacon St.)	16	Lake Crossing	1	Longwood
		18	Natick	1.5	Brookline, MA
3	University (Cottage Farm)	19.5	West Natick		
4	Allston (Cambridge Crossing)	21	Framingham (South Framingham)		64B. Highland Branch
5	Brighton	24	Ashland	0	Riverside, MA
6	Faneuil	27.5	Cordaville	1	Woodland
7	Newton (Newton Corner) (Angiers Corner)	28	Southville (Southboro)	2	Waban
		32	Westboro	2.5	Eliot
8	Newtonville	38	North Grafton (Grafton)	3.5	Newton Highlands, MA
9	West Newton	40	Millbury Jct.		
10	Auburndale	44	Worcester, MA		
11	Riverside				

64C. Newton Lower Falls Branch	1.5 Worcester St.	5 Holliston
	2.5 Cochituate	7 Metcalfs
	4 Saxonville, MA	9 Braggville
0 Riverside, MA		10 Rocky Hill
0.5 Pine Grove	**64E. Milford Branch**	12 Milford, MA
2 Newton Lower Falls, MA		
	0 Framingham (South Framingham), MA	**64F. Millbury Branch**
64D. Saxonville Branch		0 Millbury Jct., MA
	3 Whitneys	3 Millbury, MA
0 Natick, MA	4 East Holliston	

BUILT: 1832-35; Millbury Branch, 1837; Saxonville Branch, 1846; Newton Lower Falls Branch, 1847; Milford Branch, 1847-48; Brookline Branch, 1848; Highland Branch, 1886.

OPERATORS: *Boston & Worcester,* 1834-67; *Boston & Albany,* 1867-1900; *New York Central (Boston & Albany),* 1900-68; *Penn Central,* 1968-76; *Conrail,* 1976- ; *MBTA (commuter),* 1973- ;*Amtrak (intercity passenger),* 1975- .

DAILY PASSENGER TRAINS: *1869:* 19, *1893:* 31, *1919:* 47, *1935:* 44, *1950:* 39, *1960:* 12, *1971:* 4, *1981:* 2, *1994:* 12. Passenger service ended Saxonville Branch, 1936; Millbury Branch, 1941; Newton Lower Falls Branch, 1957; Brookline Branch, Highland Branch (Highland Circuit), 1958; Milford Branch, 1959.

ABANDONMENTS: Milford Branch (Metcalfs-Milford, 1972); Brookline Branch, Highland Branch (west of Woodland-Newton Highlands), 1958; Millbury Branch, Newton Lower Falls Branch, 1976; Saxonville Branch (Cochituate-Saxonville), ca. 1987.

One of New England's three initial railroads, the Boston & Worcester has always been one of the region's busiest. Chartered June 23, 1831, one year after the Boston & Lowell and one day after the Boston & Providence, the B&W was intended to link Boston with Worcester, the seat of Worcester County, and eventually, through extensions, Albany and the West. Considering the subsequent success of the line, stock sales went slowly at first.

Colonel John M. Fessenden was hired to survey the line. Local sentiment determined the alignment of the route as much as engineering considerations. Originally slated to pass through Watertown and Waltham the line was shifted southward through Newton when the former communities expressed opposition. When the owners of a turnpike company objected, the original routing through Framingham Center was also moved southward.

Construction began in August 1832 westward from Boston. The original Boston depot was on Washington Street, but this was relocated to Lincoln and Beach Streets shortly after the line was completed. The B&W crossed the then open waters of the Back Bay on a 170-foot long trestle and embankment. In the middle of the Back Bay it crossed the line of the Boston & Providence (near the site of today's Back Bay station). Construction of the two railroads greatly reduced the tidal flow of the bay and helped promote its filling in later in the century.

On April 4, 1834, a gravel train was run from Boston to Newton, the first time a steam locomotive had been operated in New England. Three days later a locomotive hauled the first passenger train from Boston to Davis Tavern, West Newton. Regularly scheduled passenger

THE BOSTON & WORCESTER RAILROAD.
FROM AN OLD PRINT.

FROM THE OUTLOOK.

service began on this route a few days later, making the B&W New England's first steam-powered railroad open for service.

In July the tracks reached Wellesley Hills (then a part of Needham), by September Ashland (Hopkinton), and by November Westborough. On July 4, 1835, the B&W opened for service between Boston and Worcester. (The original Worcester depot was on Main Street near the Common.) The Boston & Lowell and Boston & Providence were completed at about the same time, briefly making Boston the nation's leading rail center.

From the beginning the B&W was a great success, carrying heavy through and local freight and passenger traffic. Originally a single track, the line was double tracked between Boston and Framingham in 1839 and Framingham to Worcester in 1843. A new type of traffic appeared in 1843 when the B&W introduced special trains between Boston and West Newton for which one could purchase an annual season ticket for $60. Within a few years these commuter trains operated as far west as Framingham, and residential villages developed around the stations.

Traffic on the B&W received a further boost from the construction of the Western RR. Supported by many of the men who had backed the B&W, the Western opened from Worcester to Springfield in 1839 and all the way to Albany by the end of 1841. The Western became the B&W's most important feeder and the B&W the Western's. Despite bickering over the division of revenues the two roads formed a natural and mutually beneficial partnership. In 1867 the B&W and the Western finally merged to form the Boston & Albany RR.

Following the merger, the Boston portion of the line was expanded to four tracks and by 1884 the four-tracked section extended out to Riverside. In 1883 the B&A bought part of the former Charles River Branch RR between Brookline and Cook Street from the New York & New England RR and constructed the Highland Branch, a connection from Riverside to its line at Newton Highlands. This produced a second through route between Boston and Riverside via the B&A's existing Brookline Branch. This new service, the Highland Circuit, opened in May 1886.

By the end of the nineteenth century the B&A was one of New England's foremost main lines. Third and fourth tracks were laid between Riverside and Lake Crossing in 1894 and extended to Framingham in 1907. In 1900 the B&A was acquired by the powerful New York Central RR. In keeping with the practice of that company however, the B&A retained its separate identity for many years within the Central system. The B&A followed the NYC into the Penn Central in 1968, and eight years later it became part of Conrail's Boston Line.

A westbound Penn Central trailer van freight pulls out of Beacon Park Yard in the Allston section of Boston in March 1971. Trains are dispatched from here to points as far west as Elkhart, Ind.

A Penn Central freight passes through Weston on its way to Boston's Beacon Park Yard in October 1971. This site, just west of Route 128, has been a favorite of rail phographers for nearly a century.

In the twentieth century passenger service gradually declined, although freight traffic remained heavy. Commuter service dwindled to a few daily round trips between Boston and Framingham and long-distance service was eliminated altogether when Amtrak arrived in 1971. Shortly afterward Amtrak restored this service as part of a Boston-Worcester-Springfield-Hartford-New Haven-New York route. This lasted until March 1, 1975, when Amtrak once more eliminated service. On October 31, 1975, however, the Boston-Chicago *Lake Shore Limited* began operating over the B&W, and Amtrak has run trains continuously ever since, even constructing a new Worcester passenger station. (The old Worcester Union Station, now unused and badly deteriorated, awaits possible restoration.) In 1994 MBTA commuter service was extended to Worcester.

The construction of the Massachusetts Turnpike in the 1960s greatly altered the easternmost part of the B&W. The New York Central sold the Turnpike Authority its entire four-track right of way from Riverside to Boston in 1958. By 1965 the Turnpike was completed from its old terminus at Route 128 through to Boston, using the railroad right of way (the railroad reduced its tracks from four to two to accommodate the turnpike). In 1962 the third and fourth tracks were removed between Framingham and Riverside.

The B&W had a number of short branches. The Brookline Branch, always the most successful, was eventually made part of the Highland Circuit. The Circuit itself was abandoned in 1958 to make way for the MTA's Riverside light rail line, which opened the following year. (Short sections of track were retained for local freight service at both the Brookline and Riverside ends, and these survived into the 1970s.) The Saxonville Branch opened in July 1846. In the 1980s it was cut back and today extends only a short distance north of Route 9. Between 1904 and 1930 the Lower Falls Branch (built 1847) was electrified and served by a trolley car. It was abandoned when Conrail assumed the Penn Central's burden in 1976. (Since 1972 only the track between Riverside and the MBTA Riverside yards had been in service.) At the same time the three-mile long Millbury Branch (built 1837) was also eliminated, freight service having declined to only one train per week. The rails were removed in 1980. The Milford Branch, which opened in 1848, had passenger service as late as 1959. The final five miles between Metcalfs and Milford were abandoned by Penn Central in 1972, and by 1987 the line was not being operated beyond Holliston.

Beacon Park Yard, in Boston's Allston neighborhood, is one of New England's most important freight facilities. Both conventional and trailer trains are dispatched from here westward as far as Elkhart, Indiana. The B&W, remains one of New England's busiest rail lines, offering train watchers and photographers frequent opportunities to catch freight, commuter, and Amtrak trains.

Sources: Baker, *Formation*, 3-13; Harlow, *Steelways*, 93-101; Humphrey and Clark, *Boston's Commuter Rail*, 21-25; Kennedy, "Commuter Services"; Kirkland, *Men, Cities, and Transportation*, 1:115-16, 143-47; Salisbury, *The State, the Investor, and the Railroad*; U.S. Railway Association, *Final System Plan*, 2:139-40; U.S. Railway Association, *Preliminary System Plan*, 2:501-02.

65. Agricultural Branch

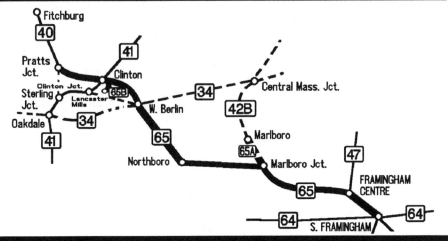

		65A. Marlboro Branch		
0	Framingham (South Framingham), MA	12	Talbot (Hospital Sta.) (State Farm)	0 Marlboro Jct., MA
1	Montwait (Lakeview)	14	Northboro	2 Marlboro, MA
2	Framingham Centre (Framingham)	17	Berlin	
		19	Carters (West Berlin)	**65B. Lancaster Mills Branch**
5	Fayville (Faysville)	21	Bolton	
6	Southboro	22	[Lancaster Mills Jct.]	0 [Lancaster Mills Jct.], MA
8	Marlboro Jct. (South Marlboro) (Marlboro)	23	Clinton	1.5 Lancaster Mills, MA
		28	Pratts Jct., MA	

BUILT: 1849-55, 1866; Marlboro Branch, 1855; Lancaster Mills Branch, 1875.

OPERATORS: *Boston & Worcester RR,* 1855-67; *Boston, Clinton & Fitchburg,* 1867-76; *Boston, Clinton, Fitchburg & New Bedford,* 1876-79; *Old Colony,* 1879-93; *New York, New Haven & Hartford,* 1893-1968; *Penn Central,* 1969-76; *Conrail,* 1976- .

DAILY PASSENGER TRAINS: *1869:* 6, *1893:* 12, *1919:* 6, *1935:* 6 (Framingham-Marlboro). Passenger service ended Marlboro Jct.-Pratts Jct., 1931; remainder of line (including Marlboro Branch), 1937. Lancaster Mills Branch freight only.

ABANDONMENTS: Marlboro Branch, 1966.

The original survey of the Boston & Worcester routed the railroad through Framingham Centre, but opposition from a turnpike company led the railroad to build through South Framingham instead. Soon after the B&W opened in 1834 residents of Framingham Centre began to regret being left off the railroad. To remedy this situation, in

Southboro station a century ago. (History of the Old Colony Railroad, *1893*).

1849 the B&W completed a short line to Framingham Centre.

Even before the construction of this branch, the Agricultural Branch RR had been chartered in 1847 to extend it westward to Northboro. Construction finally got under way in 1852. The initial segment from Framingham Centre to Marlboro (by way of the Marlboro Branch) was opened in June 1855 and the remainder of the line to Northboro the following December. The B&W immediately leased the line.

In July 1866 the line was extended north from Northboro to an intersection at Pratts Junction with the Fitchburg & Worcester, which provided access to Fitchburg. The following year the name was changed to the Boston, Clinton & Fitchburg RR, and it began joint operation with the Fitchburg & Worcester, the B&W having apparently given up its lease. In 1869 the BC&F absorbed the Fitchburg & Worcester and seven years later became the Boston, Clinton, Fitchburg & New Bedford. This in turn became part of the Old Colony system in 1879, and subsequently, the New Haven in 1893.

Passenger service ended in the 1930s, but the line has continued to carry freight. In the 1970s there were still a number of industrial customers in Northboro, Clinton, and other old manufacturing towns. In more recent years some of these concerns have gone out of business or been replaced by high-tech industries that have little need for rail service. Unlike most central Massachusetts branch lines the Agricultural Branch was transferred to Conrail in 1976 and has been operated as a CR branch ever since.

The Agricultural had two short branches. The two-mile Marlboro Branch was built in 1855, had passenger service until 1937, and was abandoned in 1966. The Lancaster Mills Branch, 1.6 miles in length, was constructed in 1875 to serve a factory. Entirely within the town of Clinton, it has always been operated only for freight.

Sources: Baker, *Formation*, 6, 25, 32-33, 36; *Chronological History of the New Haven Railroad*; Cornwall and Smith, *Names First*, 1; Humphrey and Clark, *Boston's Commuter Rail*, 22; U.S. Railway Association, *Final System Plan*, 2:142; U.S. Railway Association, *Preliminary System Plan*, 2:504-05.

66. Charles River

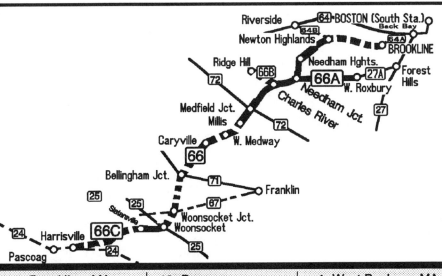

0	Brookline, MA	
0.5	Brookline Hills (Cypress St.)	
1.5	Beaconsfield	
2	Reservoir (Brighton St.)	
3	Chestnut Hill	
4	Newton Center	
5	Newton Highlands	
5.5	Cook St.	
6	Saco (Cabot)	
6.5	Newton Upper Falls (Upper Falls)	
8	Needham Heights (Highlandville) (Avery)	
9	Needham (Needham Plain) (Needham Center)	
10	Needham Jct. (West St.)	
11	Charles River (Charles River Village)	

13	Dover
16	Farm St.
17	Medfield Jct. (Medfield) (Harding)
19	Clicquot (Kimball)
20	Millis (East Medway)
22	Medway
24	West Medway (Woodside)
25	Caryville
26	North Bellingham
28	Bellingham Jct. (Bellingham) (Midland)
33	Woonsocket Jct., MA
35	Woonsocket, RI

66A. West Roxbury Extension

0	Needham Jct., MA
1	Birds Hill (Hersey)
4	West Roxbury, MA

66B. Ridge Hill Branch

0	Charles River, MA
2	Ridge Hill, MA

66C. Pascoag Extension

0	Woonsocket, RI
1	Union Valley
2.5	Forestdale
3.5	Slatersville
5	Nasonville
7	Glendale
8	Oakland Centre
9	Whipple
10	Harrisville, RI

BUILT: 1850-63; Ridge Hill Branch, 1879; Pascoag Extension, 1891; West Roxbury Extension, 1906.

OPERATORS: *Boston & Worcester,* 1852-58; *Goss & Munson (private contractors),* 1858-63; *New York & Boston,* 1858-65; *Boston, Hartford & Erie,* 1865-73; *New York & New England,* 1873-95 (Brookline-Newton Highlands to *Boston & Albany,* 1883-1900; *New York Central,* 1900-58); *New England,* 1895-98; *New York, New Haven & Hartford ,* 1898-1968; *Penn Central,* 1969-76; *Conrail,* 1976-87; *Springfield Terminal,* 1982-83; *Bay Colony,* 1984- ; *MBTA (commuter),* 1973- ; *Providence & Worcester,* ca. 1982- .

DAILY PASSENGER TRAINS: *1869:* 6, *1893:* 11, *1919:* 12, *1936:* 5 (Boston-Bellingham Jct.; Needham Jct.-Needham Heights, 22), *1950:* 5 (Boston-West Medway, via West Roxbury; Needham Jct.-Needham Heights, 19), *1960:* 2 (Boston-West Medway, via West Roxbury; Needham Jct.-Needham Heights, 22), *1971:* 22 (Needham Jct.-Needham Heights), *1993:* 30 (Boston-Needham Heights). Passenger service ended Ridge Hill Branch, ca. 1885; Pascoag Extension, 1924 or 1925; Newton Upper Falls-Newton Highlands, 1927; Woonsocket-Bellingham Jct., 1930; Needham Heights-Newton Upper Falls, 1932; Bellingham Jct.-West Medway, 1941; West Medway-Millis, 1966; Millis-Needham Jct., 1967. Passenger service not operated 1979-87.

ABANDONMENTS: Ridge Hill Branch, 1889; Woonsocket Jct.-Bellingham Jct., 1934; Pascoag Extension (Slatersville-Harrisville, 1937); Woonsocket Jct.-Woonsocket, 1938; Bellingham Jct.-Caryville, 1941; Caryville-West Medway, 1949; West Medway-Millis, 1967.

In 1848 the Boston & Worcester RR opened a three-mile branch line to Brookline Village, in one of the area's fastest-growing suburbs. The line was an instant success, and the following year the Charles River Branch RR was chartered to extend the line westward another sixteen miles to Dover. Construction began from Brookline in 1850 and the initial segment from Brookline to Newton Upper Falls opened in November 1852. By this time the railroad had been merged into another line, the Charles River RR, with authority to build all the way to Woonsocket, R.I. The Boston & Worcester operated the Charles River as an extension of the Brookline Branch.

The Charles River managed to open an additional two miles of track to Needham in June 1853, just before the railroad ran out of money and construction ceased. In 1855 the Charles River was merged into the New York & Boston RR, which had a grandiose scheme of constructing an inland route from Boston to New York City. The Charles River was the only part of the hapless New York & Boston that actually existed, and even this continued to be operated by the B&W until about 1858 when the NY&B was finally prepared to take over.

Since 1967 the Charles River line has ended just west of Millis station (shown here in August 1992). Passenger trains ceased at the same time.

During the 1850s Boston's Back Bay was still largely water, and the city fathers were looking for additional sources of fill material. They struck a deal with the firm of Goss & Munson to provide gravel for filling in the bay. The contractors bought their own locomotives and cars, and in 1858 began operating around-the-clock gravel trains from a gravel pit in Needham to the Back Bay via the Charles River and a track parallel to the Boston & Worcester. These trains, which made up the bulk of traffic on the Charles River, continued until 1863.

After many years of delay the New York & Boston finally extended the Charles River, reaching Medway in November 1861, West Medway by September the year following, and finally Woonsocket in October 1863. In 1865 the New York & Boston was absorbed by the Boston, Hartford & Erie RR, which in turn became in 1873 the New York & New England RR. The Charles River was finally part of a viable larger system, and carried commuter, through passenger and freight traffic. It formed one of the NY&NE's two main lines into Boston, although it was always the lesser of the two routes.

In 1883 the cash-poor NY&NE sold the initial nine miles of the Charles River RR, from Brookline to Cook Street, to the Boston & Albany. The NY&NE retained trackage rights into Boston, but most through trains coupled to or uncoupled from B&A trains at Cook Street. This segment became part of the B&A's Highland Circuit line, and after 1957, the MBTA's Riverside Light Rail line.

Local interests chartered the Woonsocket & Pascoag RR in 1889 to extend the Charles River from Woonsocket to Pascoag, R.I., where it would meet the Providence & Springfield RR. The extension followed an uncompleted grade built by the New York & Boston in the 1860s. Trains finally ran through to Pascoag in March 1891.

By the time it took over the Charles River in 1898 the New Haven RR found itself with numerous lines out of Boston to the South and Southwest. In order to rationalize this maze of commuter branches the New Haven in November 1906 constructed a four-mile connecting link from Needham Junction, on the Charles River, to West Roxbury, on the New Haven's Dedham Branch. This enabled Charles River trains to run to Boston without using the B&A.

Service on the Charles River declined in the 1920s. Through trains from Woonsocket to Boston (via West Roxbury) last ran in 1926, and all passenger service beyond Bellingham Junction ended four years later. Passenger service was discontinued between Needham Junction and Bellingham Junction in July 1938 but was restored in March 1940. Cutbacks and abandonments followed, until by 1967 the tracks were gone beyond Millis and passenger service was provided only between Needham Junction and Needham Heights and on the West Roxbury Extension. Reconstruction of the Boston & Providence main line into Boston caused the suspension of all service on this route from October 1979 to October 1987. Since 1982 the Bay Colony RR has operated freight service east of Medfield Junction. Conrail provided freight service between Medfield Junction and Millis until 1987, when the Bay Colony took over this service as well. The Providence & Worcester RR has operated the remaining three miles of the Pascoag Extension between Slatersville and Woonsocket since 1973.

The Charles River had but one branch. In 1879 a two-mile line was built from Charles River station to Ridge Hill Farms, the site of a recreational hotel. Regular passenger service was provided summers only for several years, ending around 1885. The NY&NE abandoned the line in 1889.

Sources: Baker, *Formation*, 4, 13, 45-47; Brown, "Charles River Line"; Harlow, *Steelways*, 198-99; Humphrey and Clark, *Boston's Commuter Rail*, 43-47; Nelligan, "Mr. Kneiling, Meet Messrs. Goss and Munson"; Poor, *History*, 110; 199 I.C.C. 697; 224 I.C.C. 50; 247 I.C.C. 93.

67. Norfolk County

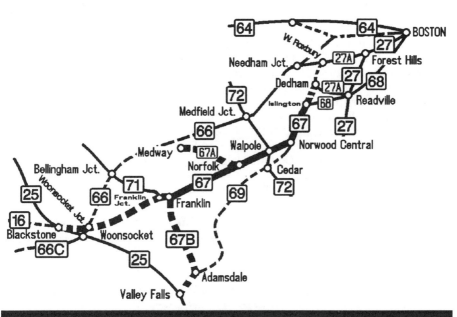

0	Dedham, MA	10	Highland Lake (Campbells) (Campbells Pond)
1	Islington (South Dedham) (West Dedham)	11.5	Norfolk (North Wrentham)
1.5	Ellis	13	City Mills
2.5	Norwood (South Dedham) (Nahatan)	16	Franklin
		16.5	Franklin Jct.
3	Norwood Central (Dedham Middle)	19	Wadsworths (Wadsworth)
4	Winslows (Durfees) (South Dedham & East Walpole)	21	Bellingham (South Bellingham)
5	Windsor Gardens	22.5	Woonsocket Jct. (Mill River)
6	Plimptonville (Tiltons) (Plymptons)	25	Blackstone, MA
7.5	Walpole		
9	West Walpole		

67A. Medway Branch

0	Norfolk (North Wrentham), MA
2	Rockville
4	Medway, MA

67B. Valley Falls Branch

0	Franklin, MA
4	West Wrentham, MA
5	Grants Mills, RI
7	Diamond Hill
8	Arnolds Mills
9	Abbotts Run, RI
11	Adamsdale Jct., MA
12	Adamsdale, MA
13	Cumberland Mills, RI
13.5	Valley Falls, RI

BUILT: 1847-49; Medway Branch, 1852; Valley Falls Branch, 1877; Islington-Dedham rebuilt 1890.

OPERATORS: *Norfolk County,* 1849-53; *Boston & New York Central,* 1853-55; *Boston & Providence,* 1855-57; *East Thompson,* 1857-58; *Norfolk County,* 1858-67; *Boston, Hartford & Erie,* 1867-75; *New York & New England,* 1875-95; *New England,* 1895-98; *New York, New Haven & Hartford,* 1898-1968; *Penn Central,* 1969-76; *Conrail,* 1976- ;*MBTA (commuter passenger),* 1973- .

DAILY PASSENGER TRAINS: *1869:* 6 (Islington-Blackstone), *1893:* 12 (Islington-Blackstone), *1919:* 8 (Islington-Blackstone), *1935:* 12 (Islington-Blackstone), *1950:* 8 (Islington-Blackstone) *1960:* 8 (Islington-Blackstone) *1971:* 8 (Islington-Franklin), *1981:* 16 (Islington-Franklin), *1994:* 30 (Islington-Franklin Jct.). Passenger service ended Dedham-Islington, ca. 1867, restored in 1880s and after 1890, discontinued 1904; Valley Falls Branch, 1930; Blackstone-Franklin, 1966. Restored Franklin-Franklin Jct., 1988.

ABANDONMENTS: ; Dedham-Islington, 1883; Blackstone-Franklin Jct., 1969; Medway Branch, 1864; Valley Falls Branch (Franklin-Adamsdale Jct., 1941; Adamsdale Jct.-Valley Falls, 1963).

In 1846 the Walpole RR was chartered to build a railroad from Dedham (on a branch of the Boston & Providence) seven miles to Walpole. A

An outbound MBTA commuter train pauses at Walpole in August 1992. The station at Walpole was built to serve the Mansfield & Framingham, as well as the Norfolk County line, which cross each other here at grade.

second company, the Norfolk County RR was chartered the year following to continue the route to Blackstone. The two companies were merged a few months later under the name of the Norfolk County RR. Construction was soon under way and the line was opened in its entirety in the spring of 1849.

The Boston & New York Central, a weak railroad with strong ambitions, took over the Norfolk County in December 1853. In January 1855 it opened its own route into Boston via Dorchester (the Midland RR), giving the Norfolk County better access to the city. Through service was offered via this route from Boston to New York, using the Norwich & Worcester RR to reach steamers on Long Island Sound. Unfortunately, various difficulties led to frequent suspensions of service on this line over the next few years.

In August 1855 the mortgage trustees of the Norfolk County took back control of the railroad and leased it for two years to the Boston & Providence. Following a year's lease to the East Thompson RR the trustees decided to operate the line themselves, and it continued under independent operation until December 1866, when it was leased to the Boston, Hartford & Erie (which did not begin operating the line until the following February). It served as the main line in and out of Boston for the BH&E, a role it retained when that railroad became the New York & New England RR in 1875. Between 1873 and 1881 the route was double tracked between Islington and Walpole, and by 1882 to Franklin. One of New England's legendary passenger trains, the New York-Boston *New England Limited*, popularly called "The White Train," ran on this route between 1891 and 1895.

Because the Midland RR route from Islington to Boston was frequently out of service, the Norfolk County had relied on its original Islington-Dedham track to reach Boston via the Boston & Providence's Dedham branch. Once the Boston, Hartford & Erie took over, however, the Midland route went into permanent operation, and the Islington-Dedham track became a seldom-used branch. In 1881 the NY&NE built a branch to Dedham from the Midland, and in 1883 the Dedham-Islington track was abandoned.

Under the New Haven RR, which took over the Norfolk County in 1898, the Norfolk County continued to see both long distance and commuter passenger trains. Service between Boston, Hartford, and

Waterbury was provided over this route until a hurricane in August 1955 took out track in Connecticut, permanently severing the line.

Commuter service continued between Blackstone and Boston until April 1966, when the New Haven was given permission to discontinue these trains. Since the outer towns served by this line lay outside the MBTA, the railroad would only continue them with local subsidies. Blackstone and Bellingham would not pay, and the route was cut back to Franklin. Three years later the line west of Franklin Junction was abandoned, leaving Franklin the terminus of freight and passenger service. In 1988 a new commuter station was opened at Forge Park three miles beyond Franklin on the Milford & Woonsocket line.

When the Norfolk County opened in 1849 it bypassed the town of Medway. Local investors obtained a charter to build a short branch line to connect their town to the Norfolk County. This line, the Medway Branch RR, was opened December 1852. The opening of the Charles River RR through Medway in 1861 eliminated the need for the Medway Branch, and the line was abandoned in 1864.

In 1875 a group of citizens of Franklin raised funds to build a rail line from their town thirteen miles south to Valley Falls, R.I. The Rhode Island & Massachusetts RR was completed in September 1877 and operated by the NY&NE as a branch of the Norfolk County. The NY&NE used it to operate through passenger service between Boston and Providence, but it was hardly competitive with the Boston and Providence. The New Haven occasionally found it useful as a detour when the Boston & Providence main line was not in service. The branch was ultimately abandoned in 1941 and the rails removed in 1942, except for the final two miles between Adamsdale Junction and Valley Falls, which long had served as an extension of the Walpole & Wrentham branch. These survived for another twenty years. The Valley Falls Branch right of way is now used by a gas pipeline.

Sources: Baker, *Formation*, 58; Cornwall and Smith, *Names First*, 16, 90; Humphrey and Clark, *Boston's Commuter Rail*, 43-47; Ozog, "Another Way to Boston"; Poor, *History*, 133; 189 I.C.C. 85; 242 I.C.C. 296.

68. Midland

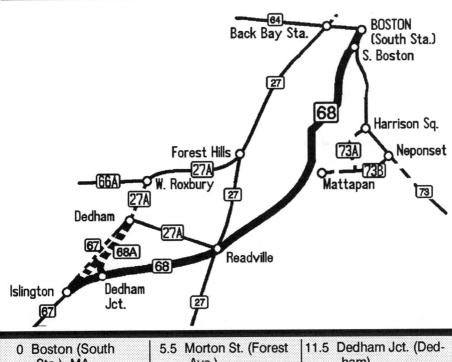

0 Boston (South Sta.), MA	5.5 Morton St. (Forest Ave.)	11.5 Dedham Jct. (Dedham)
0.5 South Boston	6 Blue Hill Ave. (Mattapan)	12 Islington (South Dedham)(West Dedham) (Springvale), MA
1.5 South Bay Jct.		
2.3 Cottage St. (Roxbury)	6.5 Rugby	
2.5 Uphams Corner (Dudley St.) (Stoughton St.)	7 River St.	
	8 Fairmount (Hyde Park)	**68A. Dedham Branch**
3 Bird St.	8.5 Glenwood Ave.	0 Dedham Jct./Islington, MA
4 Mt. Bowdoin	9 Readville	
4.5 Harvard St. (Carltons)	10 Ashcroft (Oakdale)	1.5 Dedham, MA
	10.5 Endicott (Elmwood) (East St.)	
5 Dorchester	11 Rust Craft	

BUILT: 1854-55; Dedham Branch, 1881, 1890.
OPERATORS: *Boston & New York Central, 1855-57; East Thompson, 1857-58; Boston & New York Central, 1858; Midland, 1858; Not operated, 1858-66;*

Boston, Hartford & Erie, 1867-75; *New York & New England,* 1875-95; *New England,* 1895-98; *New York, New Haven & Hartford,* 1895-1968; *Penn Central,* 1969-76; *Conrail,* 1976- ; *MBTA (commuter passenger),* 1973- .

DAILY PASSENGER TRAINS: *1869:* 8, *1893:* 36, *1919:* 11, *1936:* 6 (17 Readville-Islington), *1950:* 8 (Readville-Islington), *1960:* 9 (Readville-Islington), *1971:* 13 (Readville-Islington), *1981:* 18 (Boston-Readville, 77), *1992:* 8 (Boston-Readville, 49). Passenger service Boston-Readville suspended 1938-40; ended 1944, restored 1979. Dedham Branch service suspended 1884-88, ended 1899 (via Dedham Jct.) and 1904 (via Islington).

ABANDONMENTS: Dedham Branch, 1884; reopened 1888; abandoned 1932.

The Midland RR received a charter in 1850 to build from Boston to a connection with the Norfolk County RR at West Dedham (later Islington). The Midland would provide the Norfolk County with its own access to Boston, instead of having to use the Boston & Providence. In December 1853 the still unbuilt Midland was consolidated with the Norfolk County and another unbuilt Connecticut company to form the Boston & New York Central RR.

The B&NYC finally completed the Midland in January 1855, and immediately began to use it for through passenger trains. Six months later, however, operation of the Midland halted when Dorchester residents obtained an injunction on the grounds that its grade crossings were dangerous and should be replaced with bridges. The Midland remained out of service until the injunction was lifted in December 1856.

Despite its grandiose ambitions, the B&NYC was a marginal railroad. In March 1857 the Midland, along with the rest of the B&NYC, was transferred to the East Thompson RR, which operated the line for one year. A new Midland RR succeeded the B&NYC in 1858. By this time the line apparently was out of service or at best, operated infrequently.

Over the next few years the bankrupt Midland changed hands, but was not operated or was in service only briefly. In 1863 it was acquired by the Boston, Hartford & Erie RR, which hoped to revive the old B&NYC system. Attempts were apparently made to reopen the Midland in April 1866 from Boston to Readville, but the line was not in operation a few months later. In December the Trustees of the Norfolk County RR finally agreed to lease their line to the BH&E and the

Midland finally appears to have resumed full operation early in 1867 in conjunction with the Norfolk County.

The Midland provided the BH&E (and after 1875, the New York & New England) with direct access to Boston. Crack passenger trains like the New York-Boston *New England Limited*, popularly called "The White Train," ran on this route. Following its takeover by the New Haven RR in 1898, however, the Midland declined in importance. Most traffic used the New Haven's primary Boston access, the Boston & Providence, and the Midland was reduced to a branch. In 1899 Connecticut though trains were shifted onto the Boston & Providence at Readville, leaving only a few Boston-Readville and Boston-Franklin trains. These were discontinued in July 1938 but restored two years later. Remaining commuter service on the Midland between Boston and Readville ended in March 1944.

The short segment between Readville and Islington continued to serve both though and commuter passenger trains. Through service

Penn Central Alco locomotives pull a freight through Readville in March 1971.

to Connecticut ceased in 1955, but the commuter trains (Boston-Blackstone until 1966; since then, Boston-Franklin) have continued ever since. Passenger service made a surprising return to the Boston-Readville portion of the line in November 1979, when the start of the massive reconstruction of the Boston & Providence line between Readville and Boston caused all trains from that line, both commuter and Amtrak Northeast corridor trains, to detour onto the Midland. This continued until the completion of the MBTA/Amtrak's new Boston & Providence line in 1987. By this time commuter service on the Midland had become popular enough to justify its continuation.

In 1881 the NY&NE constructed a short branch to Dedham, closely paralleling the old Dedham-Islington route of the Norfolk County RR, which was out of service (it was removed in 1883). This branch, which provided direct access to Boston, was intended to compete with the B&P's Dedham Branch, but without success. Service was discontinued in 1884, but restored by order of the state railroad commission in 1888. In 1890 the NY&NE built a short connecting track from the branch to Islington (in effect, the west leg of a wye), for the use of trains from the Old Colony's Walpole & Wrentham line then under construction. When the New Haven RR took over in 1898, it had no use for what amounted to four branches to Dedham, and passenger service between Dedham Junction and Dedham ceased in September 1899, and from Islington in 1904. By the time the line was formally abandoned in 1932 in had been out of service for many years. Part of the right of way was used to construct Route 1.

Sources: Baker, *Formation*, 58; *Chronological History of the New Haven Railroad*; Cornwall and Smith, *Names First*, 16, 69, 114; Humphrey and Clark, *Boston's Commuter Rail*, 43-47; Poor, *History*, 133.

69. Walpole & Wrentham

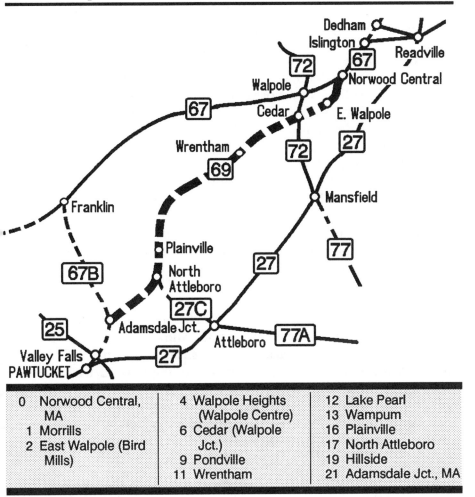

0	Norwood Central, MA	4	Walpole Heights (Walpole Centre)	12	Lake Pearl
1	Morrills	6	Cedar (Walpole Jct.)	13	Wampum
2	East Walpole (Bird Mills)	9	Pondville	16	Plainville
		11	Wrentham	17	North Attleboro
				19	Hillside
				21	Adamsdale Jct., MA

BUILT: 1890-1903.

OPERATORS: *Old Colony,* 1890-93; *New York, New Haven & Hartford,* 1893-1968; *Penn Central,* 1969-76; *Conrail,* 1976- .

DAILY PASSENGER TRAINS: *1893:* 9 (Norwood Central-North Attleboro), *1919:* 8, *1935:* 2. Passenger service ended 1938.

ABANDONMENTS: Adamsdale Jct.-Plainville, 1963; Plainville-Wrentham, 1965; Wrentham-East Walpole, 1976.

In December 1890 the Old Colony RR completed a thirteen-mile branch line from Walpole Junction, on its Mansfield & Framingham line, to North Attleboro. This extended rail service to Plainville and Wrentham, towns previously bypassed by railroads. In February 1892 another six miles from Walpole Junction to Norwood Junction (Norwood Central) were added. The Old Colony obtained operating rights over a short section of the New York & New England's Norfolk County line between Dedham and Norwood Central. Using an existing branch line between North Attleboro and Attleboro and then the Old Colony's Boston & Providence line, the OC now had a second Boston-Providence route.

Although the New Haven RR soon took over both the Old Colony and the NY&NE, it continued to run Boston-Providence trains over this route. In June 1903 it built yet another extension, from North Attleboro to Adamsdale, where it connected with other NYNH&H lines to Valley Falls and Providence. This enabled the New Haven to abandon operation of its Attleboro-North Attleboro branch, which was being operated under an expensive lease.

Service on the Walpole & Wrentham declined after the First World War, and all passenger service ended in 1938. The line between Adamsdale and Wrentham was abandoned in 1963 and 1965. (About five miles of track between Wrentham and a concrete plant near Plainville remained in service as an industrial spur until 1976.) By the early 1970s the only active shipper on the line beyond East Walpole was at Wrentham, and this only saw once a week service. The line between Wrentham and East Walpole was abandoned in 1976 at the time Penn Central departed from the rail business. The remaining portion of the line, from Norwood Central to East Walpole, was transferred to Conrail, which has continued to provide freight service.

Sources: *Chronological History of the New Haven Railroad*; Humphrey and Clark, *Boston's Commuter Railroads*, 31; U.S. Railway Association, *Final System Plan*, 2:150-52; U.S. Railway Association, *Preliminary System Plan*, 2:514-16.

70. Grafton & Upton

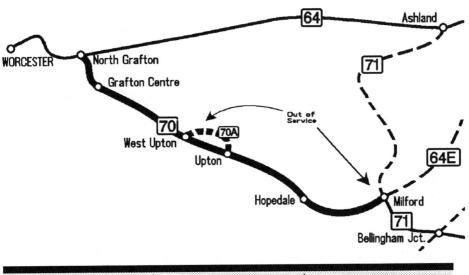

0	North Grafton, MA	7	West Upton	11	Hopedale
3	Grafton Centre	8	Upton	12	Milford, MA

BUILT: 1874-90; Upton Loop, 1898-99.
OPERATORS: *Grafton Centre, 1874-88; Grafton & Upton, 1888- .*
DAILY PASSENGER TRAINS: *1893:* 10, *1919:* Hourly electric cars.
Passenger service on Upton Loop ended 1919; remainder of line 1928.
ABANDONMENTS: Upton Loop, 1919.

The Grafton Centre RR was chartered in 1873 to build a three-foot gauge railroad from North Grafton, on the busy main line of the Boston & Albany RR, three miles south to Grafton Centre. This narrow gauge line was completed in August 1874. With one steam dummy locomotive its only rolling stock (an early type of self-propelled rail car) it was in every sense a small operation.

Most of its business consisted of hauling passengers. In 1887 the Grafton Centre converted to standard gauge and embarked on a program of expansion. Changing its name to the Grafton & Upton RR in 1888, the line was extended to West Upton in March 1889 and to

Milford in May 1890. In 1898 the railroad constructed a loop track through Upton Center from Brook Street in Upton to Williams Street, West Upton.

In 1901 and 1902 the railroad strung trolley wire above its tracks and leased trolley cars from the Milford & Uxbridge Street Railway to provide frequent passenger service. The Grafton & Upton acquired the Upton Street RR at this time, a local trolley operation that used the loop track. Freight trains operated at night using steam locomotives, with the largest customer being the Draper Corp. of Hopedale, then one of the world's largest manufacturers of textile machinery. (Draper eventually came to own the G&U.) In 1919 electric locomotives were acquired and steam operation ended.

Trolley service ended on the Upton Loop on June 1, 1919, and the tracks were removed. Passenger service over the rest of the G&U

The G&U purchased 30-ton electric locomotive number 8 from General Electric in 1918, and it continued to haul freight until replaced by diesels in 1946. (Photo courtesy Walker Transportation Collection, Beverly Historical Society & Museum.)

continued until 1928, when the Milford & Uxbridge Street Railway scrapped its trolleys and converted to buses, leaving the G&U without passenger equipment. Passenger business no longer offered enough incentive for the G&U to seek replacement for the trolleys, and all passenger service ended August 31. Electric freight continued until 1946, when diesel locomotives arrived and the wires came down.

The Grafton & Upton has continued to operate as an independent short line. Until 1968 it interchanged with two different railroads, the B&A (New York Central) at North Grafton and the New Haven at Milford; but since the merger of both into the Penn Central the interchange at Milford has been discontinued, and the line between there and Hopedale has not been in use. Until 1988 the tracks between Grafton Centre and Hopedale were used to provide access to an engine house at Hopedale. Since then the Grafton & Upton has regularly operated only between North Grafton and Grafton Centre. In the winter of 1993-94 service between North Grafton and West Upton was restored to enable the railroad to deliver rock salt.

Sources: Armstrong, *Railfan's Guide*, 31; Campbell, "Grafton & Upton"; Cornwall and Smith, *Names First*, 44; Hilton and Due, *Electric Interurban Railways in America*, 322; Lewis, *American Short Line Railway Guide*, 53.

71. Milford & Woonsocket

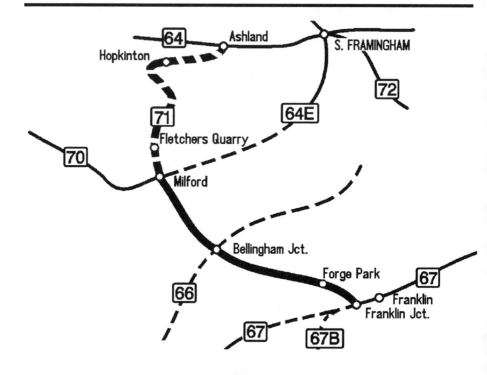

0 Franklin Jct., MA	8 Milford	13 Hayden Rowe
2 Unionville	9 Fells Ave.	15 Hopkinton
2.5 Forge Park	10 North Milford	20 Ashland, MA
5 Bellingham Jct.	(Fletchers Quarry)	
6 South Milford	11 Darlings	

BUILT: 1868-83.

OPERATORS: *Providence & Worcester, 1868-83; Milford & Woonsocket, 1883-87; New York & New England, 1887-95; New England, 1895-98; New York, New Haven & Hartford, 1898-1968; Penn Central, 1969-76; Conrail, 1976-.*

DAILY PASSENGER TRAINS: *1893:* 3 (10 Franklin-Milford), *1919:* 0 through trains (2 Franklin-Milford, 2 Milford-Ashland), *1935:* 5 (Franklin Jct.-Bellingham Jct.), *1994:* 31 (Franklin Jct.-Forge Park). Passenger service ended 1920. Restored Bellingham Jct.-Franklin Jct., 1926, discontinued 1938. Operated two months 1940. Restored Franklin Jct.-Forge Park, 1988.

ABANDONMENTS: Hopkinton-Ashland, 1938; North Milford-Hopkinton, 1953; Fells Ave.-North Milford, 1959; Milford-Fells Ave., ca. 1981.

Although the Milford & Woonsocket RR was chartered in 1855, it did not complete its three-mile line between Bellingham Junction and Milford until August 1868. This short branch gave Milford access to the Boston, Hartford & Erie's Charles River line at Bellingham Junction. Bypassed by through routes, Milford had been served by a branch of the Boston & Worcester RR since 1848. On completion, the Milford & Woonsocket was leased by the Providence & Western, probably to prevent it from falling into the hands of a competitor.

In 1869 the Hopkinton Branch RR was chartered to build a line south from the Boston & Albany main line at Ashland to Hopkinton. The following year this was consolidated with another unbuilt railroad, the Hopkinton & Milford, to form the Hopkinton RR. In December 1872 this line was opened from Ashland to Milford, where it connected with the Milford & Woonsocket. The Providence & Worcester RR leased the Hopkinton when it opened.

In 1882 the Milford, Franklin & Providence RR was chartered to extend the Milford & Woonsocket from Bellingham Junction to Franklin, on the main line of the New York & New England. This was completed in August 1883. At this time the Providence & Worcester lease ended, and the Milford & Woonsocket resumed independent operation. The M&W assumed operation of the Milford, Franklin & Providence, as well as the Hopkinton, which it purchased in May 1884. The Milford & Woonsocket now had a twenty-mile through line from Ashland to Franklin Junction. In September 1887 the entire Milford & Woonsocket operation was leased to the NY&NE, which in 1898 was absorbed by the New Haven.

The Milford & Woonsocket was a minor railroad in a region served by numerous rail lines. The old Hopkinton RR segment was particularly vulnerable. By 1914 passenger service between Ashland and Milford was reduced to a mixed train, and even this was eliminated by 1920. In 1938 the New Haven sought to abandon the entire line north of Milford, but the I.C.C. would allow only the tracks between Hopkinton and Ashland to be torn up. (They were removed in 1940.) Hopkinton still shipped and received feed, grain, coal, hay, and lumber, but after the Second World War trucks took what was left of this traditional rail traffic. Most of the remainder of the Hopkinton RR was abandoned in 1953, although the tracks from Milford to Fletchers Quarry in North Milford continued in service until 1959, and the final three-quarters of a mile to Fells Avenue, Milford, survived until around 1981.

Passenger service declined to a pair of mixed trains before being discontinued entirely in 1920. Between 1926 and 1938 the New Haven routed some Boston to Franklin trains via the Charles River line and over the M&W between Bellingham Junction and Franklin Junction. (This was also operated briefly in 1940.) Passenger service returned to the first two and a half miles of the M&W in 1988 when the MBTA opened a new passenger station at Forge Park to serve as the new terminus of the Franklin line. Freight service between Franklin and Milford has continued until the present, with Milford generating most of the traffic along this branch.

Sources: *American Railroad Manual, 1874*, 54; Baker, *Formation*, 4, 46, 72; Humphrey and Clark, *Boston's Commuter Rail*, 44-46; Ozog, "Another Way to Boston"; U.S. Railway Association, *Final System Plan*, 2:152-53; U.S. Railway Association, *Preliminary System Plan*, 2:516; 224 I.C.C. 503.

72. Mansfield & Framingham

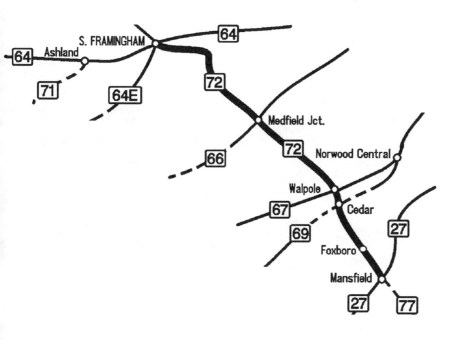

0	Framingham (South Framingham), MA	8	Medfield Jct.	16	South Walpole
		9	Medfield	17	North Foxboro
		13	Walpole	18	Foxboro
4	Sherborn	14	Cedar (Walpole Jct.)	20	Foxvale (Rockdale)
6	South Sherborn			21	Mansfield, MA

BUILT: 1867-70.

OPERATORS: *Boston, Clinton & Fitchburg,* 1870-76; *Boston, Clinton, Fitchburg & New Bedford,* 1876-79; *Old Colony,* 1879-93; *New York, New Haven & Hartford,* 1893-1968; *Penn Central,* 1969-76; *Conrail,* 1976- .

DAILY PASSENGER TRAINS: *1893:* 9, *1919:* 6. Passenger service ended 1933.

ABANDONMENTS: None.

The Foxboro Branch RR had been chartered in 1862 to construct a line from Mansfield to Walpole, but the line had never been built. In

Walpole Station, at the diamond where the Norfolk County route crosses the Mansfield & Framingham, as it appeared in August 1992. This view looks down the M&F toward Mansfield. Walpole is still an active MBTA station on the Franklin line, but passenger trains have not been operated on the M&F since 1933.

1867 the Mansfield & Framingham RR was incorporated to build a railroad from South Framingham to Walpole and was consolidated with the rights of the Foxboro Branch to extend to Walpole. By 1870, if not earlier, the Mansfield & Framingham had come under the control of the Boston, Clinton & Fitchburg RR, which operated a small system of railroads between Fitchburg, Worcester, and Framingham. The BC&F was seeking to expand, and the Mansfield & Framingham would be its vehicle.

When the Mansfield and Framingham was completed in the spring of 1870 it was immediately leased to the BC&F. The line was a success, giving the BC&F a major link between the central and southeastern regions of Massachusetts. The BC&F grew into the Boston, Clinton, Fitchburg & New Bedford in 1876, and in 1879 it became part of the Old Colony RR system, which had obtained a regional monopoly over southeastern Massachusetts. The Old Colony was swallowed, in turn, by the New Haven RR in 1893.

Passenger service did not survive the Great Depression, but the Mansfield & Framingham has remained an important freight route. It enables traffic from southeastern Massachusetts to reach the Boston & Albany main line, as well as enabling north- and east-bound traffic to bypass Boston. Today virtually all remaining rail traffic from the Old Colony region uses this Conrail branch. Special MBTA trains operating from both Boston and Providence to Foxboro Stadium use three miles of this route.

Sources: Baker, *Formation*, 6, 25, 35; *Chronological History of the New Haven Railroad*; Fisher, *Old Colony*.

73. Old Colony

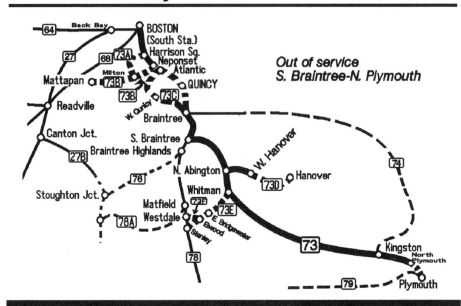

Out of service
S. Braintree-N. Plymouth

0	Boston, MA
0.5	South Boston
1	South Bay Jct.
2	Crescent Ave.
3	Savin Hill
4	Harrison Square (Dorchester)
4.5	Popes Hill
5	Neponset
6	Atlantic
6.5	Norfolk Downs
7	Wollaston Heights (Wollaston)
8	Quincy
9	Quincy Adams (South Quincy)
10	Braintree
11	South Braintree
15	South Weymouth
18	North Abington
19	Abington

21	Whitman (Whitman Jct.)(South Abington)
23	North Hanson
25	South Hanson (Hanson)
26	Burrage (Bournetown)
27	Monponsett
28	Halifax
29	Silver Lake
30	Plympton
33	Kingston
35	North Plymouth (Cordage) (Seaside)
37	Plymouth, MA

73A. Shawmut Branch

0	Harrison Square, MA
0.5	Fields Corner
0.8	Melville
1	Shawmut
1.2	Centre St.
1.5	Ashmont
2	Cedar Grove
3	Milton (Milton Lower Mills), MA

73B. Milton Branch

0	Neponset, MA
1.5	Granite Bridge
2	Milton (Milton Lower Mills)
2.5	Central Ave.
3	Mattapan, MA

73C. Granite Branch

0	Atlantic, MA
0.5	Montclair
2	East Milton
3	West Quincy
3.5	Granite
4	Washington St.
4.5	Printing Plant
5	Braintree, MA

73D. Hanover Branch

0	North Abington, MA
1	Rockland (Emerson)
3	West Hanover (Circuit St.)
4	Winslows Crossing
6	South Hanover (Perry)
7	Curtis Crossing
8	Hanover, MA

73E. Bridgewater Branch

0	Whitman (Whitman Jct.) (South Abington), MA
1	Whitman/Washington St.
2	Browns (Northville)
4	East Bridgewater
6	Elmwood (Joppa)
7	Stanley (Bridgewater Jct.), MA

73F. Elmwood Branch

0	Elmwood (Joppa), MA
2	Westdale (Satucket), MA

BUILT: 1844-46; Granite Branch, 1826, 1848,1871-76; Milton Branch, Bridgewater Branch, 1847; Gravel Branch, 1848; Hanover Branch, 1868; Shawmut Branch, 1872;; Elmwood Branch, 1885.

OPERATORS: *Old Colony*, 1845-54; *Old Colony & Fall River*, 1854-62; *Old Colony & Newport*, 1862-72; *Old Colony*, 1872-93; *New York, New Haven & Hartford*, 1893-1968; *Penn Central*, 1969-76; *Conrail*, 1976- ; *Bay Colony*, 1982-90.

DAILY PASSENGER TRAINS: *1869:* 6, *1893:* 13, *1919:* 17, *1935:* 12 (Boston-Braintree, *1950:* 6. Passenger service ended 1959. Service discontinued on Bridgewater Branch, Elmwood Branch, 1925; Shawmut Branch, 1926; Milton Branch, 1929; Granite Branch, 1940; Hanover Branch (West Hanover-Hanover, 1938; North Abington-West Hanover, 1948.

ABANDONMENTS: Neponset-Atlantic, 1960; Atlantic-Quincy, 1966; Quincy-Braintree, 1978; North Plymouth-Plymouth, ca. 1980; Shawmut Branch, Milton Branch (Central Ave.-Mattapan, 1929); Bridgewater Branch (Whitman-East Bridgewater, Elmwood-Stanley, 1937; East Bridgewater-Elmwood, 1976); Hanover Branch (West Hanover-Hanover, 1938); Granite Branch (Atlantic-Montclair, ca. 1849 (rebuilt); Atlantic-East Milton, 1941; East Milton-West Quincy, 1952; West Quincy-Granite, 1953; Granite -Washington St., 1956; Washington St.-Printing Plant, 1973); Elmwood Branch, 1976.

Inhabitants of southeastern Massachusetts proudly recalled that the land they inhabited had once been the Plymouth Colony, the first in New England. The memory of the Old Colony, as it was called, lived on long after the colony itself was merged into Massachusetts Bay in 1691. It seemed appropriate when a charter was granted in 1844 to build a railroad from Boston to Plymouth that the name selected was not the Boston & Plymouth but the Old Colony RR.

Plymouth citizens were apparently the most active in promoting this railroad. Built mostly along the coast, the line was not difficult to construct, and the railroad was completed from a temporary terminus in South Boston to Plymouth in November 1845. The original alignment through South Boston followed today's Old Colony Avenue. Three months later the Old Colony built a temporary station at Lincoln and Beach. This remained the terminus until the spring of 1847 when the line was extended a half mile from South Boston to a new station on Kneeland Street, near the depot of the Boston & Worcester RR. The Old Colony used this station until 1899 when its trains, now operated by the New Haven, were shifted to the new South Station. The new line at first was hampered by competition from coastal ships on the Boston-Plymouth route and by its propensity to build expensive branch lines; but by the 1850s it was profitable.

The Old Colony formed the nucleus of what was to become one of the state's major rail systems. Various other lines were acquired and the name was changed twice before reverting back to Old Colony RR in 1872. As early as 1848 traffic on the Boston to South Braintree portion of the Old Colony was heavy enough to require double tracking, and eventually almost the entire line to Plymouth was two tracks. From 1854 to 1893 the Old Colony operated trains on the left-hand set of tracks, contrary to the practice of nearly all other American railroads.

The first ten miles between Boston and Braintree saw especially heavy traffic, since trains from many other lines used the Old Colony to access Boston; this continued after the New Haven acquired the Old Colony in 1893. By 1913 the route between South Boston and Atlantic featured four tracks. As late as 1935 the section between Boston and Braintree saw more than a hundred daily passenger trains. With such heavy volume it is not surprising that two of New England's worst rail accidents occurred on the Old Colony: a derailment caused by a jack left on the tracks at Qunicy on August 19, 1890, killed twenty-three; and a derailment at Wollaston resulting from a mislined switch took twenty-one lives on October 8, 1878.

Even after World War II the Old Colony carried large numbers of commuters, but the railroad did not profit from them. Citing heavy losses, the New Haven in the late 1950s sought to abandon commuter service. Efforts to preserve the line by the state, local communities, and transit advocates were ineffective, and the New Haven ended all Old Colony passenger service on June 30, 1959. The following year the

*Harrison Square in the early 1890s was a busy point on the Old Colony. The tracks to the right of the station are the beginning of the Shawmut Branch to Milton. (*History of the Old Colony Railroad, *1893.)*

drawbridge that carried the tracks across the Neponset River near Atlantic station burned and was not repaired, leaving the Old Colony severed.

In 1965 the New Haven sold the Old Colony right of way between South Boston and South Braintree to the MBTA, which used it to construct an extension of its existing Dorchester rapid transit line. This new route, part of the MBTA's Red Line, was opened to Quincy Center in 1971 and to Braintree in 1980. The MBTA route included a freight track from South Boston to Neponset, but the line south of the Boston Globe plant in Dorchester is no longer in use. When Red Line construction began in 1966 freight service between Atlantic and Quincy was "temporarily" suspended but it was never restored. Freight service was provided from Braintree to Quincy until 1978. Since the late 1970s the final two miles of the Old Colony between North Plymouth and Plymouth have been out of service and the rails removed. The remaining portion of the Old Colony from Braintree to North Plymouth was operated for freight by the Bay Colony RR from 1982 until the summer of 1990 when a lack of business brought operations to an end (Conrail still operates between South Braintree and Braintree). In the early 1990s the state decided to restore commuter rail service on the Old Colony, and reconstruction of the line for this purpose has begun. The MBTA should be operating at least as far as Kingston before the end of the century.

The Old Colony built several short branch lines. Of greatest historic interest was the former Granite Branch, which incorporated the right of way of one of New England's earliest railroads. (The long-standing claim that this was the nation's first rail line, however, is not true.) In 1826 the Granite RR was chartered and constructed to transport granite from a quarry in West Quincy to a dock on the Neponset River in Milton. Here the stone was loaded onto ships for transport to the site of the Bunker Hill Monument in Charlestown. Horses provided the motive power. The Granite RR continued to operate under horse power into the 1860s. The Old Colony built its so-called Gravel Branch, a half mile of track from Atlantic to Montclair, near the Granite RR, in 1848, but abandoned it almost immediately. Finally, in 1870, the Old Colony purchased the Granite RR and rebuilt its tracks into a standard gauge steam railroad. A connection was built along the route of the old Gravel Branch in 1871 and in 1873 the Granite RR was extended southward from West Quincy to still another gravel pit near Braintree. Finally, in June 1876 the branch was extended back to the Old Colony main line just north of Braintree, making the Granite Branch into a loop. Commuter passenger service on the loop lasted until 1940, but freight trains operated until 1952, when a series of abandonments began. By 1973 only a half mile between Braintree and the Patriot-Ledger printing plant remained. Since 1976 this has been served by Conrail.

In December 1847 the Dorchester & Milton Branch RR opened its 3½-mile line from Neponset to Mattapan, the Old Colony at once taking it under lease as its Milton Branch. In December 1872 the Old Colony built another branch line, the so-called Shawmut Branch, from Harrison Square on the main line 2½ miles to the Milton Branch near Milton. The Boston Elevated Railway bought the right of way and used it for a rapid transit line to Ashmont. Service on the Shawmut Branch ended in September 1926, but continued on the Mattapan Branch until New Haven commuter trains were replaced by trolleys from Ashmont to Mattapan. This line opened in 1929, and has operated as an extension of the Boston-Ashmont rapid transit line (today's MBTA Red Line). Freight service on the Milton Branch between Neponset and Central Avenue continued until recently, but the line is no longer used.

The Bridgewater Branch was built in 1847. A short extension, the Elmwood Branch, was constructed in 1885 to enable Old Colony trains to reach Brockton from Boston by way of Abington and the Bridgewater Branch. The Elmwood Branch always was operated as a wye in conjunction with the Bridgewater Branch. In 1937 the portions of the branch between Whitman and East Bridgewater and between Elmwood and Stanley were abandoned, leaving only the section between Westdale and East Bridgewater in service, with access only from the Fall River line utilizing the Elmwood Branch. The line was last used by the Penn Central in 1976, and in 1982 it was sold to the state. Although long out of service the rails remain.

The eight-mile Hanover Branch was chartered in 1864 as the Hanover Branch RR. Opened in July 1868, it was owned by Hanover businessmen. It was operated as an independent short line until June 1887 when it was sold to the Old Colony. In 1938 it was cut back to West Hanover, and passenger service ended ten years later. It was operated for freight by the Bay Colony until around 1989, but it is no longer in service.

Sources: Baker, *Formation*, 25-26; Clark, *South Shore*; Fisher, *Old Colony*; Harlow, *Steelways*, 35; Humphrey and Clark, *Boston's Commuter Rail*, 95-96; Kirkland, *Men, Cities, and Transportation*, 1:100-01, 253; Lee, "America's Very First Railroad"; U.S. Railway Association, *Final System Plan*, 2:143-45; U.S. Railway Association, *Preliminary System Plan*, 2:506-08; 90 I.C.C. 3; 221 I.C.C. 453; 224 I.C.C. 681; 244 I.C.C. 303.

74. South Shore

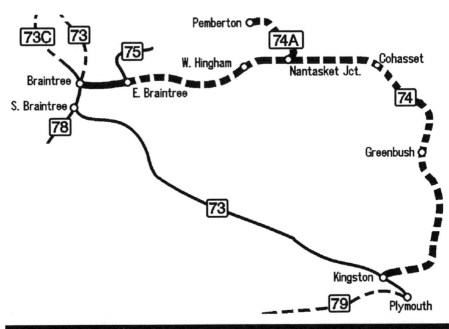

BUILT: 1847-49, 1871-74; Nantasket Branch, 1880.

OPERATORS: *Old Colony RR*, 1849-54; *South Shore RR*, 1854-77; *Duxbury & Cohasset*, 1871-78; *Old Colony*, 1877-93; *Nantasket Beach*, 1880-86; *New York, New Haven & Hartford*, 1893-1968; *Penn Central*, 1969-76; *Conrail*, 1976- ; *Bay Colony RR*, 1982-83 .

DAILY PASSENGER TRAINS: *1869:* 12 (Braintree-Cohasset), *1893:* 7 (25 Braintree-Cohasset), *1919:* 12, *1935:* 2 (29 Braintree-Cohasset), *1950* 8 (Boston-Greenbush). Passenger service ended Greenbush-Kingston, 1939; remainder of line, 1959. Regular passenger service ended on Nantasket Branch, 1932 (some summer excursion trains to Nantasket until 1936).

ABANDONMENTS: Greenbush-Kingston, 1939; Nantasket Jct.-Greenbush, 1962; Nantasket Branch, 1937; West Hingham-Nantasket Jct., 1979; East Braintree-West Hingham, 1983.

The South Shore RR was chartered in 1846 to build a line from the Old Colony RR at Braintree to Cohasset. Construction began in November 1847 and the line was completed in January 1849. The Old Colony RR operated the South Shore until 1854, when it began to operate independently.

A separate railroad, the Duxbury & Cohasset, was chartered in 1867 to extend the South Shore's route southward along the coastline. The towns of Marshfield and Duxbury were persuaded to invest $225,000 of municipal funds. During the summer of 1871 the line opened from Cohasset to South Duxbury, and in June 1874 it reached the Old Colony main line at Kingston. The Duxbury & Cohasset was backed by both the South Shore and the Old Colony but operated independently of either. The line fared poorly when the economy collapsed in the mid-1870s. In April 1877 the Old Colony acquired the South Shore, and the following year, the Duxbury & Cohasset as well.

In July 1880 the Nantasket Beach RR opened a line along the shore from in the town of Hull, without direct connection to any other railroad (steamers provided access). The following year a connection was made with the South Shore in Hingham (Nantasket Junction). The line was unsuccessful and finally closed in 1886. The Old Colony leased the line in 1888 and reopened it. When the New Haven took over the South Shore system in 1893 it soon developed ambitious plans for these lines. In June 1895 the Nantasket Beach line, now double tracked, was strung with trolley wire and streetcar service introduced. This was one of the first of many American electrified steam railroad lines.

In July 1896 the electrification was extended to the South Shore proper, from Nantasket Junction to East Weymouth, using a third rail (also a first for a surface rail line). The third rail was extended to Braintree in 1898 and to Cohasset in 1899, with the intention of

North Weymouth station around 1890. (History of the Old Colony Railroad, *1893.*)

possibly extending this to other New Haven commuter lines out of Boston. Electrification of the South Shore was short-lived: the third rail between Braintree and Cohasset was removed in 1906. The Nantasket Beach trolley operation carried heavy traffic until the Great Depression. The wires were removed in 1932, although occasional Sunday excursion trains were operated under steam to Nantasket during summers for several years. The line itself was finally abandoned in 1937.

The South Shore was one of the rare lines in New England whose passengers generated more revenue than did freight. Boston-bound commuters predominated along the northern half of the line, while south of Scituate most of the traffic came from summer visitors and property owners in coastal villages. Although commuter traffic remained heavy even during the 1930s, excursion and weekend travel to the shore resort towns had largely shifted to the highways. Passenger service south of Greenbush had dwindled to a single round trip train, and freight trains ran but three times a week. In 1937 the New Haven sought to abandon the line south of Greenbush altogether, but after howls of protests from commuters and the towns affected, the I.C.C. rejected the request. A year later, however, the great hurricane of September 1938 caused extensive damage, and the I.C.C. reversed itself. The line was abandoned in 1939.

Service on the remainder of the line continued until June 30, 1959, when all passenger trains on the entire Old Colony system were discontinued. Three years later the line was cut back to Nantasket Junction, and the tracks through Cohasset and Scituate removed. After 1982 the Bay Colony RR provided freight service on the remaining

The Nantasket Beach RR operated only between 1880 and 1886. Here locomotive number 1, an inside-connected 4-4-0, poses at the Pemberton Hotel. (Photo courtesy Walker Transportation Collection, Beverly Historical Society & Museum.)

seven miles of the South Shore, but discontinued service the following year. Conrail resumed service on the initial mile of track between Braintree and East Braintree to interchange with the Fore River RR. Today, only the first mile of the South Shore remains in service, although this may change in the near future. Recently the Quincy Bay Terminal RR (successor to the Fore River RR) has reportedly begun operating over the South Shore to interchange with Conrail at Braintree or South Braintree.

For many years proposals have been made to restore rail commuter service to the South Shore. Recently the MBTA and the state of Massachusetts have started work on rebuilding the South Shore and restoring rail commuter service to Greenbush. Still unresolved is how the tracks will pass through Hingham Center, with some local groups calling for a tunnel.

Sources: Baker, *Formation*, 25-26; Fisher, *Old Colony*; Humphrey and Clark, *Boston's Commuter Rail*, 95-96; Kirkland, *Men, Cities, and Transportation*, 2:312; Middleton, *When the Steam Railroads Electrified*, 428; Poor, *History*, 150; 221 I.C.C. 670; 224 I.C.C. 644; 230 I.C.C. 585.

75. Fore River

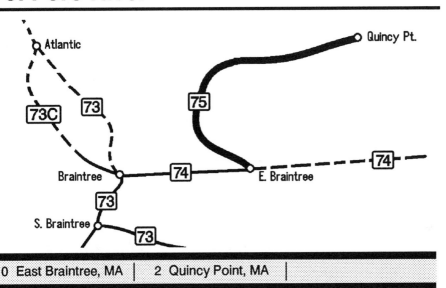

Atlantic

Quincy Pt.

73C 73 75

74

Braintree 74 E. Braintree

73

S. Braintree

73

| 0 East Braintree, MA | 2 Quincy Point, MA |

BUILT: 1902-03
OPERATORS: *Fore River Shipyards,* 1903-19; *Fore River RR,* 1919-91; *Quincy Bay Terminal,* 1991- .
DAILY PASSENGER TRAINS: Freight only.
ABANDONMENTS: None.

Alexander Graham Bell's partner, Thomas A. Watson, had used a fortune amassed in the early telephone industry to enter the shipbuilding business. Armed with a navy contract, Watson purchased land at Quincy Point to build a shipyard. It soon became apparent that the new facility needed rail service, but the New Haven RR, whose South Shore branch came within two miles of the yard, refused to build a branch to serve it.

Watson set out to construct his own railroad. No difficulties were encountered in laying out a route. Unfortunately, Watson sought to keep his business structure informal and unincorporated, and no charter was obtained for the rail line. Without the powers of eminent domain normally enjoyed by a railroad, he was forced to pay dearly for one parcel needed for the right of way. Once the land was obtained, construction proceeded rapidly and the line opened from the connection with the New Haven at East Braintree to the shipyard in June 1903.

In its early years the Fore River was operated as part of the shipyard. Small steam locomotives (some purchased from the New York City Elevated after that line electrified) hauled shipyard materials and coal into the yard. Around 1916 the shipyard and the railroad were acquired by the Bethlehem Steel Corporation. Shipyard activity was busy during the First World War. In order to accommodate the large number of shipyard workers a connection was laid with the Bay State Street Railway's trolley line and wire was strung over part of the Fore River to allow trolleys to access the ship yard. The wires came down soon after the war ended.

In 1919 Bethlehem Steel incorporated the Fore River RR as a separate entity. Business in the shipyard and on the railroad declined after World War I but picked up sharply during the Second World War. Steam locomotives were used exclusively until 1946 when the first diesels arrived. Steam was gone by 1947.

For a time the shipyard was busy, but activity had almost come to a standstill by the early 1960s. In 1963 Bethlehem Steel was on the verge of closing the yard when it suddenly sold the facility—and the Fore River—to General Dynamics Corporation. The new owners were able to secure enough government contracts to keep both the shipyard and railroad in business for many years. In 1986, however, General Dynamics closed the shipyard. Although most of the Fore River RR's business came from the shipyard, the line did serve a few customers outside of the yard, including an oil depot and a soap factory.

In 1987 General Dynamics at last found a buyer—the Massachusetts Water Resources Authority (MWRA), which was looking for land to use in conjunction with the $6-billion Boston Harbor cleanup project. The railroad was conveyed to the MWRA along with the shipyard. In 1991 the MWRA hired the Quincy Bay Terminal Company, a subsidiary of the New England Southern RR of Concord, N.H., to operate the line. In addition to the soap factory, the Quincy Bay Terminal carries MWRA sludge and occasionally brings in construction materials.

Sources: Armstrong, *Railfan's Guide to New England,* 30; Kyper, "Diminutive High Iron"; Nazarow, "From Fore River to Quincy Bay."

76. Dighton & Somerset

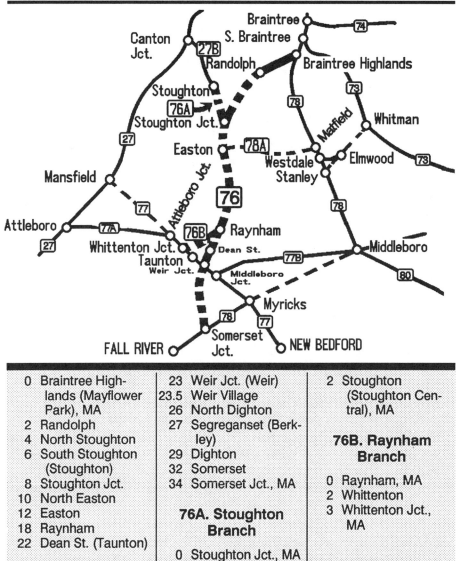

0	Braintree High-lands (Mayflower Park), MA	23	Weir Jct. (Weir)	2	Stoughton (Stoughton Central), MA
2	Randolph	23.5	Weir Village		
4	North Stoughton	26	North Dighton		**76B. Raynham Branch**
6	South Stoughton (Stoughton)	27	Segreganset (Berkley)		
8	Stoughton Jct.	29	Dighton	0	Raynham, MA
10	North Easton	32	Somerset	2	Whittenton
12	Easton	34	Somerset Jct., MA	3	Whittenton Jct., MA
18	Raynham				
22	Dean St. (Taunton)		**76A. Stoughton Branch**		
		0	Stoughton Jct., MA		

BUILT: 1863-66; Stoughton Branch, 1854-55; Raynham Branch, 1882.

OPERATORS: *Boston & Providence,* 1855-66; *Old Colony & Newport,* 1866-72; *Old Colony,* 1872-93; *New York, New Haven & Hartford* , 1893-1968; *Penn Central,* 1969-76; *Conrail,* 1976- ; *Bay Colony,* 1982- .

DAILY PASSENGER TRAINS: *1869:* 8, *1893:* 18, *1919:* 19 (Taunton-Fall River); 4 (Braintree Highlands-Taunton via Raynham Branch), *1935:* 21 (Stoughton-Raynham); 3 (Braintree Highlands-Randolph), *1950:* 6 (Stoughton-Raynham). Passenger service ended Raynham-Weir Jct., ca. 1916; Randolph-Stoughton Jct., ca. 1927; Weir Jct.-Somerset Jct., 1932; Braintree Highlands-Randolph, 1938; Stoughton-Raynham, Stoughton Branch, Raynham Branch, 1958.

ABANDONMENTS: Somerset Jct.-Dighton, Dean Street-Raynham, 1937; Randolph-Stoughton Jct., 1938; Raynham Branch, 1958; Raynham-Easton, 1966; Dighton-Weir Village, 1971; Stoughton Jct.-Easton, 1976; Stoughton Branch, 1976; Weir Jct.-Weir Village, 1982.

The Dighton & Somerset had its beginning in 1854 when the Easton Branch RR was chartered to extend an existing branch line of the Boston & Providence RR. This four-mile branch between Stoughton and North Easton was completed in May 1855 and immediately leased to the Boston & Providence.

In 1863 the Dighton & Somerset RR was chartered with authority to build a new railroad from Taunton to Somerset by way of Dighton. The following year the charter was amended to allow the Dighton & Somerset to build all the way north to Randolph or Braintree. This would enable it to build parallel to the Fall River line of the Old Colony & Newport RR and presumably divert a good portion of its traffic. The Old Colony quickly moved to eliminate this threat, and by the end of 1865 had it acquired the Dighton & Somerset.

It might be assumed that the Old Colony had no interest in completing the Dighton & Somerset, but such was not the case. The Old Colony opened the line in its entirety in September 1866. Between Stoughton Junction and North Easton it used the route of the Easton Branch RR, which the Old Colony took over from the Boston & Providence at this time. The remaining two miles of the line between the new line and Stoughton were retained as a freight branch; after the Old Colony took over the Boston & Providence in 1888 this line was double tracked and upgraded to form part of the through route to Boston. At Somerset Junction the Dighton & Somerset connected with the Old Colony's Fall River line to reach Fall River. The Dighton & Somerset gave the Old Colony a second Boston-Fall River route that was five miles shorter than the Fall River line, as well as access to Taunton and Somerset, which became an important coal port.

For many years this served as the primary Boston to Fall River route under the Old Colony, and after 1893, under the New Haven RR. Around 1882 through passenger trains were rerouted between

*Designed by H. H. Richardson, the Old Colony station at North Easton has been an architectural landmark for more than a century. (*History of the Old Colony Raiload, *1893.)*

Raynham and Weir Junction, enabling the New Haven to consolidate all passenger service in one Taunton depot. By 1895 the *Fall River Boat Train* was the only passenger train regularly using the original main line between Raynham and Weir Junction, and about twenty years later all passenger service on this segment ended. The Dighton & Somerset went into decline after the First World War. In the mid-1920s the New Haven rerouted Dighton & Somerset trains onto the Stoughton Branch and on to Boston by way of Canton Junction and the Boston & Providence. Passenger service between Randolph and Stoughton Junction ended and the tracks were eventually removed altogether. After

*Stoughton Central station circa 1890. (*History of the Old Colony Railroad, *1893.)*

1932 the tracks between Raynham and Dean Street, Taunton, were out of service, with all trains diverted onto the Raynham Branch. Passenger trains and through freights no longer used the tracks between Weir Junction and Somerset Junction after 1932 when the New Haven chose to abandon a long drawbridge across the Taunton River rather than make expensive repairs.

Between the 1930s and 1976 the remaining portions of the Dighton & Somerset lost passenger service and then were abandoned altogether, so that today only two short segments remain in service. Conrail continues to provide freight service over the initial mile of the line out of Braintree Highlands; the Bay Colony RR operates another mile in Taunton between Weir Junction and Dean Street. Apart from these the Dighton & Somerset is a ghost railroad.

Sources: Baker, *Formation*, 24-25, 30-31; Fisher, *Old Colony*; Humphrey and Clark, *Boston's Commuter Rail*, 95-96; U.S. Railway Association, *Final System Plan*, 2:149-50; U.S. Railway Association, *Preliminary System Plan*, 2:513; 221 I.C.C. 395, 421, 453; 224 I.C.C. 681.

77. New Bedford & Taunton

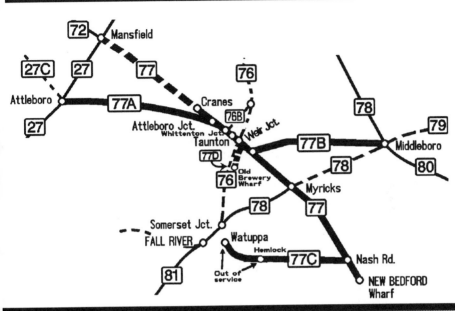

0 Mansfield, MA	
4 Norton	
7 Cranes	
8 Attleboro Jct. (Standish)	
9 Whittenton Jct.	
11 Taunton (Taunton Central)	
12 Weir Jct.	
12.2 *Weir Village*	
13 Middleboro Jct. (Cotley Jct.)	
17 Myricks	
19 Howlands	
22 East Freetown	
24 Brayleys	
28 Achushnet	
29 Nash Rd. (Weld St.)	
30 New Bedford	
31 New Bedford Wharf, MA	

77A. Attleboro Branch

0 Attleboro Jct., MA
2 Meadowbrook (Norton Furnace)
5 Barrowsville
6 Chartley
7 Bearcroft
9 Attleboro, MA

77B. Middleboro & Taunton Branch

0 Middleboro Jct. (Cotley Jct.), MA
2 East Taunton
4 Chaces
5 North Lakeville
6 Turnpike
8 Middleboro, MA

77C. Fall River Branch

0 Nash Rd. (New Bedford), MA
0.5 Mt. Pleasant
3 North Dartmouth
5 Hicksville
6.5 Westport Factory
8 Hemlock
10 North Westport
11 Flint Village (Flint)
12 Watuppa (Fall River), MA

77D. Weir Branch

0 *Weir Village, MA*
1 Old Brewery Wharf, MA

BUILT: 1835-40; Weir Branch, 1847; Middleboro & Taunton Branch, 1856; Attleboro Branch, 1871; New Bedford Wharf extension, 1873; Fall River Branch, 1875.

OPERATORS: *Taunton Branch,* 1836-40; *Taunton Branch-New Bedford & Taunton (joint operation),* 1840-74; *New Bedford,* 1874-76; *Boston, Clinton, Fitchburg & New Bedford,* 1876-79; *Old Colony,* 1879-93; *New York, New Haven & Hartford,* 1893-1968; *Penn Central,* 1969-76; *Conrail,* 1976- ; *Springfield Terminal,* 1982-84; *Bay Colony,* 1984- ; *Amtrak (passenger, summers),* 1987- .

DAILY PASSENGER TRAINS: *1869:* 7, *1893:* 16, *1920:* 22, *1935:* (Mansfield-Taunton, 1; Taunton-New Bedford, 16), *1951:* 6 (Saturdays only). Regular passenger service ended 1958. Cape Cod trains Attleboro-Middleboro, summers only, 1958-64. Amtrak New York-Hyannis trains operate summer weekends, Attleboro-Middleboro, 1987- . Passenger service discontinued on Fall River Branch, 1918; Attleboro Branch, Middleboro & Taunton Branch, 1958. Weir Branch freight only.

ABANDONMENTS: Cranes-Mansfield, 1965; Weir Branch, ca. 1873.

When the Boston & Providence RR opened in 1835 it came within eleven miles of the growing industrial town of Taunton. That year the Taunton Branch RR received a charter to build a rail line from Mansfield on the B&P to Taunton. Construction began that year and the line was completed in August 1836, making it one of the earliest railroads in New England.

In 1838 the Old Colony RR was chartered to extend the line to New Bedford. This railroad was renamed the New Bedford & Taunton in 1839 (the Old Colony name would later be taken by a different railroad) and completed to the whaling port of New Bedford in July 1840. The Taunton Branch and the New Bedford & Taunton were operated as a single railroad, although each retained its separate corporate identity. In 1874 they were finally consolidated under the name New Bedford RR.

In July 1873 the New Bedford & Taunton extended its line in New Bedford one mile to reach the wharves. Here it now connected with Long Island Sound steamers to New York and served a large coal receiving facility. The railroad had dreams of making New Bedford a major Atlantic port, unloading coal and shipping out western grain via the Boston & Albany or even the new Hoosac Tunnel. It was soon consolidated with a group of central Massachusetts railroads under the name of the Boston, Clinton, Fitchburg & New Bedford RR, giving it direct routes to Fitchburg and Lowell. This entire system was acquired by the Old Colony RR in 1879 and ultimately became part of the New Haven system in 1893.

Two branches were added to the system by the Old Colony. The Weir Branch RR was chartered and built in 1847, extending a single mile from the main line at Weir Village along the Taunton River to the Old Brewery Wharf. It served a number of factories along the river bank, and was apparently operated only for freight. It became super-

New Bedford station a century ago. (History of the Old Colony Railroad, *1893*).

fluous after 1866 when the Old Colony & Newport opened its Dighton & Somerset line through Weir Junction. This line ran parallel to the Weir Branch about a thousand feet to the west and served the same customers. The Weir River Branch was abandoned around 1873. The other line, the nine-mile Attleboro Branch from Attleboro Junction to Attleboro, was opened in August 1871 to provide better access to Providence and vicinity.

More branches were acquired by the Old Colony and operated in conjunction with the New Beford & Taunton. The Taunton & Middleborough RR had been chartered in 1848 to construct a line east from Taunton but it had never been built. In 1853 its charter was revived by the Middleborough & Taunton RR, which opened its eight-mile line from Middleborough Junction in Taunton on the New Bedford & Taunton RR to Middleboro in July 1856. Providing a connection to Cape Cod, the Middleborough & Taunton was successfully operated for many years as an independent short line until the Old Colony acquired it in April 1874.

In 1874 the Fall River RR was chartered to build between New Bedford and Fall River. This line was opened in December 1875 and leased to the Old Colony RR in 1882. The rails reached Watuppa station in Fall River but never connected with the Old Colony's Fall River line. (Watuppa is on a cliff far above the Old Colony's Fall River depot.) Several daily round trip passenger trains between Watuppa and New Bedford were operated in the 1890s before a parallel trolley line carried off most of the passenger traffic. Afterwards the line was primarily operated for freight, and passenger service was reduced to a daily mixed train before being eliminated altogether in 1918.

After 1900 the New Haven found itself with a dense network of trackage in Southeastern Massachusetts, most of it redundant; but the New Bedford & Taunton system held up well. Regular passenger service ended 1958, but summer-only Cape Cod trains used the line from Attleboro to Middleboro until 1964. In 1987 Amtrak restored summer-only New York to Cape Cod service, running weekend trains over this same route. (This was still operating as of the summer of 1994.) The only significant abandonment, the old main line between Mansfield and Cranes, resulted from a grade crossing elimination project in Mansfield in 1955 which severed the route. For some years the trackage in Mansfield was served from Taunton, but in 1965 the line between Mansfield and Cranes was abandoned.

Aside from that segment, Conrail continues to make use of nearly the entire system. Conrail suspended service on the Fall River Branch between Flint Village and Watuppa in 1980. Two years later it turned over operation of the branch west of Westport Factory to the new Bay Colony RR (which in turn subcontracted this operation to the Springfield Terminal RR until 1984). Since 1987 the end point of service has been Mid-City Scrap, just west of the old Hemlock station.

Sources: Baker, *Formation*, 25, 36-37; *Chronological History of the New Haven Railroad*; Fisher, *Old Colony*; *History of the Old Colony Railroad*, 58; Poor, *History*, 138-39.

78. Fall River

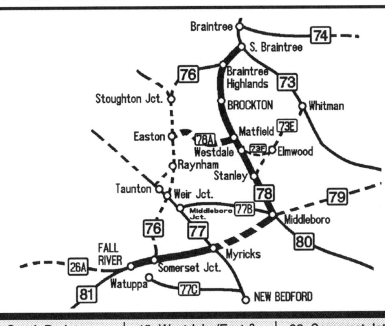

BUILT: 1844-46; West Bridgewater Branch, 1888.

OPERATORS: *United Corp.*, 1845-46; *Fall River*, 1846-54; *Old Colony & Fall River*, 1854-63; *Old Colony & Newport*, 1863-72; *Old Colony*, 1872-93; *New York, New Haven & Hartford*, 1893-1968; *Penn Central*, 1969-76; *Conrail*, 1976- ; *Cape Cod & Hyannis (passenger, summers only)*, 1984-88.

DAILY PASSENGER TRAINS: *1869:* 4 (8, S. Braintree-Middleboro), *1893:* 6 (17, S. Braintree-Middleboro), *1919:* 4 (31 S. Braintree-Middleboro), *1935:* 22 (S. Braintree-Middleboro), *1950:* 11 (S. Braintree-Middleboro). Passenger service ended Middleboro-Myricks, 1931; Myricks-Fall River, 1958; remainder of line, 1959. Passenger service ended on the West Bridgewater Branch 1925. Between 1984-88 the Cape Cod & Hyannis RR operated Braintree-Cape Cod service over the S. Braintree-Middleboro portion of this line, summers only.

ABANDONMENTS: Middleboro-Myricks, 1937; West Bridgewater Branch (W. Bridgewater-Eastondale, 1938; S. Easton-Eastondale, 1940; Easton-S. Easton, 1954; Matsfield-W. Bridgewater, 1963).

In 1844 the powerful Borden and Durfee families of Fall River obtained a charter for the Fall River Branch RR to build a line from their city to a rail connection at Myricks or Taunton. The interests of these clans included textile factories, iron forges, and steamships, all of which would benefit from a rail connection. At first their plan seems to have been to use the Boston & Providence RR (via the Taunton Branch RR) to reach Boston, but they soon struck a more satisfactory deal with the Old Colony RR. Two additional railroads, the Randolph & Bridgewater and the Middleboro, were chartered to extend the line north to South Braintree on the Old Colony.

In March 1845 the three uncompleted railroads were merged to form the "United Corporation of the Middleboro RR Corporation with the Fall River Branch RR Company and the Randolph & Bridgewater RR Corporation." Under this unwieldy banner the first segment of line between Fall River and Myricks opened the following June. In April 1846 the United was renamed—mercifully—the Fall River RR. That December the line was completed to South Braintree. The following spring the Old Colony and Fall River jointly began a daily *Boat Train* from Boston to Fall River, where it connected with steam boats for New York City. For many years this was the most popular Boston-New York route, and the *Boat Train* continued to run daily for ninety years (although over various routes after 1880).

In 1854 the Fall River and Old Colony railroads merged to form the Old Colony & Fall River RR, and the Fall River formed the backbone of the Old Colony system until it became part of the New Haven system in 1893. The opening of the shorter Dighton & Somerset line in 1866, however, diverted many through trains off of the Fall

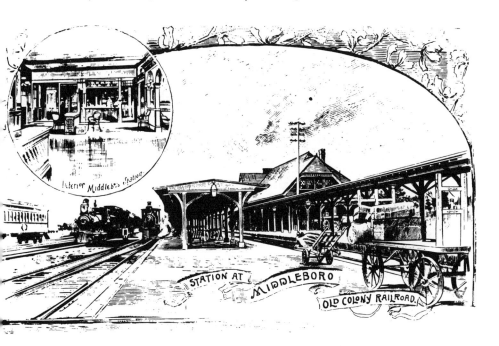

Middleboro station, the hub of the Fall River line, around 1890.
(History of the Old Colony Railroad, *1893*).

River. But the line from South Braintree to Middleboro also carried Boston-Cape Cod trains, and enough traffic used this route to justify adding a second track on this segment in 1883-84.

Under New Haven control after the turn of the century the Fall River was increasingly operated as two separate lines, South Braintree-Middleboro and Myricks-Fall River. In 1931 the New Haven ended Boston-Fall River service via the Fall River, which meant the elimination of the remaining trains on the Middleboro-Myricks segment. Freight service was suspended the year following, and the Middleboro-Myricks section was abandoned altogether in 1937. Remaining Boston-Fall River trains now used the Boston & Providence rather than the Old Colony to reach Boston. When the New Haven abandoned the Dighton & Somerset line between Taunton and Somerset Junction in

1932 all Fall River trains were routed onto the old Fall River RR between Myricks and Fall River. Passenger trains ran for many years until the end of Fall River service in September 1958 and South Braintree-Middleboro service in June 1959.

After fire destroyed a bridge over the Neponset River near Atlantic station on the Old Colony in 1960, the Fall River became the only access route for rail traffic moving in and out of the South Shore/Plymouth County region. Although rail freight from Plymouth, Braintree, Quincy, and other South Shore towns is not heavy, what remains takes the Fall River.

In June 1984 the Cape Cod & Hyannis RR restored passenger service to the Fall River between South Braintree and Middleboro and on to Cape Cod. These summer-only trains were only moderately successful, and the elimination of a necessary state subsidy (in the face of a severe state fiscal crisis) prevented their resumption in the summer of 1989. This suspension of service seems temporary given the state's commitment to bringing back commuter trains to the ex-Old Colony system. If all goes according to current plans—and construction has already begun—the MBTA will be operating passenger service to Middleboro before the end of the century.

Sources: Baker, *Formation*, 24-25, 30; Fisher, *Old Colony*; Harlow, *Steelways*, 217-19; Humphrey and Clark, *Boston's Commuter Rail*, 95-96; Poor, *History*, 121; 221 I.C.C. 411; 224 I.C.C. 681; 240 I.C.C. 377.

79. Plymouth & Middleborough

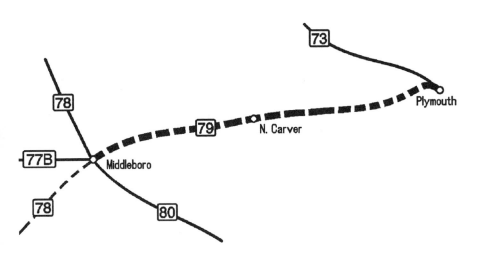

0 Middleboro, MA	5 East Middleboro	11 Darby
3 Nemasket (Put- nams)	(Mt. Carmel) 8 North Carver	16 Plymouth, MA

BUILT: 1890-92.

OPERATORS: *Old Colony*, 1892-93; *New York, New Haven & Hartford*, 1893-1939.

DAILY PASSENGER TRAINS: *1893:* 6, *1919:* 6. Passenger service ended 1927.

ABANDONMENTS: Plymouth-North Carver, 1937; North Carver-Middleboro, 1939.

The venerable town of Plymouth obtained its first rail connection in 1845 when the Old Colony RR opened its line from Boston. Nearly half a century later this remained Plymouth's only rail link, requiring all passenger and freight traffic to be routed by roundabout routes. In response to what was seen as public demand the Old Colony RR in

1890 chartered the Plymouth & Middleborough RR to give Plymouth direct access to Cape Cod, Providence, and the West. The line was completed in December 1892 and leased to the Old Colony RR. A few months later the Plymouth & Middleborough, along with the rest of the Old Colony, became part of the New Haven system.

The new railroad never generated as much traffic as had been anticipated, and it was particularly vulnerable to automobile and truck competition. Passenger service ended in 1927, and what freight traffic Plymouth generated took the Old Colony line. That left only local traffic, which by the 1930s consisted almost entirely of cranberries. In 1934 the New Haven discontinued freight service between Plymouth and North Carver (the only affected station, Darby, served a population of seventy-five) and abandoned this segment altogether three years later.

After 1934 the line was reduced to a branch line to North Carver, serving cranberry growers. Most of the traffic moved only in October, November, and December. Track conditions had so deteriorated that a 20 mph speed restriction had been put into effect. When the New Haven petitioned to abandon the line in 1938 no one showed up to protest; more and more growers were switching to trucks. The line was abandoned in early 1939, and the tracks were removed by the time of the attack on Pearl Harbor.

Sources: Baker, *Formation*, 32; Cornwall and Smith, *Names First*, 98; Fisher, *Old Colony*; 221 I.C.C. 453; 230 I.C.C. 393.

80. Cape Cod

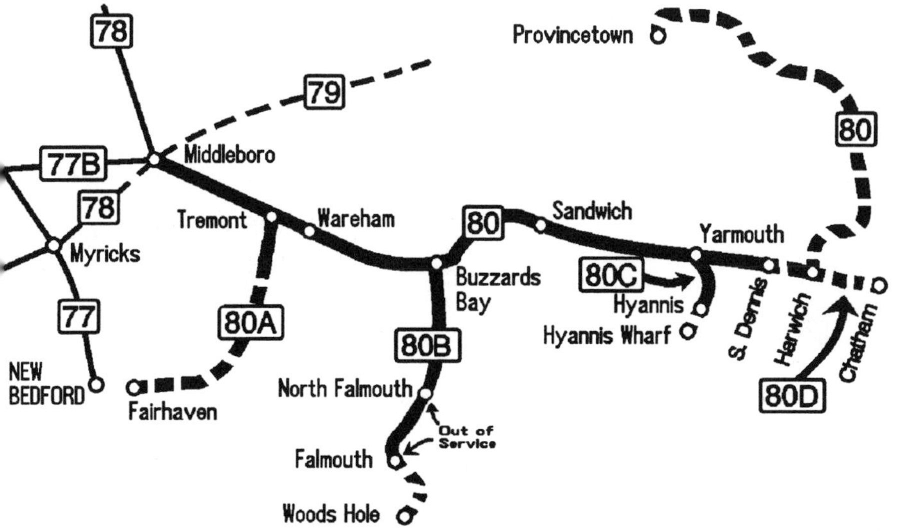

0	Middleboro, MA
5	Rock (Rock Meeting House)
7	South Middleboro
11	Tremont (West Wareham)
13	South Wareham (Burbanks)
14	Parker Mills
15	Wareham
16	Tempest Knob
17	Onset (Agawam) (East Wareham) (Onset Jct.) (Onset Bay) (Onset Beach)
19	Cohasset Narrows
20	Buzzards Bay
21	Bourne (Monument)
24	Bournedale (North Sandwich) (Sampson) (Herring River)
26	Sagamore (West Sandwich)
28	Sandwich (Webster)
31	East Sandwich
35	West Barnstable (Clement)
38	Pond Village
39	Barnstable
41	Yarmouth
44	Bass River (South Yarmouth) (East Yarmouth) (Yarmouth Farm) (North Yarmouth)
47	South Dennis (Halls)
48	North Harwich (Norman)
50	Harwich
52	Pleasant Lake
55	Brewster
58	East Brewster
60	Orleans
63	Eastham
65	North Eastham (Hastings)
69	South Wellfleet
72	Wellfleet
74	South Truro
76	Truro
77	Corn Hill
79	North Truro (Moorland)
83	Puritan Heights
86	Provincetown, MA

80A. Fairhaven Branch	4 Pocasset (Wenaumet)	1 Camp Sta.
	5 Irwin	3 Hyannis
0 Tremont, MA	6 Cataumet	4 Hyannis Wharf, MA
5 Marion	7 North Falmouth	
10 Mattapoisett	(Williams)	**80D. Chatham**
15 Fairhaven, MA	10 West Falmouth	**Branch**
	(Longview)	
80B. Woods Hole	14 Falmouth	0 Harwich, MA
Branch	17 Woods Hole	1 Harwich Centre
	(Woods Holl), MA	3 South Harwich
0 Buzzards Bay, MA		4 South Chatham
1 Gray Gables	**80C. Hyannis Branch**	6 West Chatham
1.5 Cleveland		7 Chatham, MA
2 Monument Beach	0 Yarmouth, MA	
(South Monument)		

BUILT: 1846-73; Hyannis Branch, 1853; Fairhaven Branch, 1852-54; Woods Hole Branch, 1872; Chatham Branch, 1887.

OPERATORS: *Cape Cod Branch,* 1848-54; *Cape Cod,* 1854-72; *Fairhaven Branch,* 1854-60; *New Bedford & Taunton,* 1860-74; *Cape Cod Central,* 1865-68; *Old Colony,* 1872-93; *New Bedford,* 1874-76; *Boston, Clinton & Fitchburg,* 1876-79; *Chatham,* 1887-88; *New York, New Haven & Hartford,* 1893-1968; *Penn Central,* 1969-76; *Conrail,* 1976-82; *Bay Colony,* 1982- ; *Cape Cod & Hyannis (passenger),* 1982-88; *Amtrak (passenger, summer weekends only),* 1987- ; *Cape Cod Scenic (excursion passenger),* 1989- .

DAILY PASSENGER TRAINS: *1869:* 4 (Middleboro-Orleans), *1893:* 4, *1919:* 6, *1935:* 2, *1950* 8 (Middleboro-Hyannis). Passenger service ended Yarmouth-Provincetown, 1938 (restored temporarily 1940); remainder of line 1964; restored, Middleboro-Hyannis, 1982-88; since 1988, summer weekends only. Passenger service ended Fairhaven Branch, 1935; Woods Hole Branch, 1964 (restored 1982-88); Hyannis Branch (Hyannis-Hyannis Wharf, 1931; remainder of branch, 1964; restored, 1982; summers only since 1988); Chatham Branch, 1931.

ABANDONMENTS: North Eastham-Provincetown, 1960; South Dennis-North Eastham, 1965; Chatham Branch, 1937; Hyannis Branch (Hyannis-Hyannis Wharf, 1937); Fairhaven Branch, 1953; Woods Hole Branch (Falmouth-Woods Hole, 1968).

The Cape Cod Branch RR received a charter in 1846 to construct a line from Middleboro (on the Fall River RR) to Sandwich on Cape Cod. The Fall River RR backed the new line, but it never took it over as was apparently the original intention. The initial fifteen-mile segment from Middleboro to Wareham opened in January 1848, and the remainder of the line was completed to Sandwich by May. At first the new railroad did not prosper. Adding to its difficulties was the fact that it reached only the first two towns on the Cape, which were on the north shore, away from the islands of Nantucket and Martha's Vineyard, and the fact that it made only a single connection (with the Fall River RR at Middleboro).

The first problem was addressed when permission was secured in 1850 to extend the Cape Cod Branch RR. A dispute arose over whether the line should turn directly south for the port of Hyannis, where steamers could reach the islands, or swing further to the east to serve Barnstable and Yarmouth and then back to Hyannis. The longer route prevailed, and the rails reached the docks of Hyannis in July 1854. By this time the Cape Cod Branch had been renamed the Cape Cod RR.

For several years Yarmouth was the furthest rails went on the Cape. In 1861 the Cape Cod Central RR was chartered to extend the tracks from Yarmouth to Orleans. The Civil War delayed construction, but this nineteen-mile extension finally opened in December 1865. The Cape Cod Central operated independently for only a short period before being purchased by the Cape Cod RR in 1868. Tracks were extended to Wellfleet in January 1871 and to Provincetown in July 1873. By this time the Cape Cod had become part of the Old Colony RR.

In July 1872 the Woods Hole branch was completed, and the ferries to Nantucket and Martha's Vineyard were moved here from Hyannis. For nearly a century trains from Boston and New York discharged passengers at Woods Hole to the island ferries. After passenger service on the branch ended in 1964 the last few miles into Woods Hole saw little traffic, and the line between Falmouth and Woods Hole was abandoned in 1968. In recent years this right of way has been converted into a popular bicycle trail. The tracks between North Falmouth and Falmouth have been out of service since 1990.

The Fairhaven Branch RR was chartered in 1849 to construct a line from the Cape Cod Branch RR at Tremont to Fairhaven, where steamers would connect it with New Bedford, across New Bedford Harbor. The Cape Cod and the Old Colony RR supported this scheme to expand their traffic. Construction began in 1852 and the line was completed October 1854, including ferry service to New Bedford.

Unfortunately, the line never met expectations, and a few years later the Old Colony and the Cape Cod sold their interest in the line to the New Bedford & Taunton RR. Although it had no direct rail connection (only a ferry) with the rest of the New Bedford & Taunton, it continued to be operated as a part of that system and its successors until 1879, when along with the rest of the Boston, Clinton, Fitchburg & New Bedford system, it once more became part of the Old Colony system. The entire branch was abandoned in 1953, although the first few miles out of Tremont remained in service as a private spur line to a sandpit near Marion until 1976. The tracks are still in place.

The Onset Bay Grove Association built a 1.3-mile rail line from the ex-Cape Cod RR station at Onset Bay to Shell Point, where the association owned a Methodist camp-meeting site. Since the association owned all of the property along the line, it did not incorporate as a railroad. The town of Wareham complained, forcing the association to organize the Onset Bay Grove RR. The following year a new charter was obtained as the Onset Bay Street Railway. Self-propelled ("steam dummy") cars were used, on what was essentially a street car operation. The cars ran summers only until 1890, when the line was sold to a competing horsecar line, which abandoned all but a short section from Onset Avenue to Onset Bay. Horsecars continued to operate on this portion of the line until 1901, when it too was scrapped.

The Chatham RR was chartered by local interests to build a seven-mile branch line from the Cape Cod RR at Harwich to Chatham. The Old Colony agreed to lease the line on completion. Construction began in May 1887 and was finished six months later. Passenger service continued until 1931, and the line was abandoned in 1937. Two of the stations survive.

The construction of the Cape Cod Canal necessitated a major relocation of the tracks between Buzzards Bay and Sagamore and the first mile or so of the Falmouth Branch. This reconstruction, which took place between 1909 and 1911, included a bridge to carry the Cape Cod RR across the canal at Buzzards Bay. When the canal was deepened and widened in the 1930s a new bridge was required, and the present vertical lift bridge opened in 1935. As late as 1955 it was the world's longest vertical lift bridge, with a span of 544 feet and a lift that can clear 130-foot high ships. The bridge is kept raised except when approached by a train.

The automobile cut especially deeply into shore-bound passenger traffic, although rail service persisted longer here than to most other resort areas. By the 1930s the outer cape was served, even during the summer, by only a single daily round trip train (a second was added during summer weekends), and even this was gone before the Second World War. Hyannis was the terminus of passenger service on the Cape until service ended in 1964. By 1965 the tracks were cut back to South Dennis.

Since 1982 freight service on the remaining portions of the Cape Cod has been provided by the Bay Colony RR. In 1982 the Cape Cod & Hyannis RR began operating excursion trains during the summer and fall between Sandwich and Hyannis. In 1984 the state of Massachusetts contracted with the line to extend passenger service to Braintree (the terminus of the MBTA's Red Line rapid transit), to provide alternative transportation for commuters while the Southeast Expressway was being rebuilt. Since 1986 Amtrak has operated New York-Providence-Hyannis service during the summer. (A single train operates from New York Friday night and returns Sunday.) The termination of the state subsidy torpedoed the Cape Cod & Hyannis in February 1989. That summer the Cape Cod RR, a subsidiary of the Bay Colony, began operating excursion passenger service. This has continued in subsequent summers (most recently, 1994), with trains running between Hyannis and Sagamore behind vintage FP10 diesel locomotives.

Sources: Baker, *Formation*, 25, 29-31; Cornwall and Smith, *Names First*, 26; Farson, *Cape Cod Railroads*; Fisher, *Old Colony*; Harlow, *Steelways*, 226-27; Humphrey, "Onset Bay 'Dummy Railroad'"; Trencansky, "Cape Cod Railroad"; U.S. Railway Association, *Final System Plan*, 2:246-49; U.S. Railway Association, *Preliminary System Plan*, 2:509-13; 221 I.C.C. 663; 222 I.C.C. 397; 324 I.C.C. 615.

81. Newport & Fall River

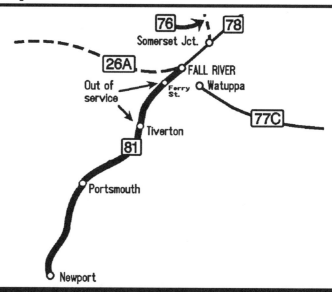

0	Fall River, MA	6	Bristol Ferry	13	Mellville (Port-
1	Ferry St. (Fall	9	Coal Mines		smouth Grove)
	River), MA	11	Portsmouth	16	Middletown (Law-
4	Tiverton, RI	12	Coreys Lane		tons)
4.5	The Hummock			19	Newport, RI

BUILT: 1862-64.

OPERATORS: *Old Colony & Newport*, 1864-72; *Old Colony*, 1872-93; *New York, New Haven & Hartford*, 1893-1968; *Penn Central*, 1969-76; *Conrail*, 1976- ; *Providence & Worcester*, 1982-ca. 1990; *Old Colony & Newport (excursion passenger)*, 1979-.

DAILY PASSENGER TRAINS: *1869:* 6, *1893:* 12, *1919:* 22, *1935:* 4. Passenger service ended 1938. Excursion and dinner train serivice (Newport-Portsmouth) since 1979.

ABANDONMENTS: None.

As early as 1846 the Newport & Fall River RR was incorporated to build a railroad to Newport, R.I. As if to underscore the decline of what once had been New England's second greatest port, it took another eighteen years before the rails reached Newport. Despite strong support from Newport, the powerful Borden family of Fall River blocked the construction of this line, fearing that Fall River would become a way station on a route to the steam ships at Newport.

After many delays the Old Colony & Fall River finally took the project under its wing, merging in 1863 with the uncompleted line (then under construction by a second Newport & Fall River RR, a different company from the first) to form the Old Colony & Newport RR. Under this name the line was opened to Newport in February 1864, although regular operation did not start until December. For a few years Newport did become the terminal for the New York steamers, but in 1869 the ships returned to their previous base in Fall River. Although the boats continued to stop at Newport, allowing passengers the choice of boarding for New York at either Newport or Fall River, most seemed to prefer a longer boat ride and shorter rail journey.

Passenger service finally ended in 1938, and Newport generated only modest rail freight. In 1973 the Penn Central applied unsuccessfully to abandon the segment between Portsmouth and Newport. By this time the line south of Portsmouth was seeing only weekly service and the track was said to be in terrible condition. After Conrail took over from Penn Central in 1976 the line south of Portsmouth was sold to the state of Rhode Island, and the section between Portsmouth and Fall River passed to Conrail. The state in turn leased its portion in 1979 to a new tourist line, the Old Colony & Newport, which has operated summer excursions ever since between Newport and Portsmouth (and occasionally all the way to the bridge at Tiverton). A second tourist operation, the Newport Star Clipper Dinner Train, also shares the tracks with the Old Colony & Newport.

The line between Portsmouth and the Rhode Island-Massachusetts state border was bought by the Providence & Worcester RR in 1982 (with trackage rights over Conrail to reach this isolated segment). A collision with a barge took the bridge at Tiverton out of service for several years ago, and the Providence & Worcester no longer operates this line. For a time the P&W actually paid Conrail to service customers in Tiverton. At present the line between Ferry Street Station in Fall River and the Tiverton Bridge is out of service.

Sources: Baker, *Formation*, 25, 30; Fisher, *Old Colony*; Harlow, *Steelways*, 228; Kirkland, *Men, City, and Transportation*, 1:255-56; Nelligan, "Whatever Happened to the New Haven?"; U.S. Railway Association, *Final System Plan*, 2:483-84; U.S. Railway Association, *Preliminary System Plan*, 2:801-02.

82. Martha's Vineyard

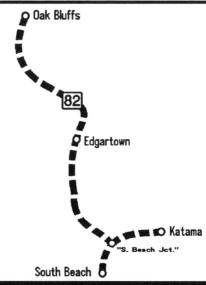

0 Oak Bluffs, MA 5 Edgartown 8 ("South Beach Jct.") 8.5 Katama, MA	82A. South Beach Branch 0 ("South Beach Jct., MA")	0.5 South Beach, MA

BUILT: 1874; South Beach Branch, 1876.
OPERATORS: *Martha's Vineyard*, 1874-96.
DAILY PASSENGER TRAINS: Summers only. Service ended 1896.
ABANDONMENTS: Entire line, 1896.

In 1873 promoters secured a charter for the Martha's Vineyard RR. This three-foot narrow gauge line was opened from the steamer wharf at Oak Bluffs to Katama in August 1874. The initial motive power was a steam "dummy" engine (as was used in some cities), but this soon proved to be too light, and a ten-ton locomotive from Pennsylvania was obtained. In July 1876 a half-mile extension from Katama to South Beach was completed.

The small railroad was modestly profitable in the 1880s. It appears to have been operated only in summer, and it carried no freight except perhaps local express. Most of its business was conveying passengers to and from steamships. Its entire rolling stock consisted of a single locomotive, three passenger cars, and one other car. The railroad was controlled by investors from Boston and its suburbs.

Conditions for this diminutive line worsened in the 1890s. In May 1892 it was sold under foreclosure to the Old Colony RR, which quickly resold it to one Joseph M. Wardwell of Edgartown. In 1894 it showed a $94 profit, but in 1896 it registered a $1,000 loss. With steamers now stopping at South Beach as well as Oak Bluffs, there was little reason for it to continue. Maintenance had deteriorated by July 1896 to the point where the state railroad commissioners declared the line unsafe. The railroad was abandoned and the tracks removed. A century later almost all traces of the line are gone.

Sources: Blackwell, *Tracing the Route*; Cornwall and Smith, *Names First*, 65; Farson, *Cape Cod Railroads*, 111-20; Humphrey and Clark, *Second Section*, 3; Mass. Railroad Commissioners, *Annual Report*, 1875, 1877; *Poor's Manual of Railroads, 1883-98*.

Martha's Vineyard narrow-gauge locomotive number 1, Active, *meets a steamer at the Oak Bluffs wharf in 1881. (Photo courtesy Walker Transportation Collection, Beverly Historical Society & Museum.)*

83. Nantucket

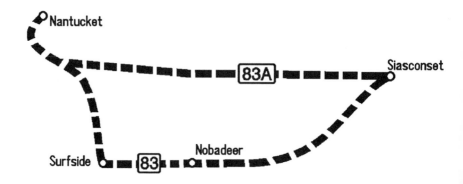

		83A. New Route
0 Nantucket, MA	11 Siasconset, MA	
3 Surfside		0 Nantucket, MA
4 Nobadeer		8 Siasconset, MA

BUILT: 1880-84; relocated, 1895.

OPERATORS: *Nantucket,* 1881-94; *Nantucket Central,* 1895-1905, 1907-09; *Nantucket,* 1910-17.

PASSENGER TRAINS: Summers only, 1881-1905; not operated 1906; operated summer and winter 1907-08; summers, 1908-17; passenger service ended 1917

ABANDONMENTS: Original route, 1894; entire line, 1918.

Philip H. Folger, a Bostonian of Nantucket origins, helped induce other Boston-area investors to launch the Nantucket RR in 1879. From the beginning the plan was to construct a three-foot narrow gauge railroad to provide passenger service for summer visitors and not incidentally, to help promote sales of land owned by the investors. The proposed route was surveyed in August 1879, then resurveyed in February 1880. A charter was obtained in April and construction began the following month.

On July 4, 1881, the Nantucket RR celebrated the opening of its initial segment from Nantucket village to Surfside, where the promoters had launched a major land development. In September the line suspended service, and it was not resumed until the following June. With only a few exceptions, the Nantucket RR continued this pattern of summers-only operation until its demise.

At first the line seemed successful. In 1882 a land boom swept Surfside, with the promoters selling 300 lots. During the 1882-83 off-season a large hotel was moved from the mainland and reconstructed along the ocean a mile east of Surfside, and the tracks were extended to serve it when it opened in 1883. In March 1884 the railroad began to construct an extension along the coastline from the hotel to Siasconset, and this was completed in July. When the railroad first opened it had but one locomotive, the *Dionis*, a Baldwin formerly used in Illinois, and two passenger cars; a second locomotive, formerly owned by the Boston, Revere Beach & Lynn RR and another passenger car were added in 1885.

But expansion appears to have been costly for the railroad, since it failed at the end of the 1886 season. The bondholders took control and reopened the line as usual in the spring of 1887. The continuous pounding of the Atlantic and severe winter storms took their toll on the coastal route, and in 1894 the line between Surfside and Siasconset was abandoned. At the end of the 1894 season the Nantucket RR once more was broke. The property was sold under foreclosure in October.

In March 1895 the Nantucket Central RR was organized to succeed the Nantucket RR. In August the Central opened a new direct route from Nantucket to Siasconset (avoiding the difficult shore line) and abandoned the old line, which had not been used in a year. This was the last narrow gauge common-carrier rail line to be built in southern New England. Without rail service, Surfside rapidly declined, the destruction of the grand hotel in 1899 marking the end of that era. Despite its new route, the Nantucket Central carried even fewer riders than its predecessor. By the end of 1905 it was clearly in trouble, and it never operated at all in 1906. Sold to new owners, it resumed service in July 1907.

In October 1907 the Central replaced steam locomotives and passenger cars with motor rail cars and trailers, and commenced year-round operation, which lasted until the fall of 1908. In May 1909 the Central was bankrupt, and new management brought back the steam locomotives. In 1910 the Central was reorganized as the Nantucket RR (the original name, but a new company). Although improved

The Nantucket Railroad obtained the narrow-gauge 0-4-4T locomotive number 1, Sconset, from the Boston, Revere Beach & Lynn. It is shown here at Siasconset in 1886. (Photo courtesy Walker Transportation Collection, Beverly Historical Society & Museum.)

service in 1913 brought in more revenue, the line could not generate enough profit to satisfy investors. The entry of the United States into the First World War in April 1917 hurt the tourist trade that summer, and when the line shut down in September 1917 for the season it never reopened. The following January the company sold its rails and rolling stock, and the tracks were gone by the summer of 1918.

Sources: Farson, *Cape Cod Railroads*, 123-37; Humphrey and Clark, *Second Section*, 3; Lancaster, *Far-Out Island Railroad*.

Appendix A

Other Southern New England Railroads

Branford Steam RR. In 1903 Louis Fisk, the owner of a trap rock quarry in North Branford, Conn., obtained a charter to build a railroad to serve it. The line began operation in 1914 and has continued to operate ever since. This 6.2-mile long railroad has always been operated privately solely for the transport of rock.

Source: McBride, "Steam in Name Only."

Cape Ann Granite RR. In 1894 this railroad was chartered to construct a 1.5-mile line between the quarries of the Cape Anne Granite Company and Pigeon Cove Harbor in Gloucester, Mass. The road opened in 1895, failed in 1902, and was sold to the New England Granite Company in 1904. It continued to haul granite, its only traffic, for several more years until it was abandoned.

Source: Cornwall and Smith, *Names First*, 22.

Flynt's Granite Branch RR. This obscure two-mile quarry railroad was built in 1875 and operated for several years. Located in the town of Monson, Mass., it connected the granite quarries of William N. Flynt & Co. with the tracks of the New London Northern.

Source: Cornwall and Smith, *Names First*, 41.

Hampden RR. In 1910 the New Haven RR, led by its president, Charles S. Mellen, obtained a charter to construct a link between itself and the Boston & Maine east of Springfield, Mass. At this time Mellen and his banker, J.P. Morgan, controlled both railroads and sought to strengthen the physical connections between them. Construction of the fifteen-mile Hampden RR began in 1911 and the line was virtually completed by 1913. Built to high standards, it extended from Athol Junction on the Boston & Albany (in East Springfield) to a connection with the B&M's Central Massachusetts line two miles east of Bondsville, Mass. By the time the line was completed, however, the B&M and New Haven were no longer controlled by the same interests, and the new management of each road wanted nothing to do with this expensive and now unnecessary line. Neither would operate it, and so the line sat completed but unused for many years. Finally, in 1926, the property was sold to a scrap dealer who removed the rails and structures; he in turn sold the right of way to an electric company in 1929. During the 1950s the Massachusetts Turnpike utilized five miles of the railroad's right of way in Ludlow. Today, many signs of the Hampden can be found along its path.

Sources: Brown, "Unused Hampden Railroad"; Greene, *Hampden Railroad*; Wroe, "Hampden Railroad."

Lancaster RR. This eight-mile long railroad between Lancaster and Hudson, Mass., was completed in 1873, but plans for it to be jointly operated by the Fitchburg RR and the Worcester & Nashua RR were never put into effect. Sold at foreclosure in 1883, the rails were removed sometime afterwards. It never operated for revenue.

Sources: *Central Mass.*, 131-32; Cornwall and Smith, *Names First*, 59.

Southern New England Railway. In 1910 the Grand Trunk Railway of Canada, led by Charles M. Hays, announced plans to construct a new railroad to Providence, R.I., breaking the New Haven RR's monopoly on rail service to that city. The Southern New England

Railway would extend from Palmer, on the Grand Trunk-controlled Central Vermont, seventy-five miles through Southbridge, Webster, Blackstone, and Woonsocket, to Providence. Permission from Massachusetts and Rhode Island was obtained, and the right of way was acquired in 1911. In April 1912 the Grand Trunk's president, Hays, went down with the *Titanic*. Contrary to myth, this did not immediately spell the end to the project; construction did not actually begin until the following month. But the new president of the Grand Trunk did decide to halt construction in November, after the GT struck a deal with the New Haven. A year later construction resumed, only to end for good at the end of 1915, the First World War by now having absorbed all available Canadian and British investment capital. Although about fifty-eight miles of right of way was graded, no steel structures were built or any track actually laid. Today parts of this right of way are visible near Palmer, Southbridge, Webster, and Millville, Mass., the latter the site of what would have been a triple level rail crossing.

Sources: Allen and Wood, "Bit of Railroad Construction in 1910"; Lowenthal, "Southern New England."

Worcester & Shrewsbury RR. This short (2.7-mile) railroad was chartered in 1872 and opened July 31, 1873, the first narrow-gauge railway in Massachusetts. It extended from Union Station (Washington Square) to Lake Quinsigamond. Hauling only passengers and using "steam dummy" locomotives, it was more urban transit line than railroad. Steady lake excursion traffic ensured its success, and locomotives and passenger cars later replaced the dummies. In 1896 it was leased by the Worcester Consolidated Street Railway and four years later converted to a standard-gauge trolley line. This line was used by the Boston & Worcester Street Railway as part of its Boston-Worcester interurban trolley route from 1903 to 1925. The tracks were removed around 1930.

Sources: Cornwall and Smith, *Names First*, 131; Cummings, *Trolleys along the Turnpike*, 10, 36; Humphrey and Clark, *Second Section*, 2.

Appendix B

Historical and Railfan Organizations Active in Southern New England

Boston & Maine Railroad Historical Society, Inc.
P.O. Box 2936
Woburn, MA 01888

Boston Street Railway Association, Inc.
P.O. Box 102
Cambridge, MA 02238

Central New England Railway Association
P.O. Box 8073
Worcester, MA 01614

Mystic Valley Railway Society
P.O. Box 486
Hyde Park, MA 02136-0486

Boston Chapter, National Railway Historical Society
P.O. 252
New Town Branch
Boston, MA 02258

New Haven Railroad Historical & Technical Association
13 Franklin St.
New Haven, CT 06473

Massachusetts Bay Railroad Enthusiasts
P.O. Box 8136
Ward Hill, MA 01835

Railway & Locomotive Historical Society
P.O. Box 1418
Westford, MA 01886

Appendix C

Southern New England Rail Museums and Tourist Railroads

Berkshire Scenic Railway
P.O. Box 2195
Lenox, MA 01240
(413) 637-2210

Cape Cod Railway
252 Main St.
Hyannis, MA 02601
(508) 771-3788

Conneticut Trolley Museum
P.O. Box 360
East Windsor, CT 06088
(203) 627-6540

MassCentral Railroad—The Ware River Line
1 Wilbraham St.
Palmer, MA 01069
(800) 892-3829

Newport Star Clipper
102 Connell Highway
Newport, RI 02840
(800) 834-1556 (RI)
(800) 462-7452 (Outside RI)

Old Colony & Fall River Railroad Museum
P.O. Box 3455
Fall River, MA 02722
(508) 674-9340

Railroad Museum of New England
P.O. Box 97
Essex, CT 06426
(203) 395-0615

Shore Line Trolley Museum
17 River St.
East Haven, CT 06512
(203) 467-6927

Valley Railroad Co.
P.O. Box 452
Essex, CT 06426
(203) 767-0103

For up to date information on tourist railroads and museums see the latest annual *Steam Passenger Service Directory: A Comprehensive Listing of Tourist Railroads and Museums in North America,* available from Great Eastern Publishing, P.O. Box 246, Richmond, VT 05477 (phone 800-356-0246).

Bibliography

Ackerman, John H. "Meet Oscar Greene, Railroad President." *Trains* 27 (June 1967): 46-49.

Adams, Robert B. "Born and Buried in Six Months." *Trains* 19 (September 1959): 34-39.

Allen, Charles F. H., and Wood, William E. "A Bit of Railroad Construction in 1910." *National Railway Bulletin* 43 (no. 6, 1978): 28-33, 46.

Allen, Richard Sanders. "The Great Bore." *Trains* 20 (June 1960): 18-25.

Armstrong, Jack. *Railfan's Guide to New England.* Adams, Mass.: Armstrong, 1987,

Bachelder, J. Leonard. *The Half-Century Limited: Celebrating 50 Years of Rare Mileage: August 26, 1934-August 26, 1984.* Ward Hill, Mass.: Massachusetts Bay Railroad Enthusiasts, 1984.

Baker, George Pierce. *The Formation of the New England Railroad Systems: A Study of Railroad Combination in the Nineteenth Century.* Cambridge: Harvard University Press, 1937.

Blackwell, Walter. *Tracing the Route of the Martha's Vineyard Railroad, 1874-1896.* Miami: Englehart Printing Co., 1971.

Bradlee, Francis B. C. *The Boston and Lowell Railroad, the Nashua and Lowell Railroad, and the Salem and Lowell Railroad.* Salem, Mass.: Essex Institute, 1918.

Bradlee, Francis B. C. *The Boston and Maine Railroad: A History of the Main Route with its Tributary Lines.* Salem, Mass.: Essex Institute, 1921.

Leading a Boston-New York Amtrak train, a massive GG-1 locomotive pauses at Norwalk, Conn., around 1971. (Photo by Roger Yepsen.)

Bradlee, Francis B. C. "The Boston, Revere Beach, and Lynn Narrow Gauge Railroad." *Essex Institute Historical Collections* 57 (1921): 273-80.

Bradlee, Francis B. C. *The Eastern Railroad: A Historical Account of Early Railroading in Eastern New England.* 2nd ed. Salem, Mass.: Essex Institute, 1922.

Brown, C. A. "The Charles River Line." *Shoreliner* 13 (no. 3, 1982): 25-36.

Brown, C. A. "Wood River Branch." *Shoreliner* 19 (no. 3, 1988): 30-39.

Brown, C. A. "The Unused Hampden Railroad." *Shoreliner* 22 (no. 1, 1991): 6-15.

Brown, Ed. "The Gloucester Branch." *B&M Bulletin* 13 (Winter 1983-84): 20-25.

Byron, Carl R. *A Pinprick of Light: The Troy and Greenfield Railroad and Its Hoosac Tunnel.* Brattleboro, Vt.: Stephen Greene Press, 1978.

Cady, John H. *The Civic and Architectural Development of Providence, 1636-1950.* Providence: The Book Shop, 1957.

Campbell, Victor J. "Grafton & Upton." *Railroad Enthusiast* 2 (1964-65): 5-11.

Carman, Barnard R. *Hoot, Toot & Whistle: The Story of the Hoosac Tunnel & Wilmington Railroad.* Brattleboro, Vt.: Stephen Green Press, 1963.

The Central Mass.. N.p.: Boston & Maine Railroad Historical Society, 1975.

Chronological History of the New Haven Railroad. N.p.: New Haven Railroad Athletic Association, [1952?].

Clark, Bradley H. *South Shore: Quincy-Boston.* BSRA Bulletin 12. Cambridge: Boston Street Railway Association, 1972.

Cornwall, L. Peter. "Danbury and Norwalk Railroad: A Successful Enterprise." 5 parts. *Shoreliner* 16 (no. 4, 1984): 22-27; 17 (no. 1, 1985): 6-11; (no. 2, 1985): 6-15; (no. 3, 1985): 6-10; (no. 4, 1985): 23-30.

Cornwall, L. Peter, and Smith, Carol A. *Names First—Rails Later.* Stamford, Conn.: Arden Valley Group, 1989.

Coyne, Terrence E. "The Hoosac Tunnel: Massachusetts' Western Gateway." *Historical Journal of Massachusetts* 23 (Winter 1995): 1-20.

Cramer, F. M. "Hoosac Tunnel." *Trains* 2 (February 1942): 28-37.

Crouch, H. Bentley. "Two Branch Lines Placed out of Service." *B&M Bulletin* 11 (Summer 1981): 6.

Crouch, H. Bentley, and Conard, R. Richard. "The Central Mass. Revisited." *B&M Bulletin* 14 (December 1985): 17-24.

Crouch, H. Bentley, and Frye, Harry A. "Worcester, Nashua & Portland: Part 1, The Phantom Division; Part 3, All Those Branches." *B&M Bulletin* 9 (Summer 1979): 5-14; (Winter 1979-80): 21-33.

Cummings. O. R. *Trolleys along the Turnpike.* BSRA Bulletin 12. Cambridge: Boston Street Railway Association, 1975.

Day, Theodore. "Georgetown, Mass.: Another Rural Junction That Is Now Just a Memory." *B&M Bulletin* 7 (Fall 1977): 5-10.

Ente, Bernard. *New England Railfan Timetable: A Compendium of Railroad Employee Timetables*. Maspeth, N.Y.: Ente, 1994.

Farnham, Elmer F. *The Quickest Route: The History of the Norwich & Worcester Railroad*. Chester, Conn.: Pequot Press, 1973.

Farrell, Joseph F., Jr. *Railfan's Guide to Conrail in Massachusetts*. Worcester: Farrell Railroad Consulting, 1991.

Farson, Robert H. *Cape Cod Railroads: Including Martha's Vineyard and Nantucket*. Yarmouth Port: Cape Cod Historical Publications, 1990.

Fisher, Charles E. *The Story of the Old Colony Railroad*. Taunton: Hack & Son, 1919.

Francis, W. L. "Oscar Greene's 9/10 of a Mile." *Yankee*, June 1966, 26-32.

Galvin, Edward D. *A History of Canton Junction*. Brunswick, Me.: Sculpin, 1987.

Gladulich, Richard M. "Exploring Metro-North." *Railfan & Railroad* 13 (June 1994): 54-67.

Goodwin, Dana D. "Ashburnham Hill." *B&M Bulletin* 6 (Fall 1976): 7-29.

Greene, J. R. *The Hampden Railroad: A Reprint of a 1913 Article with Historical Notes*. Athol: Transcript Press, 1992.

Greene, Shirley M. "The Warwick Railway." *Rhode Island Yearbook*, 1970, pp. 19-20.

Grow, Lawrence. *On the 8:02: An Informal History of Commuting by Rail in America*. New York: Mayflower Books, 1979.

Harlow, Alvin H. *Steelways of New England*. New York: Creative Age Press, 1946.

Henwood, James N. S. *Short Haul to the Bay: A History of the Naragansett Pier Railroad*. Brattleboro, Vt.: Stephen Greene Press, 1969.

Hill, Benjamin T. *Beginnings of the Boston & Worcester Railroad*. Worcester: n.p., 1901.

Hilton, George W., and Due, John F. *The Electric Interurban Railways in American*. Stanford: Stanford University Press, 1960.

History of the Old Colony Railroad. Boston: Hager & Handy, 1893.

Hoisington, Richard A., and Hornsby, E. Robert. "The Amesbury and Merrimac Branches—And Never the Trains Shall Meet." 2 pts. *B&M Bulletin* 10 (Spring 1981): 19-26; (Summer 1981): 7-12.

Humphrey, Thomas J. "The Onset Bay 'Dummy Railroad.'" Unpublished paper.

Humphrey, Thomas J., and Clark, Norton D. *Boston's Commuter Rail: Second Section*. BSRA Bulletin 20. Cambridge, Mass.: Boston Street Railway Association, 1986.

Humphrey, Thomas J., and Clark, Norton D. *Boston's Commuter Rail: The First 150 Years*. BSRA Bulletin 19. Cambridge, Mass.: Boston Street Railway Association, 1985.

Jones, Robert C. *The Central Vermont Railway: A Yankee Tradition*. 6 vols. Silverton, Colo.: Sundance, 1981.

Judkins, Harold I. "I Remember Reformatory Station." *B&M Bulletin* 9 (Spring 1980): 25.

Karr, Ronald Dale. *Lost Railroads of New England*. Pepperell, Mass.: Branch Line Press, 1989.

Kennedy, Charles J. "Commuter Services in the Boston Area, 1835-1860." *Business History Review* 36 (1962): 153-70.

Kennedy, Charles J. "Railroads in Essex County a Century Ago." *Essex Institute Historical Collections* 95 (1959): 137-48.

Kirkland, Edward Chase. *Men, Cities, and Transportation: A Study in New England History, 1820-1900*. 2 vols. Cambridge: Harvard University Press, 1948.

Kistler, Thelma M. *The Rise of Railroads in the Connecticut River Valley*. Smith College Studies in History, vol. 23, nos. 1-4. Northampton: Smith College, 1938.

Kyper, Frank. "The Diminutive High Iron of Massachusetts Bay: The Fore River Railroad Corporation, The Union Freight Railroad Company." *Railway & Locomotive Historical Society Bulletin* no. 120 (1969): 7-29.

Kyper, Frank. *The Railroad that Came Out at Night: A Book of Railroading in and around Boston*. Brattleboro, Vt.: Stephen Greene Press, 1977.

Lancaster, Clay. *The Far-Out Island Railroad: Nantucket's Old Summer Narrow Gauge, 1879-1918*. Nantucket, Mass.: Pleasant Publications, 1972.

Lee, James E. "America's Very First Railroad." *Trains* 35 (April 1975): 28-32.

Lee, James E. "The Dedham Branch." *Shoreliner* 18 (no. 1, 1987): 6-17.

Lee, James E. "More North of Northampton." *Shoreliner* 21 (no. 1, 1990): 31-33.

Lee, James E. "North of Northampton." *Shoreliner* 20 (no. 2, 1989): 7-19.

Lewis, Edward A. *American Short Line Railway Guide*. Strasburg, Pa.: Baggage Car, 1978.

Lewis, Edward A. *The Blackstone Valley Line: The Story of the Blackstone Canal Company and the Providence & Worcester Railroad*. Seekonk, Mass.: Baggage Car, 1973.

Lewis, Henry P. *Ware and the Railroads*. Ware, Mass.: Lewis, 1967.

Long, Henry Follansbee. "The Newburyport and Danvers Railroads: An Account of the Construction and Early Working of Railroads in Central Essex County." *Essex Institute Historical Collections* 46 (1910): 17-55.

Lovett, Robert W. "The Harvard Branch Railroad, 1849-1855." *Railway & Locomotive Historical Society Bulletin*, no. 113 (October 1965): 43-65.

Still in New York Central paint, a Penn Central switcher works the Beacon Park Yard in Boston in March 1971.

Lowenthal, Larry. "The Southern New England—'the Old Grand Trunk.'" *Shoreliner* 21 (no. 2, 1990): 6-11.

Massachusetts Railroad Commissioners. *Annual Reports.*

McBride, Bill. "Steam in Name Only." *Railfan & Railroad* 9 (April 1990): 54-61.

McLaughlin, D. W. "Poughkeepsie Gateway." *Railway & Locomotive Historical Society Bulletin,* no. 119 (October 1968): 6-32.

Merriam, Frank E. "Early Danvers Railroads." *Historical Collections of the Danvers Historical Society* 33 (1945): 50-57.

Middleton, William. *When the Steam Railroads Electrified.* Milwaukee: Kalmbach Books, 1974.

Milmine, Charles. "The History of the C.N.E." In *Central New England Railroad,* pp. 41-53. Salisbury, Conn.: Salisbury Association, 1972.

Mitchell, Walter. "Providence, Warren, Bristol." *Shoreliner* 7 (Winter 1976): 3-13.

Molloy, Peter M., ed. *The Lower Merrimack Valley: An Inventory of Historic Engineering and Industrial Sites.* Washington, D.C.: Historic American Engineering Record, National Park Service, 1976.

Moody, Linwood W. *The Maine Two-Footers: The Story of the Two-Foot Gauge Railroads of Maine*. Berkeley, Calif.: Howell-North, 1959.

Morgan, Philip M. "The Boston, Barre, & Gardner Railroad." *Worcester Historical Society Publications* 3 (1964): 59-68.

Mrazik, John I. "Webster, on the Norwich-Webster Branch." *Shoreliner* 21 (no. 2, 1990): 13-35.

Nazarow, Greg J. "From Fore River to Quincy Bay." *Railfan & Railroad* 13 (May 1994): 48-56.

Nelligan, Tom. "Mr. Kneiling, Meet Messers. Goss and Munson." *Trains* 37 (October 1977): 28-30.

Nelligan, Tom. "The Short Lines of Samuel Pinsly." *Bulletin of the National Railway Historical Society* 34 (no. 3, 1969): 36-41.

Nelligan, Tom. "Whatever Happened to the New Haven?" *Trains* 42 (September 1982): 16-17.

Northey, Richard P. "A Brief History of the Essex Railroad." *B&M Bulletin* 19, no. 2 (1990): 12-15.

Ozog, Edward J. "Another Way to Boston: The New York & New England in Northern Rhode Island." 3 pts. *Shoreliner* 21 (no. 3, 1990): 28-38; (no. 4, 1990): 6-38; 22 (no. 1, 1991): 23-38.

Patch, David. "Connecticut's Shore Line East." *Railfan & Railroad* 12 (October 1993): 60-67.

Patch, David. "The Housantonic Railroad Story." *Railpace Newsmagazine* 12 (August 1993): 14-23.

Patton, Ken. "Old Colony Northern Division." *Shoreliner* 19 (no. 1, 1988): 16-35.

Pierce, Merle. "The Newport and Wickford Railroad and Steamboat Company." *Shoreliner* 15 (no. 4, 1984): 37-39.

Poor, Henry V. *History of the Railroads and Canals of the United States . . .* New York: Schultz & Co., 1860.

Reed, Robert C. *Train Wrecks: A Pictorial History of Accidents on the Main Line*. Seattle: Superior, 1968.

Roy, John H., Jr. "Providence & Worcester Succeeds on Service." *Railfan & Railroad* 11 (November 1992): 54-61.

Sanderson, Edward P. "Railroads of Massachusetts." *Trains* 4 (March 1944): 14-25.

"The Saugus Branch: A Commuter's Line." *B&M Bulletin* 8 (Spring 1979): 21-27.

Schermerhorn, Gary R., and Armstrong, Jack. "The Historic Housatonic." *Railfan & Railroad* 13 (February 1994): 49-58.

Shaugnessy, Jim. "The Short Line They Call the Hoot, Toot & Whistle." *Trains* 22 (September 1962): 25-28.

Shaw, Robert B. *A History of Railroad Accidents, Safety Precautions, and Operating Practices.* N.p.: Shaw, 1978.

Smith, Henry H. "The End of the Line." *Rhode Islander (Providence Sunday Journal),* October 26, 1947, pp. 4, 6, 8.

Snow, Glover A. "Meriden, Waterbury & Connecticut River Railroad." *Transportation: Official Publication of the Connecticut Electric Railway Association* 7 (August 1953): 1-37.

Stanford, R. Patrick. *Lines of the New York, New Haven and Hartford Railroad Company.* N.p.:n.p., 1976.

Stanley, Robert C. *Narrow Gauge: The Story of the Boston, Revere Beach & Lynn Railroad.* BSRA Bulletin 16. Cambridge, Mass.: Boston Street Railroad Association, 1980.

Stilgoe, John R. *Metropolitan Corridor: Railroads and the American Scene.* New Haven: Yale University Press, 1983.

Story, Dana A. "A Recollection of the Essex Branch." *B&M Bulletin* 6 (Winter 1975-76): 5-15.

Symmes, Richard W., and Munroe, Jr., Russell F. "The Great Salem Tunnel Relocation Project." *B&M Bulletin* 5 (Fall 1975): 5-11.

Trencansky, Tom. "Cape Cod Railroad." *Railpace Newsmagazine* 11 (October 1992): 24-30.

Turner, Gregg M., and Jacobus, Melancthon W. *Connecticut Railroads: An Illustrated History.* Hartford: Connecticut Historical Society, 1986.

U.S. Railway Association. *Final System Plan for Reconstructing Railroads in the Northeast and Midwest Region Pursuant to the Regional Rail Reorganization Act of 1973.* 2 vols. Washington, D.C.: USRA, 1975.

U.S. Railway Association. *Preliminary System Plan for Reconstructing Railroads in the Northeast and Midwest Region Pursuant to the Regional Rail Reorganization Act of 1973.* 2 vols. Washington, D.C.: USRA, 1975.

Valentine, Donald B., Jr. "A Brief History of the Cheshire Railroad." *New England States Limited* 1 (Summer 1977): 20-29.

Walker, Mike. *Steam Power Video's Comprehensive Railroad Atlas of North America: North East U.S.A.* Kent, England: Steam Powered Publishing, 1993.

Wellner, John L. *The New Haven Railroad: Its Rise and Fall.* New York: Hastings, 1969.

Wilder, H. Arnold. "The Stony Brook Railroad." *B&M Bulletin* 8 (Spring 1979): 5-14.

Withington, Sidney. *The First Twenty Years of Railroading in Connecticut.* Connecticut Tercentenary Commission. New Haven: Yale University Press, 1935.

Wroe, Lewis. "The Hampden Railroad." *Railroad Enthusiast,* November 1959, 2-6.

Station Index

Connecticut

Passenger trains have not stopped at Palmer, Mass., where the Central Vermont (New London Northern) crosses the Boston & Albany, since the 1960s. (Photo taken in September 1994.)

Massachusetts

Tewksbury, 51
Tewksbury Centre, 51D
Tewksbury Jct., 51D, 56
Texas, 29A
Thayer, 41
Thorndike, 36
Thornton, 61A
Three Bridges, 14
Three Rivers, 14, 35
Thwaites, 78
Tiltons, 67
Titicut, 78
Titicut & North
	Middleboro, 78
Tobeys, 27
Toll Gate, 27, 27A
Topsfield, 54
Touisset, 26A
Tower Hill, 34
Townsend, 43
Townsend Centre, 43
Townsend Harbor, 43
Tremont, 80, 80A
Trinity Place/Hunting-
	ton Ave., 64
Truro, 80
Tufts College, 51
Turners Falls, 7E, 31B
Turners Falls Jct., 31,
	31B
Turnpike, 49, 77B
Tyngsboro, 48
Union Market, 42A
Union Sq., 42
Unionville, 71
United Shoe Machin-
	ery Co., 58
University, 64
Uphams Corner, 68
Upper Falls, 66
Upton, 70, 70A
Uxbridge, 25
Van Deusenville, 3
Vesper Club, 48
Vose, 43
Waban, 64B
Wachusett, 31
Wadsworth(s), 67
Waite, 37

Wakefield, 52
Wakefield Centre, 54,
	55
Wakefield Jct., 52, 54,
	55
Walnut Hill, 27A, 51
Walnut St., 51
Walpole, 67, 72
Walpole Centre, 69
Walpole Heights, 69
Walpole Jct., 69, 72
Waltham, 34, 42, 42A
Waltham Highlands, 34
Waltham North, 34
Wamesit, 51D, 52C
Wamesit-on-Mace, 51D
Wampum, 69
Ward Hill, 52
Ware, 34, 36
Wareham, 80
Warren, 29
Washacum, 40
Washington, 29
Washington St., 73C
Water Place, 51
Water Shops, 18
Water St., 18
Waterford, 25
Waters River, 57
Watertown, 42A
Waterville, 36
Watuppa, 77C
Waveland, 74A
Waverley, 34, 42
Wayland, 34
Wayside Inn, 34
Webster, 15, 16A, 29A,
	80
Webster Jct., 29, 29A
Webster Mills, 29A, 29B
Webster Place, 74
Wedgemere, 51
Weir, 76
Weir Jct., 76, 77
Weir River, 74A
Weir Village, 76, 77,
	77D
Weld St., 77
Wellesley, 64

Wellesley Farms, 64
Wellesley Hills, 64
Wellfleet, 80
Wellington, 52
Wellington Hill, 42
Wenaumet, 80
Wendell, 31
Wenham, 58, 58E, 58F
Wenham Rd., 54
West Acton, 42
West Andover, 51D
West Auburn, 29A
West Barnstable, 80
West Bedford, 50
West Berlin, 34, 65
West Berlin Jct., 34,
	34A
West Boylston, 34, 41
West Bridgewater, 78,
	78A
West Brimfield, 29
West Brookfield, 29
West Cambridge, 42,
	42A
West Chatham, 80D
West Chelmsford, 45
West Concord, 42, 47
West Danvers, 54, 56
West Dedham, 67, 68
West Deerfield, 31
West Dudley, 16A
West Everett, 60
West Falmouth, 80B
West Farms, 59
West Fitchburg, 31
West Gloucester, 59
West Graniteville, 46
West Greenfield, 31
West Groton, 43
West Hanover, 73D
West Hingham, 74
West Leominster, 40
West Lynn, 58, 58B, 60,
	61
West Manchester, 59
West Mansfield, 27
West Medford, 51
West Medway, 66
West Natick, 64

Rhode Island

Errata

The following are corrections of errors that have come to light since the first printing.

Pp. 33, 36: The track north of Plainfield, CT, has not been abandoned.

P. 69, station list: "Hamdem Plains" should read "Hamden Plains."

P. 144, line 5: "1937" should be "1938."

P. 145, line 21: "July 1937" should be "September 1938."

P. 177, line 3: After "85;" add "Central Massachusetts, 1885-1886;" and change "Boston & Lowell, 1885-87" to "Boston & Lowell, 1886-87."

P. 181, line 3: Change "1872-73" to "1872-79" and delete "Fitchburg, 1873-79."

P. 182, lines 12-13: Delete "In 1873 the railroad's directors contracted with the Fitchburg RR to operate the line."

P. 183, lines 5-6: Delete "The Massachusetts Turnpike was built over part of the right of way near Ludlow."

P. 201, line 2: "1845" should be "1849."

P. 201, line 13: Add "Hudson-Marlboro, 1980."

P. 211, line 30: "1982" should be "1981."

P. 223, line 2: "1886-87" should be "1885-87."

P. 226, line 9: Add "Somerville Jct.-North Cambridge, 1927."

P. 230, line 14: "Tewksbury" should be "Tewksbury Centre."

P. 238, line 7: "Wilmington Jct." should be "Ballardvale."

P. 250, line 11: "1885" should be "1884."

P. 257, line 9: Delete "(partially rebuilt ca. 1918)."

P. 275, line 6: Add "Lowell & Fitchburg Jct.-East Somerville, 1969."

P. 288, lines 4-5: Change "1865-73; New York & New England, 1873-95" to "1865-75; New York & New England, 1875-95."

P. 289, line 13: Change "1873" to "1875."

P. 292, line 13: Delete "restored in 1880s and after 1890, discontinued 1904."

P. 311, station list: Change "6 Elmwood" to "5 Elmwood," "7 Stanley" to "6 Stanley," and "2 Westdale" to "1 Westdale."

P. 324, line 14: Add "Randolph-1 mi. west of Braintree Highlands, 1982."

P. 329, line 3: "Old Colony" should be "New Bedford & Taunton."

P. 332, line 16: "Matsfield" should be "Matfield."

P. 338, line 1: "1853" should be "1853-54."

Notes